D1480564

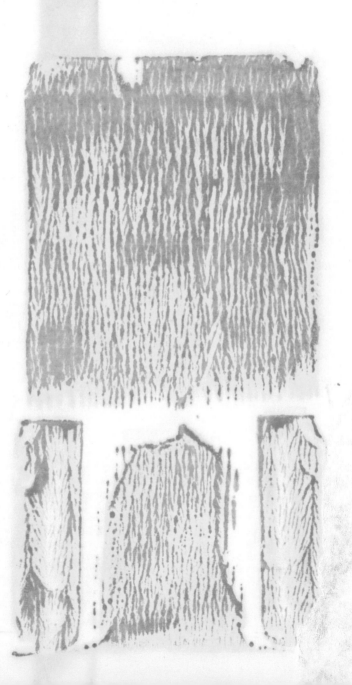

Folk-Songs of the Southern United States

(Folk-Songs du Midi des États-Unis)

Publications of the American Folklore Society
Bibliographical and Special Series
General Editor, Kenneth Goldstein
Volume 19 · 1967

Folk-Songs of the Southern United States

(FOLK-SONGS DU MIDI DES ÉTATS-UNIS)

by
JOSIAH H. COMBS

edited by
D. K. Wilgus

PUBLISHED FOR THE AMERICAN FOLKLORE SOCIETY BY
THE UNIVERSITY OF TEXAS PRESS, AUSTIN & LONDON

Originally dedicated to
Raymond Weeks, Columbia University
and
R. Huchon, University of Paris

This edition dedicated to
Charlotte Combs
whose devotion to her husband made it possible

FOREWORD

Folk-Songs du Midi des États-Unis is a rare book—in more than one way. And it was written by a rare individual. This new edition is long overdue.

American folklorists have been closer to their material than have their European colleagues, but few have been closer than Josiah H. Combs. And few have come as far—from informant to scholar, from the Highlands of eastern Kentucky to the Sorbonne and beyond.

Josiah Henry Combs was born January 2, 1886, at Hazard, Perry County, Kentucky—the heart of what he was later to call "the pure feud belt"—where his father was sheriff during the French-Eversole "war." Combs grew up in Hindman, Knott County, among members of a "singing family." The song and speech of his culture were never to leave him, but he took the first steps of a long journey when, in 1902, he trudged barefoot to the newly established Hindman Settlement School. There even the old songs of this sixteen-year-old Highland youth were well received by the "fotched-on" women who—unlike many other Kentucky "educators"—had respect for some of the esthetic elements of Highland folk culture. At least some of the songs sent by Katherine Pettit for publication in the *Journal of American Folklore* in 1907 were Josiah's.[1]

---

[1] Evelyn K. Wells, *The Ballad Tree* (New York, 1950), p. 261. Which of the texts in "Ballads and Rhymes from Kentucky" (ed. George Lyman Kittredge, *Journal of American Folklore*, XX, 251 ff.) were from Combs is difficult to determine. "My love sat down in a sad condition" and "Sail around the ocean in the long summer day" are virtually identical with Nos. 288A and 289 in the Combs Collection. It is quite possible that Combs did not write down texts which were his own— and we know the two aforementioned were his because he sent copies to B. A. Botkin (*The American Play-Party Song* [Lincoln, Nebraska, 1937], pp. 216–217, 320). Therefore the "lost texts"—conjectured on the basis of notes in the Combs Collection—of "Lord Thomas and Fair Annet" (No. 18), "Barbara Allen" (No. 24B), and "The Drowsy Sleeper" (No. 93) may simply have been in Combs' memory and therefore are those printed in the *Journal of American Folklore*. Further, we cannot conjecture.

By the time the texts of these songs appeared, however, Combs had already taken his next step. In 1905, as he told the story later, he arrived at Transylvania University in Lexington with a dulcimore and a corncob pipe, and without five dollars in his pocket. At the gates he set down his "old valise over the turnstile and crawled under the turnstile to enter the campus. Right off a senior asked me if I had 'matriculated.' I started to hit him, but catching a friendly look in his eyes, I held back." He did matriculate, "under suspicion," and again found academic sympathy, this time in the person of Dr. Hubert G. Shearin, who stimulated Combs' scholarly interest in folksongs.[2] Their joint efforts produced *A Syllabus of Kentucky Folk-Songs* (Lexington, Kentucky, 1911).

After graduating from Transylvania, Combs taught in high schools and colleges in Kentucky, Tennessee, Virginia, and Oklahoma from 1911 to 1918. During this period he published his pamphlet on *The Kentucky Highlanders* (1913); an anthology of Kentucky verse, *All That's Kentucky* (1915); and contributed to *The Journal of American Folklore* and *Dialect Notes*. Furthermore, he took time out for lecture tours and folksong recitals. Typical of this period is the outline for a series of five lectures from a brochure of about 1915:

I. FOLK-LORE: Dulcimer and Ballad Recital.
   1. The Rich Margent (Traditional).
   2. Sweet William and Fair Margaret (Traditional).
   3. Hiram Hubbert (Civil War).
   4. Florella (Traditional)?
   5. Jackaro (Traditional).
   6. Pretty Peggy-O (Colonial)?
   7. Lord Thomas and Fair Ellender (Traditional).
   8. Pretty Maumee (Colonial).
   9. William Baker (Modern).
  10. Sweet Birds (Traditional)?
  11. William Hall (Traditional).
  12. Barbara Allen (Traditional).
  13. Jiggs, Ditties, Nonsense Rimes.

II. FOLK-LORE: Folk-Lore of the Southern Mountains.
   1. Folk-Songs, Traditional and Modern.
   2. British, Largely English in Origin.
   3. Method of Transmission.

---

[2] See D. K. W., "Leaders of Kentucky Folklore," *Kentucky Folklore Record*, III (1957), 67 ff.; Josiah H. Combs, "Some Kentucky Highland Stories," *ibid.*, IV (1959), 46 ff.; Ed Kahn, "Josiah H. Combs," *ibid.*, VI (1960), 101 ff.; D. K. Wilgus, "Josiah H. Combs, 1886–1960," *Journal of American Folklore*, LXXV (1962), 354 f.

Here one can see much of *Folk-Songs du Midi des États-Unis* in outline. While "furriners" like Cecil Sharp and Loraine Wyman were

---

[3] Cf. Josiah H. Combs, "Spellin' 'em Down in the Highlands," *Kentucky Folklore Record*, III (1957), 69 f.

tracking down the "lonesome tunes" in the Highlands, a young mountain boy was bringing them to the lowlands with a blend of defensive-
ness and self-criticism, grounded in hard-won learning but salted with
folk attitudes and anecdotes. And the concerts of unarranged folksongs
were well ahead of their time.

World War I found Combs serving in an army hospital unit in England.[4] After the war he journeyed to the Continent, where he married
a charming French woman in 1920. He served as publicity director for
the YMCA attached to the Czechoslovak Army, 1920–1921, and edited
the *Czechoslovak-American*, Prague, 1921. Returning to the United
States, he became Professor of French and Spanish at West Virginia
University, 1922–1924. After study at the University of Paris, he received a doctorate *mention très honorable* in 1925—his thesis was
Folk-Songs du Midi des États-Unis.

In his ensuing academic career, Combs was Professor of French and
German, University of Oklahoma, 1926–1927; head of the Department of Foreign Languages, Texas Christian University, 1927–1947;
head of the Department of French, Mary Washington College of the
University of Virginia, from which he retired in 1956. Although he
contributed song texts to *Folk-Say* (1930) and to B. A. Botkin's *The
American Play-Party Song* (1937), and published *Folk-Songs from
the Kentucky Highlands* (1939), his scholarly energies were devoted
largely to study of the American language.[5] For, as H. L. Mencken
wrote, Combs belonged to "that small minority of American scholars
who took the national language seriously and gave it scientific study."[6]
Much of his work remains in manuscript, including his monograph,
The Language of Our Southern Highlanders.[7]

After his retirement, Combs turned again to folksong—arranging

___

[4] For a humorous account of this service, see his *The Siege of Sarisbury Court*
(Hindman, Kentucky, [1921?]).

[5] See especially "The Language of the Southern Highlanders," *PMLA*, XLVI
(1931), 1302 ff.; "Radio and Pronunciation," *American Speech*, VII (1931), 124 ff.;
"British and American Usage," *ibid.*, XVI (1941), 153; "A Word-List from the
Southern Highlands," *Publications of the American Dialect Society*, No. 2 (Nov.,
1944), pp. 17 ff.; "Indecent Words," *ibid.*, No. 23 (April, 1955), pp. 33 f. See also
George P. Wilson, "Josiah H. Combs and Folk Speech," *Kentucky Folklore Record*,
VI (1960), 104 ff.

[6] *The American Language*, 4th ed., (New York, 1936), p. 53.

[7] Of his publication difficulties, Combs wrote, "When the final hour arrives for
me to shove off into the Great Unknown, I want my earthly remains cremated, and
the ashes molded into bullets and shot at publishers. If my wishes are carried out,
it will comfort me on the scaffold, and console me in hell" (Letter, January 5,
1960). Alas, Josiah is buried in San Antonio and the publishers are unscathed.

for the disposition of his collection and contributing his wisdom, experience, and folk humor to the students who sought him out. They heard him reminisce of John Harrington Cox (who had "long since swallowed the canes of Gummere and Kittredge"), John A. Lomax, Louise Pound, Jean Thomas, *et al*. Much was insightful and humorous. Not all is publishable. For Josiah H. Combs was outspoken and "salty."[8] Many who disagreed with his pronouncements had the greatest appreciation of his character. Combs was a "mountain man" to the end. Indeed, the characteristics of the Highlanders that he analyzes[9] include many of his own traits. Although he lived elsewhere—in Texas by preference—he remained stubbornly loyal to his native Highlands, to the ideals and prejudices of his people. I shall never forget our first meeting. Entering his home in Fort Worth, I found the *savant*, his fractured leg in a cast, ensconced behind a low table liberally laden with bottles of bourbon in anticipation of a visit from an erstwhile Kentuckian. And the ultimate disposition of his folksong collection illustrates his generosity and his continuing resentment of affronts to his pride and dignity. His material was spontaneously and freely

---

[8] I am reminded of his story of "Black" Shade Combs, "a picturesque mountaineer, whose long black beard descending swept his rugged breast. 'Black' was merely a pseudonym, for Shade was white, with no great claim to education and culture, but blessed with much native wit and intelligence. Shade and some other mountaineers found themselves in Frankfort, stopping at the Capitol Hotel, frequented by the Senators and Representatives, and by the elite. It was dinner time. Directly across the table from Shade sat an elegantly dressed woman, of easy morals and notorious reputation. A waiter comes to the table to take the orders. He addresses the courtesan:

"Waiter: What will you have, Lady?

"Courtesan: First bring me a thimbleful of honeyed and spiced nectar, as sweet and soothing as an infant's cordial; second, bring me a tiny bowl of potage, seasoned with mushrooms and nightingale tongues; third, bring me a modest portion of asparagus tips, gently smothered with vinaigrette sauce; fourth, bring me a small beefsteak as tender as a chicken's breast; fifth, bring me a soft silk napkin to spread upon my bosom—and please inform me who the gentleman is that sits opposite me.

" 'Black' Shade was thinking, and thinking fast. He drank in the whole import of the woman's obvious satire and contempt. By the time the waiter got around to him he was ready with a retort stinging and terrible:

"Waiter: And what will you have, Sir?

" 'Black' Shade: First, fetch me a pint of moonshine liquor as clear as crystal and as strong as hell; second, fetch me a big bowl of onion soup full of hog kidneys and 'mountain oysters'; third, fetch me a bowl of hominy swimmin' in hog grease; fourth, fetch me a hunk of beefsteak as tough as a saddleskirt; fifth, fetch me a burlap sack to spread over my hairy breast—and (pointing straight at the woman of easy morals opposite him) please inform me who the God damned chippy is that sits opposite me."

[9] See below, pp. 6, 18, 46–50.

placed in the Western Kentucky Folklore Archive with no restrictions on use or publication—excepting the proviso that none of his collection was ever to reach the University of Kentucky, the Filson Club, or Indiana University. The rivalry between Transylvania University and the once-arrogant state university, the exclusiveness of the historical club of Louisville's first families, the impolite rejection of a scholarly note—these could not be forgotten.

On May 14, 1960, Josiah H. Combs tuned his dulcimore and again sang his Kentucky folksongs for a gathering at the home of his friend Dr. Jerrell Bennett. On June 2, while I was en route to record his performances, Josiah H. Combs was dead. His dulcimore and his collection of folksongs are now in the Western Kentucky Folklore Archive at UCLA. His memory is green and his work is still vital to the student of American folkways.

Folk-Songs du Midi des États-Unis, published at the University of Paris in 1925, has been somewhat neglected by students of American folksong because it has been difficult of access and because it was not in English. (I once saw its citation in a bibliography of French folksong.) The form of the present edition has been determined by a variety of circumstances. Our first plan was to reprint the original French edition, with an appendix listing the items in the Combs Collection deposited in the Western Kentucky Folklore Archive in 1957. We later realized, however, that the relatively simple language barrier which has separated Combs' work from the consideration of many folksong students should be removed. Yet a retranslation of *Folk-Songs du Midi des États-Unis* might resemble Mark Twain's hilarious rendering, "The Frog Jumping of the County of Calaveras." Fortunately, Combs' English manuscript of his thesis survived and, through the courtesy of Mrs. Combs, was used as the base text of this new edition. It is, however, only the "base," as it is not a precisely parallel form of the French. The difference between the two texts is one of the conditions which have necessitated difficult editorial decisions.

The English version is obviously little more than a draft. Literal adherence to its readings would have been a disservice to its author. The absence from the French text of passages in the English manuscript may be due to Combs' own second thoughts or to the decision of his Sorbonne *conférencier,* who did indeed reject one entire chapter, "The Highlander's Music" which subsequently appeared in French in *Vient de Paraître*.[10] This chapter has been restored in this edition essentially in the English version authorized by Combs and published in the *Kentucky Folklore Record*.[11] Most other passages in the English version which were not included in the French form of the text have been added, but placed in brackets. Additions and changes made by Combs for the French version have been included in my English translation. My own additions or editorial comment is so indicated. The two texts have been carefully collated; mechanics and documentation have been made to conform to current American editorial standards, although certain usages reflecting the time of publication (for example, *folk-song*) have been retained.

The English form of the headnotes to song texts did not survive, and I am responsible for the translations. The notes have not, however, been altered to incorporate current knowledge and research, except to provide references to current syllabi. My few additions, for clarity or reference, are placed in brackets. A bracketed number after the title of each text refers to the Appendix, which is an annotated list of the entire Combs folksong collection, including significant information relative to many texts. Throughout the volume I have omitted footnotes glossing Americanisms unfamiliar to the French reader.

Folk-Songs du Midi des États-Unis must be evaluated in terms of its time and the limitations placed upon it. Forty years ago perhaps no more nonsense about the nature of the folk and folksong was in general circulation than exists today; but it was a different kind of nonsense. Still of prime importance in 1925 was the alleged relationship of the English and Scottish traditional ballads to "primitive poetry," their origin in communal composition. When contemporary evidence was admitted or adduced, it was generally treated—and sometimes dubiously treated—by "outsiders" not fully acquainted with the folk cultures. Josiah H. Combs, with an intimate knowledge of one continuing folk culture and with a grasp of the scholarly literature, approached the matter with sturdy common sense as well as with some of the heat generated by the controversy. As I have elsewhere[12] surveyed this controversy and indicated to some extent Combs' place in the "ballad war," it might be better to allow him to speak. His November, 1925, *soutenance* of his thesis before the University of Paris

[10] "La Musique du Highlander des États-Unis," *Vient de Paraître*, Vol. VI, No. 50, pp. 24 ff.
[11] VI (1960), 108 ff.
[12] *Anglo-American Folksong Scholarship Since 1898* (New Brunswick, New Jersey, 1959), especially pp. 2–122, 143, 148, 151–152, 156, 178, 197–198, 340.

"jury" of Émile Legouis, René Louis Huchon, and Aurélien Digeon
would have served as an admirable introduction to the published
volume, as pertinent passages will show.

> Chapters I and II of this thesis . . . are included for the simple reason that
> a study of the folksong is incomplete without a consideration of the topo-
> graphical features of the country and an inquiry into the nationality or
> ancestry of the people. . . . Here, as elsewhere, I go directly to the folk for
> much of my information, allowing the songs, language, names, customs,
> etc. of the people to help settle the problem of ancestry. . . .
>   . . . The study of mere song texts (largely from collections made in the
> British Isles long ago) is insufficient in the matter of determining origins.
> And so, I have gone to the people for more tangible evidence, to the folk,
> who, in the Southern highlands of America, still make and still sing bal-
> lads. . . . I have seen fit to question erstwhile definitions of "folksong," or
> "ballad," which, it now appears, no longer hold good. . . . Because of its
> seeming mystery (if there be any), the question of authorship has been
> thrown out of focus for a century; thus causing the sixteenth- and seven-
> teenth-century British ballad to become too closely linked up with remote
> and almost prehistoric song and dance origins; which origins should be
> considered apart from the epic or narrative song of a later age. Communal
> origin is untenable; we must accept individual authorship.
>   . . . The contention that the making of songs and the singing of songs
> among the folk are "lost arts," or "closed accounts," is denied. The discov-
> ery of the Highlands has been the chief factor in destroying the conten-
> tion. . . . Most collectors in America have made the mistake of following
> some old trails; they should record ALL songs, whether identified with
> Child or not. In my personal experiences among the folk—which were
> many—I met with some evidence, perhaps, that all ballads were not sung
> originally. In brief, a conscientious study of the lore of the folk cannot be
> dissociated from the folk itself.[13]

One does not have to agree with all of Combs' conclusions to recog-
nize their value. His assertion of "the baneful influence of the banjo-
picker upon traditional song" may be questioned. But by "traditional
song" he seems to have meant largely the older folksongs, and it is the
influence of the banjo picker "as a true conservator of words and airs,"
that he is denying. In any event, Combs testified to the influence—for
good or ill—of instrumentalists in an area and at a time when their
existence had been virtually denied by the most renowned collector of
Appalachian folksongs.[14] Although Combs could not then foresee the

---

[13] From a typescript sent me by Combs in 1960.
[14] Cecil J. Sharp, *English Folk-Songs from the Southern Appalachians* (New
York, 1917), p. 10; (London, 1932), I, xxvii. Sharp's comments are echoed to this
day, particularly in English publications.

development from the banjo picker to the professional hillbilly musician (he later noted some of the effects), he saw clearly that the "contention that the traditional song, because of its superiority over the later lyric or love song, will outlive the later song is not well founded."

It is not the intent of this edition, however, to judge Combs' remarks and opinions in the light of current scholarship. Rather, the aim has been to preserve the original integrity of the work in a more readily available and usable form. I have consequently been content to add relatively few notes for clarification and explanation of Combs' discussion.

The collected texts in Part II of *Folk-Songs du Midi des États-Unis* must be approached in the knowledge that, apparently at the eleventh hour, Combs was not allowed to include any British or American song if "one or more versions, sometimes quite different and inferior, had already been published in America." The "line" was not tightly held —witness the inclusion of "John Henry"—but it shaped the collection.

This enforced concentration on "new finds" caused Combs, in this collection, to depend a good deal on the recently gathered West Virginia material (of the sixty-one texts, twenty-seven are from West Virginia), most of which he seems to have acquired from secondary sources. Having left his own community, Combs functioned generally as an "academic collector," depending largely on subcollectors, often students or colleagues. Among the student-collectors was one Carey Woofter, whose contributions bulk large in *Folk-Songs du Midi des États-Unis*, though less in the total Combs Collection. Both in *FSMEU* and in the Combs manuscript collection, the original informant is often credited without record of the contributor; consequently the immediate or intermediary source is not always clear. But of the twenty-seven West Virginia texts in *FSMEU*, thirteen are clearly from Woofter, seven probably, and five possibly. It is necessary to point up this situation in reference both to the contents of *FSMEU* and to the total Combs Collection because of the nature of many of the Woofter contributions—which Combs accepted but for which he does not bear ultimate responsibility. I have discussed the problem elsewhere[15] in particular relation to the issues raised by the Woofter text of "Edward" (Appendix, No. 7), but the problem must be surveyed briefly here.

The late Carey Woofter was a student at West Virginia University during the 1922–1924 faculty residence of Combs. He received his B.A. and M.A. degrees from the University and subsequently became

[15] "The Oldest (?) Text of 'Edward,'" *Western Folklore*, XXV (1966), 77 ff.

Dean of West Virginia State College at Glenville. He contributed a few texts to the collection of John Harrington Cox[16] and was reputed to have a large unpublished collection. Combs, in his last letter to me, described Woofter as "an eccentric West Virginia mountaineer, as eccentric as his name sounds . . . an avid student and collector of folk-songs and Highland dialect; [he] enjoyed getting Cox in deep water" (the last statement refers to disputes with John Harrington Cox). Woofter himself apparently published only a word list in *American Speech* (II, 347 ff.) in 1927. We have, then, as evidence of Woofter's collection, only the texts he contributed to the Cox and Combs collections, and I doubt that all items supplied to Combs are so identified. There are eighty-five texts in the Combs Collection explicitly credited as Woofter contributions, and seven others (Appendix, Nos. 10, 11, 16, 19B, 26, 89, and 121) can be attributed to Woofter on the basis of other evidence. Twenty-nine other texts in the Combs Collection could have been contributed by Woofter—and I am convinced that almost half of them were.

To judge the character of the complete Woofter collection—assuming that there was a "complete" collection—by the identifiable items in the Combs Collection might be highly unjustified. Woofter may have been selecting on the basis of rarity and the interest of the recipient. If we assume that the full Woofter collection had the miscellaneous character of the average Appalachian collection, he was practicing a good deal of selection (as Combs was forced to practice in his own selections for *FSMEU*). Of the ninety-four items that are assuredly from Woofter, thirty-eight are of the prized Child variety. On the other hand, the range of contributions extends to a large number of play-party songs.

Many, perhaps most, of the Woofter texts occasion no question. They seem—with no implied criticism—run-of-the-mill Appalachian material. Some of the rare texts inspire confidence as the product of an uninhibited native collector supplying unexpurgated texts to an uninhibited archivist. Consider a stanza of the Woofter text of "The Farmer's Curst Wife" (Child No. 278; Appendix, No. 40A):

> 7. And when he came to hell's great door
>   Says, "Get off of my back, you damned old whore."

Rare texts may occasion suspicion, yet Woofter's "Johnny Collins"

---

[16] *Folk-Songs of the South* (Cambridge, Massachusetts, 1925), Nos. 35G; 162G; 185; *American Speech*, II (1927), 226–227.

text of "Lady Alice" (Child 85; Appendix, No. 25B) was contributed before its significance was apparent.[17] A unique local item such as "River Song" (Appendix, No. 205) beginning

> Pork and beans and eggs to fry
> Doughnuts, kraut and apple pie
> We'll hit Gilmer by and by.

seems to bear its own warrant.

On the other hand, a number of Woofter's contributions merit distrust. Louis W. Chappell pointed out variations in printings of "The Yew-Pine Mountains," which Woofter supplied to both Combs and Cox.[18] The variations are slight, and Chappell was using them to attack Cox's editing, pointing out also that Cox apparently made alterations in printing a Combs text of "John Henry."[19] But we note that Woofter contributed to Cox a text of Child No. 275 credited to Mrs. Sarah Clevenger of Briar Lick Run, near Perkins, Gilmer County. "She learned it from her grandmother, Mrs. Rebecca Clevenger, who came from London County, Virginia, seventy-eight years ago, as the date in the family Bible gives it." Woofter contributed to the Combs Collection a text identical but for a transposition in one line, and indicated the source as David Chenoweth, Gip, Gilmer County, West Virginia (Appendix, No. 38). To Chenoweth is also credited the unique textual form of "The Cruel Brother" (Appendix, No. 5), which Woofter annotates as "doctored by one Daniel De Weese."

To prove an alleged traditional text fraudulent (i.e., deliberately altered or re-created to deceive the student of folksong) is not always easy. Unless one can obtain from the alleged informant a denial that he furnished the song to the alleged collector—as Vance Randolph was able to do when investigating John Robert Moore's collecting of a version of Child 218[20]—he can judge the validity of the variant only by relating it to the known history of the song, which can be established largely by a study of its variants. The process is indeed almost circular. But, despite a memorat even more convincing than that supplied for the text of Child No. 275 quoted above, I believe I have demonstrated that the Woofter text of "Edward" is a clever conflation of

---

[17] For discussion and reference see Tristram P. Coffin, *The British Traditional Ballad in North America* (rev. ed., Philadelphia, Pennsylvania, 1963), pp. 86 f.

[18] *John Henry* (Jena, Germany, 1933), pp. 3 f.

[19] *Ibid.*, pp. 2 f. Cf. Appendix, No. 81.

[20] *Journal of American Folklore*, LX (1947), 117.

Child's A and B texts.[21] In a similar study, to be published in *Western Folklore*, Bernth Lindfors has shown that the West Virginia text of Child No. 2 in the Combs Collection (Appendix, 1A; not identified as a Woofter contribution, but alleged to be from a Gilmer County informant) is a palpable fraud—palpable only to the student who has made a meticulous study of the tradition of the ballad.

When a song text has little traditional status, one must be wary of an alleged recovery from a folksinger. We therefore must at least note that the Woofter text of "Ranting Roving Lad" (p. 149) is almost identical to that printed in Allan Cunningham's *The Songs of Scotland* (pp. 208 f.). One swallow does not make a summer—but Woofter also contributed "The Old Wife" (pp. 135 f.), which is quite similar to "The Auld Wife Beyont the Fire" in Allan Ramsay's *Tea Table Miscellany* (1871 ed., I, 103 ff.), where it was published as an old song with additions. For the Scots euphemism for sexual intercourse, *snishing*, the Woofter text substitutes *spruncin*. Aside from a version of "The Old Wife" on a recent recording[22] certainly derived from Combs' printing, the only other notice of *spruncin'* (*sic*) is in a localization of "The Gypsy Laddie" (Child No. 200; Appendix, No. 33B) contributed by Carey Woofter.

We must grant at this point that many Woofter texts must be accepted as traditional variants. But the literary connections and internal evidence of some of Woofter's dubious texts furnish touchstones for a number of items not credited to Woofter yet possibly from his collection. (Items possibly attributable to Woofter are those assigned to informants in Gilmer and adjacent counties.) The geographical pattern of contribution to the Combs Collection automatically suggests as Woofter contributions "The Rantin Laddie" (pp. 127 f.) and the two texts of "Bonnie James Campbell" (pp. 126 f.). The fact that recoveries are unusual (as is certainly true of these texts) proves nothing, except that it adds to the stature of Woofter as a collector of texts rare —almost unique—in the United States. But from within Woofter's collecting area comes "The Gowans Grow Gay" (pp. 142 f.), uncomfortably close to the *Tea Table Miscellany* text (II, 214 ff.).[23] Certain

---

[21] See Appendix, No. 7.

[22] Paul Clayton, *Unholy Matrimony*, Elektra 147, 12″ LP.

[23] It is indeed ironic that "the gowans grow gay" is the unique refrain of the Buchan "Lady Isabel and the Elf Knight" (Child No. 4A) which Holger O. Nygard has demonstrated to be a "forgery" (*The Ballad of Heer Halewijn* [Knoxville, Tenn., 1958], pp. 311 ff.). One is reminded of John Pinkerton's "discovery" of the second part of "Hardyknute" (see Sigurd Bernhard Hustvedt, *Ballad Criticism in*

texts from Woofter's area which do not have such obvious literary sources do have common patterns of localization and rationalization. Fair Annie (pp. 114 ff.) is stolen away by the Indians; Lord Harry ransoms this unknown girl and she lives with him in a "mansion-house," but never tells her name. When Lord Harry is later bedded with a new bride, "Fair Annie took a banjo on her hand/To play the two to sleep." This is the kind of rationalization which should happen in an American text, but seldom does. It happens also in the Woofter text of "Edward" when the protagonist desires to "paddle the boat over the old mill dam"; and in the localization of "Prince Robert" (p. 121 ff.) at Nicut Hill (Nicut is in southeast Calhoun County, West Virginia, near the Gilmer County line). Localization does not impeach a text, but there can be too much of a good thing.

I have been less than happy to introduce these remarks into this introduction, particularly as they might seem to destroy the validity of the Combs Collection and impugn the integrity and knowledge of Josiah H. Combs. They do not. The West Virginia texts—of which Woofter's contributions are only a part—constitute little more than a third of the Combs Collection, which is seven times larger than *Folk-Songs du Midi des États-Unis*. Largely on the basis of subsequent collection and experience one can question the Woofter contributions, and whatever tentative judgments I have made here must be supported or rectified by future students, using the collected materials I have made more readily available. But the efforts of these students—like my own—will be based upon those of a pioneer American *savant*.

I am particularly grateful to Claude M. Simpson, Jr., for the extensive advice and aid provided in the final stages of editing this volume. And without the courtesy of Charlotte Combs the publication of this edition would have been impossible.

Los Angeles, California   D. K. WILGUS

Scandinavia and Great Britain during the Eighteenth Century [New York, 1916], pp. 87 f. and *passim*).

PREFACE

The songs presented in this volume have been selected from about two hundred which I have collected during the last fifteen years. Most of them have been recovered from the folksingers themselves. The states represented are: Kentucky, Virginia, West Virginia, Tennessee, Arkansas, Oklahoma, and Texas. My collection includes forty-three Child ballads, ten of which are included in the present work.

With great pleasure I express my extreme gratitude to my many friends who by their valuable contributions or by their encouraging suggestions have made this work possible, especially to my mother, Mrs. J. W. Combs, to Mr. Carey Woofter of West Virginia, to Professor J. H. Cox of West Virginia University, and to Professor G. L. Kittredge of Harvard University.

J. H. C.

Paris, July, 1925

CONTENTS

Native American Songs

APPENDIX

PART I

CHAPTER I

Topography of the Southern Highlands

IF THE STUDENT of ethnology or of anthropogeography would arrive at conclusions approaching accuracy, he must examine certain physical features of the region, or of the people, under consideration. The culture of the Highlander has always shown a marked contrast with that of the dweller in the lowlands. Physical features have a bearing on this contrast which cannot be disputed. It is said that a young Colonial officer of Virginia once paid a visit to Dr. Johnson, in London, and, in the course of a conversation with the learned Englishman, remarked on the barren features of western Virginia (now West Virginia), where a number of Scotsmen had settled. "Why, sir," replied Dr. Johnson, "all barrenness is relative; the Scotch will never know that it is barren." A brief description of the topography of the Southern Highlands in the United States may not seem out of place, with a view not only toward a better understanding of their people, but also toward establishing some possible folk-song relationships. An understanding of the principal physical features of this extensive region may aid in throwing light on certain vague anomalies and anachronisms of the folk-song, and even on the difficult question of origin or authorship.

It must be said, in the beginning, that the terms "Southern Highlands," and "Southern Highlanders," are those which we shall use most frequently with respect to the region and its people. The Southern Highlands appear to be the great reservoir for the quest of the folk-song in the English-speaking world. Some of the songs here printed or discussed were found in Louisiana, Arkansas, Oklahoma, and Texas; but the majority belong to the Highlands, and it is the Highlands which required our attention This great upland region of the United States has until recent years been almost unknown to the outside world. Even now it is not generally known, except through the fantastic columns of newspapers, which are heavily charged with sensationalism, and through the pages of third-rate fiction, whose authors adopt it because it is so far away that they know nothing about it.

The accounts of early historians, romancers, poets, scientists, and travelers coming into this region, while interesting, are not always trustworthy, since they are either too local in character, or were made upon hasty observation. In 1794 André Michaux, the French botanist, scaled the summit of Grandfather Mountain, North Carolina, and wrote: "Monté au sommet de la plus haute montagne de toute l'Amérique Septentrionale, chanté avec mon compagnon-guide l'hymne de Marseillais, et crié, 'Vive la liberté et la Republique française'!" It will be observed that Michaux speaks of Grandfather Mountain as the highest in North America. It is not even the highest in this region! Early French travelers over the mountains have left many impressions of the country. Jean Louis Bridel published his "Le Pour et le Contre," Paris, 1803; Pierre S. Maréchal wrote his *Voyage au Kentouckey*, Paris, 1821; "The Ancient Annals of Kentucky" was written by C. S. Rafinesque, Frankfort, Kentucky, 1824; *Guide des émigrans français dans les États de Kentucky et d'Indiana* was published in Paris, 1835; A. E. Rouquette has left us "Souvenir du Kentucky," from his book, *Les Savanes, Poésies Americaines*, published in Paris, 1841. In one of these poems he speaks of Kentucky:

> Ah! dans le Kentucky les arbres sont bien beaux;
> C'est la *terre de sang*, aux indiens tombeaux,
> Terre aux belles forêts, aux séculaires chênes,
> Aux bois suivis de bois, aux magnifiques scènes;
> Imposant cimetière, où dorment en repos
> Tant de *rouges-tribus* et tant de *blanches-peaux*.

The term "Southern Highlands" has been chosen as the best designation of the region under discussion. "Mountains" and "hills," often employed, hardly seem adequate, since the vast upland section consists of mountains, hills, valleys, and plateaus. This region comprises the southern part of the great Appalachian province, which reaches from central Alabama into New York State, cut in twain, for purposes of geographic convenience, by the famous Mason and Dixon Line. Such designations as "Southern Appalachians," "Allegheny Mountains," the "Cumberlands," "Southern Mountains," "Appalachian America," "Shakespeare's America," and "Elizabethan America" are often heard. However, we feel safe with the designation, "Southern Highlands."

If an aviator should take the air at Frederick, Maryland (near the Pennsylvania line), and fly in a southwesterly course through Lynchburg, Virginia, thence through Ashville, North Carolina, thence to Spartanburg, South Carolina, thence to Cartersville, Georgia, and on to Coosa County, Alabama, he would mark roughly the eastern, or southeastern boundary of the Southern Highlands. Continuing his course in a northwesterly direction to Decatur, Alabama, thence in a northeasterly direction through Tullahoma, Tennessee, and Richmond, Kentucky, to Wheeling, West Virginia, thence eastward to Frederick, he would roughly mark the remaining boundaries of the region. The territory thus described embraces most of West Virginia, the western sections of Maryland, Virginia, the Carolinas, northern Georgia, northeastern Alabama, and the eastern sections of Tennessee and Kentucky. In area this territory almost equals Great Britain and Ireland, covering about 112,000 square miles.

The mountains of this section appear to be of great antiquity, even antedating, some geologists think, the Himalayas, the Andes, and the Rockies. Agassiz believes that they were the first to appear "above the waters," and that the earliest race of men lived here. There seems to be some evidence that the Highlands were the battleground of prehistoric races, succeeded by very ancient races of Mound Builders, who in turn were exterminated by races of Indians too prehistoric to have left numerous relics of their existence.

If the vision of our aviator were far-sighted enough, he would mark on his course three distinct parallel "belts" lying lengthwise, northeast to southwest. The western belt is known as the Appalachian Plateau, the eastern as the Blue Ridge; and between these two lies the Greater Appalachian Valley. The central section is rather a depression, made up of valley ridges. Numerous mountain peaks of the Blue Ridge belt rise to an altitude of more than 6,000 feet. Unlike mountains in many other sections of the world, the ranges of the Southern Highlands are well wooded to the top, and afford a spectacle of great beauty, as well as a splendid opportunity for the setting up of "moonshine" stills. Certainly here, in the dark recesses of this far-flung wilderness, the vendetta reached its zenith, and collapsed. The conditions were ideal. With the exception of the central belt, or Greater Appalachian

Valley, hill and mountain slopes comprise a remarkably large area of the soil—in many sections as much as ninety percent. The meagre crops or harvests of the Highlander are produced for the most part on the hill- and mountainsides. Some of the cornfields slope at an angle of fifty degrees. The Highlander, with his dry humor, often speaks of a neighbor "falling out of his cornfield and breaking his neck"; or of the ox which "fell out of the pasture" and down the great chimney of the cabin below; or of "shooting" his seedcorn into the steep hillside. The sombre valleys and majestic mountains, with their strange mystery and boundless solitude, naturally breed superstition and emotionalism in the Highlander, and add to his previous store of traditional folk-lore. His environment compels him to live close to nature, and to read daily her open manuscripts. The rugged nature of this enforced environment has often caused his ideas, nature-made, to conflict with those of a faraway, centralized government, man-made, which, he thinks, has no right to interfere with a little illicit distilling of corn whiskey.

All the Southern Highlands are not an unbroken succession of hills, ridges, and mountains. Streams and rivers are numerous enough, and the Greater Appalachian Valley contains much plateau country, with a number of enterprising cities in Tennessee, Kentucky, and the Valley of Virginia. Nor must the population of these more prosperous centers be confused with that of the more remote, isolated sections, which will be discussed later. Bad roads and primitive means of transportation are a bane to the country. Most of the roads in the remote sections follow the beds of streams, or else cross the streams too often. During the winter months they are almost impassable. Rough "jolt-wagons" carry merchandise, and often passengers, in this "far country." In many sections these wagons, drawn by oxen, horses, or mules, go forty and fifty miles for merchandise with which to stock the village shops, crossing three or four mountains en route, and requiring a week or more for the journey. The best means of travel is by horseback, which is certainly the safest and the speediest.

The nomenclature of the Highlands is elemental and simple, and shows the result of the mountaineer's close contact with nature and the soil. His long and unequal struggle with the elements of nature has placed the Highlander under the necessity of dealing with conditions as he finds them, and he has formulated his nomenclature in strict accordance with the maxim, "Necessity is the mother of invention."

The names of mountains, hills, ridges, streams, roads, and post offices form an integral part of Highland culture. Natural phenomena and physical characteristics often determine place-names. Streams and mountains sometimes take their names from birds and fowls, sometimes from the names of persons. In the strange medley of names that dot the country, one section has resorted to an arrangement which is at the same time highly logical and suggestive. This section has a stream called Cow; a little further on there is Bull, and nearby, Calf! Such striking place or stream names may or may not account for the Highlander's predilection for personal combats and vendettas, but a Highland barrister thinks it possible, and has put into verse the names of some of the streams:

> When Red-Eye into Hoss-Neck pours
> Its measly moonshine tide,
> Big Stinking scatters as she goes
> Old Hell-fer Sartain wide;
> When Bull-Skin into Cut-Shin runs,
> And Cut-Shin into Goose,
> No wonder people get their guns—
> And sometimes turn them loose.

A traveler enquiring his way over this strange country comes into possession of information which is worthy of safeguarding as a priceless heirloom. [Let us conjure up an imaginary request of a traveler thus seeking his way.

[TRAVELER—"How does one get to Mr. So-and-So's, on Jones' Fork?"

[HIGHLANDER—"Jist ye foller right on up Carr's Fork till ye come to Arshman Creek, on the left-hand side, 'bout the rise o' four mile. Turn up that creek and go two mile, till ye come to two big beech trees and a hog-pen on the right. Then turn to the left, up the branch, till ye come to a calf-path leading up the mountain. Foller it to the other side, and strike down Perkins Branch, till ye come to the main road, on Troublesome Creek. Turn up Left Fork and go two mile, till ye come to the mouth o' Mill Creek. Turn to the left and go straight ahead to the mountain. On the other side is Jones' Fork. Old man Triplett lives with his gal, and ye'll find their house on the third branch on the right-hand side, under a big sycamore at the foot of the cove."][1]

---

[1] [Passages in brackets are from Combs' English MS and do not appear in the French translation.—D. K. W.]

Communities and villages are not characteristic of the Highlands, as they are of European countries. Habitations consisting of one- or two-room cabins, usually constructed of rough, unhewn logs, and the more pretentious and modern, framed farm houses, are scattered far and wide over this vast country. Often a large family inhabits a one-room cabin. Highland families are large. An old Highland lady, when asked how many children she had, replied: "Only ten; hit jist looks like a body ort to have at least a dozen." There is one village or small town in each county, and it is the county seat. Such isolation and lack of communication and social intercourse, rare in Western Europe, make the Highlander complete master of his household, and lord of his premises. The little "grave-yards," or cemeteries, at once arrest the attention, being situated on an elevation, or small hill, often under the trees. They are badly kept, and the graves are sometimes covered with tiny, painted, latticed houses; truly a picture of desolation and neglect. They are seldom visited except at a burial, or at a "funeral," which is usually preached many years after the burial.

The dense thickets and underbrush which characterize the Highlands in so many places lead one to draw certain parallels between this country and the *maquis* of Corsica. The topography of the country is especially adapted to the vendetta and to the distillation of moonshine whiskey. Kentucky has had some remarkable feuds, which the Highlander calls "wars," but they have been overdrawn by the outside world.[2] The purely transversal vendetta has been rare, yet it offers certain parallels with that of Corsica. In one of these Kentucky feuds Tom Baker, a feudist, had been shot and killed as he was leaving a tent guarded by troops sent by the governor to prevent bloodshed at Baker's trial. Captain Bryan asked the widow of the murdered chieftain why she did not leave that country of feuds and teach her children to forget. "Captain Bryan," she replied, "I have twelve sons. It will be the chief aim of my life to bring them up to avenge their father's death. Each day I shall show my boys the handkerchief stained with blood, and tell them who murdered him." In the same feud, "Big" John Philpotts, though severely wounded, fought from behind a log and killed four of his adversaries. The mountaineer's code does not require that he come out in the open to fight his enemy; he may take advantage of him, foul or fair, as did the Corsican feudists. [The recent passage of the pro-

[2] See Charles G. Mutzenberg, *Kentucky's Famous Feuds and Tragedies.*

hibition laws in America has greatly increased illicit distilling in this region, contrary to report of prohibition officials. For the same reason, murder and crime have increased in many sections. The advent of railroads here and there to tap the rich coal and mineral fields is bringing into the Highlands an undesirable population and increasing lawlessness.]

CHAPTER II

Ancestry of the Highlanders

"Je me souviens aussi d'etranges histoires sur ces Ragged Mountains (Montagnes Déchirées), et de races d'hommes bizarres et sauvages qui habitaient leurs bois et leurs cavernes." The above is one of the earliest literary references to the "strange and savage men" of the Southern Highlands. It is from one of Poe's stories, "Les Souvenirs de M. Auguste Bedloe," translated by Baudelaire.[1] Poe, who was more of a literary artist than an accurate historian, made this early estimate of the Highlanders while he was a student at the University of Virginia, which is in close proximity to the Highlands. The Highlanders are not savage, nor did they ever inhabit caves. An understanding of their ancestry should precede a study of their folk-songs. Who are the Southern Highlanders, and whence their ancestors? The Highlands have been inhabited for a century and a quarter, certainly not a long lapse of time in the history of a people; yet the question of Highland ancestry has become as mysterious as has the origin or authorship of the popular ballad. Five and a half millions of people are unable to determine accurately the nativity of their forebears, and historians and students are trying to do it for them.

The Highlander was first discovered during the Second War with England (1812–1815). Commodore Perry placed him in the rigging of his ships in the Battle of Lake Erie, to pick off British officers of the

---

[1] ["I remembered, too, strange stories told about these Ragged Hills, and of the uncouth and fierce races of men who tenanted their groves and caverns" (Edgar A. Poe, "A Tale of the Ragged Mountains," *The Complete Poems and Stories of Edgar Allan Poe*, ed. Arthur Hobson Quinn and Edward H. O'Neill [New York, 1946] I, 517). Poe's tale was first printed in *Godey's Lady's Book*, April, 1844. The French translation is from *Histoires Extraordinaires* (Paris, 1856).—D. K. W.]

opposing fleet; also, it is said, to prevent his running too far into the British lines, in the infantry, and disobeying orders! He won the Battle of New Orleans, where his aim was deadly. But he continued to lie dormant, in a long, Rip van Winkle sleep—until the guns of later wars awakened him, as they have never failed to do. Almost alone, as in the Second War with England, he won the Mexican War (1846–1848), while the New Englander was trying his best to lose it. The Civil War (1861–1865) aroused him again from his lethargy, and, like a long, keen sabre, he cut deep into the vitals of the Southern Confederacy. Almost 180,000 Highlanders enlisted in the Union Armies, because they had no slaves, and because the idea of secession from the Union was foreign to them; not because they loved the Negro, whose servility they detested. When Lincoln first called for volunteers to put down the Rebellion, some Highland counties were depleted of men between the ages of fifteen and sixty. In 1918 Marshal Foch decorated a Tennessee Highlander, Alvin C. York, as the greatest individual hero fighting in any of the Allied Armies. Such are some of the outstanding facts concerning a people who are more truly American than the rest of the country, and more truly English than England; a people in whom the American government has shown but slight interest, choosing rather to busy itself with undesirable types of foreigners in the slums of the greater American cities.[2] Too long have our "contemporary ancestors, beleaguered by nature," been the stock-in-trade of scurrilous, yellow journalists and cheap motion-picture film producers. We are to deal with the major part of more than five millions of one hundred percent pure Americans, whose ancestors, we shall attempt to prove, were recruited largely from the great English commons. It is a difficult question, but one which is not impossible of solution.

Some of the difficulties might be summarized as follows. The basic problem is that the Highlander himself knows nothing of his ancestry, for good reasons. Three hundred years have passed since the beginning of English colonization in America. For nearly two centuries the Highlander's ancestors, carving out a new nation, fighting Indians, and trying to protect themselves against a most unfavorable environment, were too busy to build up and preserve family trees. All that was left to the "F.F.V.'s," or the First Families of Virginia. Then came the

[2] At the beginning of the present century less than 5 percent of the Highlanders dwelt in cities of 8,000 or upwards. Out of 3,000,000 (the population exclusive of cities and towns), less than 20,000 were of foreign birth, or less than 1 percent. The Negro population is small, being about 11 percent of the whole.

great migrations over the mountains, westward, a century and a half
ago. Few of these pioneers stopped in the mountains, but kept on, till
they reached the lowlands. A quarter of a century later, or around the
beginning of the nineteenth century, the Highlands began to receive
a considerable influx of population. If the lot of the earlier pioneer was
difficult, that of the Highland pioneer was desperate. The latter was
lucky if he succeeded in preserving his skin, not to mention family
trees. Besides, had he not come to a new world to leave behind the Old
World and many of its traditions? He became sidetracked in the great
Highland wilderness, marooned and benighted in spite of himself,
while the tide of migration swept on to the lowlands and to the plains.
It is hardly to be wondered at, then, that the Highlander knows nothing of his ancestry beyond his grandfather or great-grandfather. Until
recent years no records of vital statistics have been made and preserved in the Highlands. Intermarriage among relations has long been
common, for obvious reasons, and has served to complicate further an
already difficult question. A mountaineer put it very well in this way:
"They are all Smiths, Joneses and Browns, married and intermarried,
cousin to cousin, second cousin to second cousin, and so on, till every
mother's son of them is his own grandmother, if he only knew how to
figure out the relationship."

Generally speaking, there appear to be two distinct classes of Highlanders: the typical, isolated Highlanders, and the plateau and valley
Highlanders. The first of these two classes, comprising about three
millions of inhabitants, is to demand our attention in this chapter,
since it is this class which is contributing much to folk-lore. The second
type of Highlanders consists of those inhabiting the prosperous cities
and towns, particularly in the Shenandoah Valley of Virginia, and in
Tennessee, Kentucky, West Virginia, and elsewhere. It is not necessary to dwell long on how the Highlanders found themselves in the
remote fastnesses of this region—whether it was because of the abun-
dant game and water, or because a member of the family fell ill en
route over the mountains, or because a wagon wheel broke down; they
are there, for better or for worse, and that is the point of interest. Much
has been written of the three great "reservoirs" from which the early
pioneers are often said to have migrated, central and western Pennsylvania, and the Piedmont section of North Carolina. The assumption
that the early pioneers did come from these reservoirs throws no light
on the ancestry of the Highlanders, since no evidence indicates that
the former, pushing their way southwestward from Pennsylvania,

stopped to reside in the mountains; they sought the smiling, level country farther west, in Kentucky and Tennessee. The further assumption that the early pioneers were of Scottish, or of Scottish-Irish extraction, which is improbable, leaves the question still unsolved, since, as has been remarked above, the Highlands had no noticeable population before the year 1800.

The theories of ancestry so far advanced by students and investigators are based largely upon conjecture, tradition, and hearsay. Absence of accurate data and records of nationality has left most of these theories unstable and untenable. Except for some general historical facts, we shall confine much of this discussion of ancestry to a study of the Highlander himself, his folk-lore and his surnames, and his language.

The Scottish and Scottish-Irish theories are the ones most commonly accepted, because they antedate the others, and have been widely advertised. The Anglo-Saxon theory has gained headway in recent years, although the term "Anglo-Saxon" is misleading and indefinite. Like "Anglo-Celtic," it is too vague. Let us examine some of the conclusions reached heretofore as to the ancestry of the Highlanders. If our discussion may appear to be too polemical, it is because we are trying to get at the truth of the matter. Fiske is of the opinion that the Highlanders are of Scottish-Irish ancestry.[3] The proponents of this theory seem to take Ulster (northern Ireland) as their starting point, transfer its inhabitants to the New World, people the original colonies with them, settle the entire Highland country, penetrate the mountains, and open up the great West. This is a remarkable feat for a few counties of northern Ireland; these counties had only a million and a half population even as late as 1910, including Scottish and Irish. The "Ulsterites," of Scottish extraction, have long been termed Scottish-*Irish*, which is a misnomer, since the majority of them went to Ulster from Scotland in the reign of James I. Almost no amalgamation, seemingly, occurred between the Scottish and the Irish in Ulster. The term was employed in the Scottish universities to distinguish the Scottish students of Ulster from those of Scotland. Says Fiske: "From the same prolific hive [Ulster] came the pioneers of Kentucky and Tennessee with their descendants through the Mississippi and beyond." Roosevelt also makes colonizers of the Ulsterites: "Though mingled with the descendants of other races, they were nevertheless the predominant

[3] John Fiske, *Old Virginia and Her Neighbors*, p. 394 and *passim*.

stock which formed the kernel of this distinctively American race who were the pioneers of our people in their westward march, the vanguard of the army of fighting settlers who with ax and rifle made their settlements in the mountains."[4] One is led to wonder when the Scots became such colonizers, and from whence so many of them came, outdistancing even the English. [The Scottish and Irish tendency to advertise their feats and accomplishments is well known, which may account for the splendid propaganda which they have for so long maintained and fostered.]

No note is taken here of the various "estimates" of the Scottish-Irish population of the Highlands. It is well known that most of the colonies, including Pennsylvania and North Carolina, kept no census records. But to return to Ulster. It appears that the Scottish Protestants had little success in converting or Protestantizing Ireland, and that they became dissatisfied with taxes imposed upon them by the British government, in consequence of which many of them began to migrate to the colonies. This migration began around 1727, and continued until the middle of the century. It is "estimated" that at the beginning of the American Revolution (1775) the Scottish-Irish in the colonies numbered 500,000—although no authoritative statistics are available. The population of the entire thirteen colonies at the time was under 3,000,000. For 155 years (1620–1775) the English had been keeping up a steady migration to the colonies. At the outbreak of the Revolution the predominant strain in *all* the colonies, Pennsylvania not excepted, was English. The only peoples other than the English who had migrated to the colonies were the Dutch and Belgians in New York, the Swedes in Delaware, and some French Huguenots in the Carolinas. But at the outbreak of the Revolution all these were overshadowed by the English.

Mr. Horace Kephart, like Fiske, Roosevelt, and others, assigns to the Scottish-Irish the important role of making the New World, and brings them out of Ulster to settle the Highlands. "One thing is certain: if any race was ordained to exterminate the Indians, that race was the Scotch-Irish."[5] Mere conjecture. It was the English who colonized the eastern part of the United States, who peopled the Highlands, who drove the Indians westward, as no serious historian disputes. In those days the English seem to have been adept not only at alienating the affections

[4] Theodore Roosevelt, *The Winning of the West*, I, 106.
[5] Horace Kephart, *Our Southern Highlanders*, p. 362.

of their colonies, but also at exterminating other races. Kephart makes much of the Ulster contribution. The Ulsterites were almost entirely Scottish Presbyterians. If the Highlanders are the descendants of these people, it is significant that there were no Presbyterians among them until Presbyterian missionaries came, along with Methodists, Baptists, and others. The religious faith of the Highlanders, where they live today, has always been, and is, that of the Primitive Baptists. Kephart remarks that the Scottish-Irish were Washington's favorite troops, that they carried the day in three great battles: Saratoga, Cowpens, and King's Mountain. Conjecture again, for obvious reasons: there were not enough of them. Besides, the assertion has no bearing on Highland ancestry, since the Highlands had no noticeable population during the Revolution. However, Mr. Kephart splendidly refutes the worn-out theory that the Highlanders are descendants of "poor whites" and criminals who escaped into the Highlands.

[A Mr. Perrow, of Louisville, Kentucky, falls into the "poor whites" and criminal theory.[6] He adds that "adventurous spirits" threaded their way through the mountain defiles to what was then the west, early after the settlement of eastern Virginia and North Carolina. As a matter of fact, this "threading" did not begin, to any appreciable extent, until a century and a half later, or until the Revolution, and therefore cannot be introduced as evidence. Even then the "adventurous spirits" did not settle in the Highlands. Mr. Perrow, in the article cited above, is one of the worst offenders: "Almost every affair of life" (among the Highlanders), says he, "is regulated in accordance with the sign of the moon." He also says that it is a custom to "sit up" with a dead body for *several* days. The "sign of the moon" superstition is not general, and the "sitting-up" accusation is ridiculous.]

The Reverend Samuel T. Wilson, in a book on the Southern Highlanders, also becomes entangled with the Ulster element, and thinks that the Scottish-Irish form at least fifty percent of the population. He says that this is "proved" by history, by tradition, and by the family names prevailing in the mountains; that Huguenot, Welsh, and German names are "numerous."[7] More conjecture, since the "proofs" mentioned by the Reverend Mr. Wilson appear to prove, to the contrary of his assertions, that the Southern Highlanders are rather of old

---

[6] [E. C. Perrow, "Songs and Rhymes from the South," *Journal of American Folklore*, XXV (1912), 137.]

[7] Samuel T. Wilson, *The Southern Mountaineers*, pp. 11–25.

English ancestry, as we shall try to demonstrate. The Huguenot, Welsh, and German names are rare, except in a few localities in North Carolina, Kentucky, and Virginia, and even there they are insignificant in number. Mr. Wilson is a Presbyterian minister. He discovered that such given names as Andrew, Hugh, James, John, and Samuel are common on the streets of Londonderry (Ulster), and also among the Highlanders, reasoning from this that the Highlanders are Scottish-Irish. Now, such names are common in England and France and elsewhere, and are purely and simply Biblical names, with the exception of Hugh, and consequently add nothing to the argument one way or the other. With respect to surnames, the Celtic, or Gaelic, patronymics represented by such words as "McCoy," "MacDaniel," "MacIntosh," and a few others may or may not suggest Scottish ancestry; however, such patronymics are in the minority.

The Scottish-Highlander theory can be dismissed briefly, since it never had any particular *raison d'être* in the first place. The mere fact that the Southern Highlander inhabits highlands, as does the Scottish Highlander, that he has had considerable advertising as a feudist, like the Scottish Highlander, that he is hardy and brave, like the Scottish Highlander, proves nothing. Such fallacious logic could as easily make Corsicans of the Southern Highlanders! Statistics of the British Isles show that the Highland population of Scotland was never extensive, at any time; the few Scottish Highlanders who migrated to America settled in Nova Scotia and Newfoundland, principally in the *lowlands*.

No attempt is made here to ignore the Scottish and Irish elements in the United States. There is no reason to doubt that considerable numbers of both migrated from the British Isles, the Scottish before the Revolution, and the Irish during the nineteenth century. But the number of Scottish has always been overestimated, and the importance of their exploits exaggerated. It is freely admitted that the majority of Scottish immigrants probably came from Ulster, and that they settled largely in Pennsylvania, later *crossing* the mountains to the south, but not *settling* in the Highlands, with the exception of parts of West Virginia, the Shenandoah Valley of Virginia, and a few counties of western Maryland. But the population of these same sections today is more English than Scottish. While not germane to our discussion, it may be well to note here that Daniel Boone, the celebrated pioneer, was not of Scottish-Irish extraction, as has so often been said, but of English. Likewise was Washington of English extraction.

By far the most authoritative work which has yet appeared on the Southern Highlanders is *The Southern Highlander and His Homeland*, by the late John C. Campbell of the Russell Sage Foundation, New York. It represents a study of twenty years among the Highlanders themselves, and approaches the subject with sympathy and understanding. Mr. Campbell leaves the question of ancestry unsolved, but admits that the *present* Highland population is probably English. He thinks that the early settlers, however, were Scottish-Irish.[8]

Most of our discussion of Highland ancestry up to this point has been a matter of refutation, a destructive method of criticism. We now approach a constructive method, and shall attempt to build up what seems to be the most plausible theory, the Old English. With the data at hand it certainly seems the most logical. Every man that is not ashamed of his family bears his family name. In this respect the mountaineer himself speaks loudest in the matter. Admittedly, a study of cognomens may not always prove to be absolute and conclusive, but in the absence of recorded facts one must lend a certain weight to them. Names belonging to Scotland, and which are Scottish beyond cavil, are in the great minority in the Southern Highlands. The percentage is around four or five to one in favor of names which the genealogist would record as English. The early petitions made by Transylvania County of Virginia (now Kentucky) to the State of Virginia before 1792 are often cited as evidence in favor of the Scottish-Irish theory, because a number of Scottish names appear in the petitions. This adds no evidence, since the Highlanders had nothing to do with the petitions, the Highlands at that time not even being inhabited. The petitions came from central and northern Kentucky.

An examination of the telephone directories in Highland towns reveals a great preponderance of English names here, as elsewhere over the South. Among the Highlanders one meets with such historic first names as Cicero, Virgil, Homer, Napoleon, etc. There is at least one Highlander who manages to struggle along under the flamboyant praenomen of "Cecil Calvert Lord Baltimore," and his cognomen is "Noble"! However, these historic first names throw no light on the question, since the Highlander likes to find names for his children in "hist'ry books," which are almost the only books he reads, when he reads at all. Reading fiction is against his principles, because, says he, "Hit ain't so."

[8] John C. Campbell, *The Southern Highlander and His Homeland*, pp. 50–71.

Undoubtedly the Highlander's surname demonstrates his English ancestry; so do his traditions, his dialect, his folk-lore, including folk-songs, play and dance songs, children's games and songs. In the far reaches of this vast region one hears no tales of early romance transported from Scotland, of clansmen and chieftains battling for their family's honor; no recounting of their forebears' deeds of valor along the English-Scottish border. One listens in vain for the wild, irregular pibroch of the bagpipe, for it is not there, nor does the Highlander have any traditions of it. The Scottish kilt is as foreign to the Southern Highlander as a Turkish fez. The Highlander's temperament is not Scottish in any respect, but English. It is that of a taciturn and conservative race, phlegmatic in character whenever the Highlander is face to face with an outsider.

There are few survivals of the Scottish vernacular among the Highlanders. These same survivals, with few exceptions, are also heard in England, and cannot be said, at this time, to be the exclusive property of the Scottish. On the other hand, Early and Elizabethan English are common, and even many Old English survivals have been noted.[9] A comparison of the Highlander's vernacular with Abbott's *A Shakespearian Grammar* demonstrates clearly that Highland speech belongs to the Elizabethan age. A few conversations with the Highlander seldom fail to reveal much of the vocabulary and idiom of Chaucer, Spenser, Cotgrave, Beaumont and Fletcher, and Shakespeare. There is also no inconsiderable amount of slang which belongs to the Elizabethan age, some of it being survivals of cant.[10] Doubtless more of this slang could be identified as belonging to the Early English period, were it not for the fact that slang does not appear to have been *written* so freely then as now. Compound nouns and expressions, a characteristic of Old English, are quite common.[11]

[The Highlander's folk-lore, particularly his folk-songs, throw some light on his ancestry. It may be argued that this is not convincing, since so many songs belong to the British Isles in general, and even to countries in Continental Europe, and since a number of the Highlander's songs are undoubtedly of Scottish origin. But the Scottish songs sung by the Highlander have been sheared of their former Scottish vo-

---

[9] Josiah H. Combs, "Old, Early and Elizabethan English," *Dialect Notes*, IV, 283 ff.

[10] J. H. Combs, "Early English Slang Survivals," *Dialect Notes*, V, 115 ff.

[11] Those interested in the Highlander's language as portrayed in fiction are referred to the stories of Will N. Harben, Charles Egbert Craddock, John Fox, Jr., and Lucy Furman.

cabulary, because they probably came from versions of the songs which were quite common in England also. The same process has been applied to children's songs, play-party songs, and others. If the Highlander were Scottish, the Scottish dialect would characterize his songs.]

Mr. Cecil J. Sharp, the greatest authority on English folk-music and folk-dance, thinks that "The strongest argument in favor of this view [English] is based on the character of the traditional songs and dances, which seem to me to be saturated with the Anglo-Celtic idiom to the exclusion of every other."[12] Mr. Sharp spent some time in the Southern Highlands and states that their predominant culture is overwhelmingly Anglo-Saxon; that the Highlander's everyday manners, habits, and customs are demonstrably Anglo-Saxon; that an analysis of his traditional songs, ballads and dances, singing-games, etc., and his physical characteristics demonstrate this.[13]

[An examination of the following Scottish songs surviving in the Highlands shows almost no traces of the Scottish dialect: "The Cruel Brother"; "Lord Randal"; "The Lass of Roch Royal"; "Little Musgrave and Lady Barnard"; "Bonny Barbara Allan"; "Mary Hamilton"; "Our Goodman." However, a few songs in the Scottish dialect have been found in West Virginia. The music of the Highlander's folk-songs appears to be English rather than Scottish. It has more affinity with the normal English folk-tune than with that of the Gaelic-speaking (Scottish) Highlander.[14]]

The most logical conclusion, then, is that the Southern Highlanders are of pure English extraction; that most of them are descendants of English colonists who were recruited largely from the great English commons. The ancestors of some of them may have migrated to the colonies in the eighteenth century. However, whatever nationality or ancestry one may ascribe to the English commons of the seventeenth and eighteenth centuries, whether Anglo-Saxon or otherwise, the same nationality may be applied to the Southern Highlanders in the United States. The Highlanders descend from neither Cavalier nor Puritan; they are not of noble lineage, probably, because it has never been established that the nobility of England in the sixteenth and seventeenth

[12] Letter to John C. Campbell, in *The Southern Highlander and His Homeland*, pp. 69–71.
[13] See also Cecil Sharp, *The Country Dance Book*, Part V.
[14] [See the introduction to *English Folk-Songs from the Southern Appalachians* by Olive Dame Campbell and Cecil Sharp.]

centuries sang ballads, preferring to listen to them, until royal edict interfered with the wandering minstrel and ballad singer. The Southern colonists descending from noble lineage have always as a rule known more or less about their ancestors, while the Highlander knows nothing of his. From what colonies, or states did the Highlander's forebears come? Doubtless from Virginia, Maryland, and the two Carolinas, from where they slowly pushed into the upland wilderness, where game and water were plentiful, and where the highland fastnesses offered protection and defense against the elements of nature and the attacks of the redmen.

CHAPTER III

The Question of Origin or Authorship

"ORAL LITERATURE" is no longer a contradiction in terms. The origin of much of it, however, is shrouded in mystery, and will always be. The student who launches himself out in an attempt to account for it finds himself therefore in uncharted waters. He arrives at conclusions which can be only theoretical or conjectural, although apparently buttressed by arguments which on the face of them may seem sound and reasonable. But things are not always what they seem to be, nor are they always what reason and logic would make them. If they were thus, many difficult questions would have been disposed of long ago, and Delphic utterances, long since dark oracles, would have ceased to be dark and vague. With the limitations incident to such a discussion, we approach the dangerous terrain of folk-song origin cautiously, with a certain amount of fear and trembling. The question has not been settled, nor is it likely that it will ever be settled. Our modest excuse for a few opinions, then, may carry with it something approaching justification.

[By way of introduction, it may be well to review some opinions hitherto set forth relative to the provenance of the traditional folk-song. The question may be said to have had its inception, indirectly, with F. A. Wolf's attack on the authorship of the Homeric poems, in 1795. This attack led to a consideration of the origin of the popular ballad, or folk-song. Percy and Ritson in England had commenced just previous to this a serious study of British folk-songs, but the question of origin was, for the most part, held in abeyance. In 1812 it received an impetus hitherto unknown in the hands of Jakob Grimm, the German philologist and folk-lorist. Up to the time of Grimm our popular folk-songs were assumed to be the productions of individual authors (unknown), as are the poems of artistic composition. Such an assumption had been accepted without much question. Grimm's theory, epitomized in the dangerous phrase, *das Volk dichtet,* is that the *people,* as a whole, composes poetry. However this dark oracle may be interpreted, and its interpretation has doubtless often gone awry, the major portion of folk-song criticism has followed in the footsteps of Grimm ever since. In one way or another, the question of origin has shifted from individual authorship to *popular,* or *folk,* origin; these terms, as we shall see, may easily be dangerous. The theory of minstrel authorship for British folk-songs has gradually played out and is no longer seriously considered.]

At the outset it appears that research and scholarship have conspired to saddle the folk-song with paraphernalia that it was never meant to carry, by introducing a mass of material which is too far removed to have a direct bearing on authorship. One condition is made to fit another, one age to coincide with another, with an amazing gesture of accuracy and cocksureness. Apparently everything but the *truth* has been established beyond all cavil. The very "mystery" of the question has added to its momentum, until the defenseless folk-song and its origin seem to have been completely thrown out of focus. Now it is the communal throng, with a voice in unison, that is producing the folk-song; now it is the folk or communal dance; now it is the European peasants of the Middle Ages; now the savage Botocudos of South America, who "never sing without dancing, never dance without singing"; now it is the Färöe Islanders, thronging around the returned fisherman and improvising songs about him; now a leprous monk of the fourteenth century, living on the banks of the Rhine and making songs for all the people: "There!" exclaims Böhme, in his *Altdeutsches Liederbuch,* "we have the secret about the origins of popular poetry," etc.; now it is the British minstrel, who was a worse rhymester than musician.

It is unsafe to accept as postulates conditions or things which are merely hypotheses, wanting in direct and conclusive proof. There is no reason for going too far beyond the *folk-song itself,* as it exists today, for a probable explanation of its origin or authorship. The conditions that produced it may not, after all, be so mysterious. Certainly the subject matter is neither ancient nor vague, in most cases. For it the folk has drawn upon the simple events of human experience, and in this respect a simple folk does not change materially, since it lives, loves, passes through the usual routine of earthly vicissitudes, sees good and bad, grows old and dies, very much as it always has done. [Its songs are merely an expression of its outlook on passing events. In this restricted sense they may be said to be of popular or folk origin. But, we say, a poem implies authorship; that much is reasonable, and easily within the bounds of common sense. It must have had a beginning; still easier of belief, else the poem would not have existed. The exact method of composition of the folk-song, as it has come down to us today, is another matter. Another thing is absolutely certain: the folk-song is the exclusive property of the folk, as opposed to the poem of artistic production, whose author we know, with pen in hand. The latter does not necessarily voice the sentiments of the community, but rather those of *himself*. Artistic poetry is, then, for the most part, *personal*, although it sometimes represents the feelings of a race, or nation, as in national anthems and epics. The folk-song on the other hand is not usually personal, for its author is speaking for the folk as a whole.]

Here we are led into a definition of the folk-song. Professor Kittredge defines it as "a short narrative poem, adapted for singing, simple in plot and metrical structure, divided into stanzas, and characterized by complete impersonality so far as the author or singer is concerned."[1] This appears to be a splendid definition. However, perhaps too much has been made of the elements of "narration" and "impersonality" in the folk-song. All folk-songs, as we know the term today, are not narrative; doubtless the earlier ones were, for in them the lyric element is rare. Many traditional songs of the people which have come down to us have an overwhelming lyric quality; others are equally divided between lyric and narration. Nor are all folk-songs impersonal. Even many traditional songs savor of the personal element "I," with moral reflections at the close. In many cases these elements are the work of the minstrel, for we know that this individual tampered with songs as he pleased. What could be more natural than a minstrel infusing a little of his personality into a song before an audience? Songs of more recent origin have much of the personal element in them, and are strongly lyric in many cases. If we measure the folk-song by standards of narration and impersonality, then its scope must be narrowed down to the earlier types, and we are not ready to admit that these are the only types which deserve the name of folk-songs. The term "folk-

[1] George Lyman Kittredge, Introduction to the abridged edition of Child's *English and Scottish Popular Ballads*, p. xi.

song," like many others, must in time lose its restricted significance, and come to be applied to the songs of the folk, whether narrative or not, impersonal or not. Not all of the present collection, by any means, are ballads, if the iron-clad rule of narration and impersonality is to be applied to them. They are included because they belong to the folk.[2]

[Most of the studies of the folk-song that have been made in America are based on Child's great compilation, and the songs in that work have come to be those by which others are measured. Professor Kittredge himself admits that not all Child songs are folk-songs, if they be measured by his own views in the matter. There is no reason for classing the Robin Hood cycle of poems as folk-songs, for various reasons. They are rather a cycle of metrical romances, perhaps never sung, except, in isolated instances, as fragments. Certainly their length would indicate that they were never sung. There is not any too much evidence that "A Geste of Robyn Hode" (Child No. 117) is "composed from *several ballads*," as Child thinks.[3] If one of the qualities of a folk-song is that it must have been *sung* to be called thus, many poems of the Child collection, as far as we know, would have to be omitted. *Is there any evidence that all these pieces were* SUNG? The fact that an anonymous poem of popular origin has been recovered from an ancient manuscript is not necessarily proof that it was ever sung. That is why some of the Child "songs" appear suspicious. "Riddles Wisely Expounded" (No. 1) bears the earmarks of antiquity rather than of a folk-song. It is probably nothing more nor less than a clever riddle poem, which poems were once common. I refer to Version A* among the variants. In the category of popular verse, not song, could also be classed the poems of sacred tradition in the Child collection: "St. Stephen and Herod," "Judas," "The Cherry-Tree Carol," "The Carnal and the Crane," and "Dives and Lazarus." "Judas" is the oldest of the songs in the Child collection, as far as manuscripts go, dating from the thirteenth century. It is probably a popular piece of folk verse.]

We are not here concerned with the antiquity of the British folk-song, whether or not it antedates the thirteenth century, whether its

---

[2] Under Kittredge's definition, the following songs in the Child collection might be questioned: Nos. 78, 84, 219, 292, 295, as well as other lyric songs.

[3] *Piers Plowman* mentions the Robin Hood poems, in no complimentary terms, in the latter half of the fourteenth century. They were evidently circulating at that time, but not as folk-songs.

origin must be associated with that of the epic, or whether it is older than the metrical romance.[4]

It is not a question of what remote conditions may or may not have had to do with certain vague origins. Those things would lead us too far afield of our study. The folk-song must be approached as we have it today—along with songs which have sprung up in recent years. Folk music has certainly existed from a very remote period; nobody doubts this. But this does not argue the folk-song of equal antiquity with it. Are we to return to such remote periods in order to obtain a perspective for the folk-song of the sixteenth and seventeenth centuries in the British Isles? But in order to examine certain opinions which have long been in vogue, it is necessary to touch briefly on some of these things.

Both Gummere and Grundtvig set much store by a simple incident related by the chronicler, Thomas of Ely, in his *Historia Eliensis*, written in the second half of the twelfth century.[5] King Canute (1017–1035) paid a visit to Ely and the church, according to the chronicler, and composed a song, the first and only remaining stanza of which has since occasioned much comment among scholars, relative to folk-song origins. The mysterious stanza follows:

> Merie sungen the Muneches binnen Ely,
> Tha Cnut ching rew ther by.
> Roweth, cnihtës, noer the land,
> And herë we thes munechës sang.

Gummere thinks these four lines are the first glimpse of ballad structure, that the missing verses were probably epic, relating Canute's conquest—a chronicle ballad in the grand style. Evidently the four lines have been given a prominence which they never deserved. The passage of the king by Ely was probably a mere incident not worthy of the grand epic, a visit made to the church. The lines have little or nothing to do with the history and authorship of the folk-song. If the chronicler has not lied, the king made the song himself, a fact which hardly coincides with Gummere's theory of authorship, that of communal composition. Canute's verse, like that of most kings, does not seem to have had merit enough to live, even among the folk. Besides,

---

[4] Frank Sidgwick thinks that it is a genre older than the epic, than tragedy, than literature, than the alphabet! (*The Ballad*, pp. 7, 39). Mere conjecture, since there is no evidence whatsoever for such an extreme opinion.

[5] Francis Barton Gummere, *The Popular Ballad*, pp. 58–60; Svend Grundtvig, *Danmarks gamle Folkeviser*, p. ix ff.

had the simple occasion produced a "grand ballad epic," that late in history, it is probable that we should have it today.

We turn now to an examination of the theory of throng or communal improvisation or composition for the folk-song [—a theory, which like many others "Made in Germany" is too feeble to stand upon its own legs. It has, to use the words of Lincoln, been "bounded on the north, south, east and west," until it has come to be too commonly accepted, although lacking in conclusive evidence]. Because of it the folk-song has been made a legitimate offspring of the singing or dancing throng, the two being inseparable, one and indivisible. The theory is too well known to require excerpts from the opinions of those who champion it. Yet it needs explanation in order to avoid possible confusion or vagueness. It is held that the traditional British folk-song, as we now have it, is the work not of an individual, but of a community, or throng, either in dancing or singing, or both. Corollary to this extreme view is the one less extreme: that the community or throng played a prominent part in the making of the song, in one way or another; that an individual made the song, which was later taken up by the throng, or vice versa, that the individual singer adopted it after the throng had made it. However tenable or untenable any of these views may be, we must not misunderstand their proponents; some of these scholars doubtless did not intend to convey the impression that the folk-song *extant* is the actual production of the throng, but rather that the song may be traced back to the singing, dancing throng. Kittredge had made this clear in his Introduction to the Child songs. If *communal* is to be applied to a throng gathered together for the purpose of singing, dancing, or both, at which gathering folk-songs are made (presumably by improvisation), then the issue is clear-cut. Evidently a number of scholars construe the term in this way. If *communal* has reference to the folk public merely, individuals of which give different variants of songs, each in his own way, because of oral transmission, then the theory begins to appear more reasonable: namely, that the folk-song originally had an individual composer, whose identity is long since lost, the song becoming, so to speak, the property of the *folk*. This seems to be the opinion of certain American scholars, among whom are Phillips Barry, C. Alphonso Smith, Louise Pound, and possibly G. L. Kittredge.

However, the phrase "individual authorship plus communal recreation" may not be entirely clear. That depends on the construction or meaning of the word "communal." Here C. J. Sharp does not make himself clear, although he does not use the phrase referred to.[6] After saying that the folk-song must have been originally the work of an individual, he continues: "Whether or not the individual in question can be called the author, is another matter altogether," etc. Later he says: "The folk-song is therefore communal in two senses; communal in authorship, and communal in that it reflects the mind of the community." On page 93 he again says that the ballad was perhaps communal in performance, as in authorship. On page 31 he says: "Communal composition is unthinkable. The community plays a part, it is true, but it is at a later stage, after, and not before the individual has done his work and manufactured the material." On this point one is led to wonder who deserves the credit for the folk-song, its original, individual composer (granting that he made the song) or the folk who changed it after him, to suit the conditions. The bare fact remains that without the individual composer we perhaps should not have had the song. However much transformation it has undergone in language is secondary, provided the thread of the story and its principal incidents remain intact. [The ways of verse are different from the ways of the prose narrative. For example, *A* returns to the community and relates in his simple folk language the story of an unusual incident that has just taken place on the public highway. It at once becomes the story and the property of the whole community, and nobody attempts to remember the exact words used by *A*, but only the story. After a reasonable length of time the story is forgotten; that is, by the community as a whole. *B* returns to the same community and relates the same story, let us say, in his own way. He is so moved by the incident that he writes (or makes orally) a song about it. The song becomes the property of the folk, and even spreads to distant communities. Now, common sense compels us to accord to *B* the authorship of the song, even though the song has undergone some changes.]

Returning to the question of communal composition by *improvisation*, the favorite theory of Gummere, we are confronted by an opinion that does not, so far as we know, hold good for any one of the three hundred and five songs of the Child collection. On the face of the matter, it is difficult to understand how such an ancient institution as the singing, dancing throng could have produced the finished folk-songs of the sixteenth and seventeenth centuries. With very few exceptions, there is no proof that these songs antedate the centuries

---

[6] Cecil J. Sharp, *English Folk-Song: Some Conclusions*, p. 10.

mentioned—and we must study the question from the age that gave them to us. If the Angles and Saxons had folk-songs in abundance when they invaded Britain, none of them have come down to us, nor do we know that they were songs of the types under discussion. What concerns us is that which *exists*, and not what *may have been* at a remote period. Practically all the manuscript evidence available indicates that the epic or metrical romance antedates the folk-song as we now have it. It is not denied that the throng improvised, and even that it improvised songs; there is ample proof of this. But it is vigorously disputed that such a process produced the folk-songs of the sixteenth and seventeenth centuries; for we know that the subject matter of some of these songs is not older than those centuries. The throng, so far as we know, had absolutely nothing to do with the composition of those later songs. Significantly, the earliest ballad scholars, such as Percy and Ritson, make no mention of such a process of composition, although they lived at a time which was not far removed from the seventeenth century, a period which produced many folk-songs.

Gummere thinks that European peasants in the Middle Ages improvised ballads (folk-songs) in song and dance, thus establishing a type of balladry superior to and having more vitality than anything of the kind which had its origin in individual ownership. Aside from the bald hypothesis introduced in this statement with respect to mode of composition, we have no tangible evidence of such a superior type. Now, those songs that do result from communal improvisation—and evidence is not lacking here—cannot be placed alongside our folk-songs, nor do they deserve the name of folk-songs of the Child type. Could the serious student attempt to compare the crude improvisations of the Färöe Islanders, or the Negro spirituals, with the finished products, "Mary Hamilton," "Sir Patrick Spens," and "The Golden Vanity"? Or with any of the better Child songs? As to the vitality of the improvised song little needs to be said—for it has never known much vitality when compared with the folk-song.

Many aboriginal peoples have been summoned to the tribunal to testify in behalf of the theory of communal composition, including especially the Färöe Islanders and the Botocudos of South America. In addition to the probability that such aboriginal improvisations have little bearing on British balladry, it might be mentioned that another aboriginal people, the North American Indians, makes songs, but there is no record of communal improvisation among them. Their songs are

individual, as Louise Pound has pointed out.[7] More research has perhaps been made among the North American Indians than among
any other aboriginal people.

It remains to go into detail as to the relationship which ballad structure, and particularly a process of repeating known as "incremental
repetition," bears to folk-song origins, especially to communal composition. For such repetition seems to be one of the chief features of the
songs of primitive peoples. Briefly explained, the process consists of
the repetition, in each stanza of a given song, of the substance of each
preceding stanza, with some variation which advances the story.[8] Its
origin may go back to the singing, dancing throng, which evidently
developed song before the individual. Gummere devotes fifteen pages
to a discussion of this primitive process of song in support of his theory,
using "The Maid Freed from the Gallows" as a type.[9] Kittredge comments on the song, but adds, ". . . we are here concerned not with
'The Hangman's Tree' itself, but with *what it stands for.*"[10] He is evidently of the opinion that our popular folk-songs originated in the
throng, but says that such a method of composition cannot be proved
for any of the English and Scottish ballads.

It must be borne in mind that "incremental repetition" is not the
chief feature of all our popular folk-songs, or even of many of them,
but only of a few of them. It may be that it owes its existence to the
communal throng; but does this prove a similar genesis for the folk-
song in general? One type of composition or literature may consciously
or unconsciously influence another without being the source of authorship of the later type itself. In this instance the folk-song may
easily be indebted to the communal throng, without having been produced by it. And if we assume that the throng developed music and
song before the individual, borrowing on the part of the folk-song is
not difficult to understand. However, we speak of a principle, and not
of the direct borrowing of stanzas. For it is not probable that any of
our fine stanzas of incremental repetition were taken over directly
from the throng. But the integrity of the principle involved may not
be affected, one way or the other. If incremental repetition produced
our folk-songs, the principle ought at least to apply to all or most of

[7] Louise Pound, *Poetic Origins and the Ballad*, pp. 13–22.
[8] Cf. the Negro songs in the present collection, as well as others.
[9] Gummere, *The Popular Ballad*, pp. 117–132, and elsewhere in his works.
[10] Kittredge, Introduction to Sargent-Kittredge, p. xxvi.

them. It applies only to a few. Such a process of composition, then, may be said to be only an incident in the development of the folk-song, and not evidence for the source. [It may be significant that not one traditional British folk-song, as far as we know, is an essential part of, or is even used in a single play-party or dance in the United States. And the American play and dance songs are almost without exception British in origin. Newell discovered an isolated instance, however, in New England, of a party of children who sang "Barbara Allen" in one of their gatherings.[11] But the song fits in with no particular children's games or movement songs. There is no evidence that *any* of the British folk-songs were ever used as dance or play songs.[12]]

Throng improvisations are of necessity hasty, and are arrived at with no thought or deliberation. One wonders how our finished folk-songs could descend from them. The proponents of the theory like to contend that the throng takes its inspiration from incidents, real or imaginary, that have transpired in or near the community. If such be the process, what are we to say about certain songs that have enjoyed great currency not only in the British Isles, but over Europe in general, and even in Asia? Reference is made of course to the story embodied in these songs. The stories thus told are not likely to have inspired the singing, dancing throng to sudden outbursts of song, since they are of little interest to the community, and may be said to have no direct bearing on its own peculiar methods of improvisation.[13] Nor are songs with such stories likely to be improvised by the singing, dancing throng of the Färöes, whose members make merry around the returning fisherman!

An almost painful simplicity marks improvisation, especially incremental repetition. Our folk-songs contain many stanzas which it is difficult to believe came to us in this way; stanzas that are highly artistic (though perhaps unconsciously so), and which are almost certain to be those of some individual, part and parcel. [They appear in earlier song, and in later ones.] The worn-out expression that our folk-songs are artless does not hold good; but their art is of course not the

---

[11] [W. W. Newell, *Games and Songs of American Children*, pp. 78–79—D. K. W.]

[12] [Louise Pound ably supports this view in *Poetic Origins and the Ballad*, pp. 81–82, by reference to *The Complaynt of Scotland*, (1549). In this book a throng is made to sing a number of songs, some of them Child songs, after which the company dance in a ring, where not one Child song is sung.]

[13] Some of the songs of wide currency are: "The Elfin Knight," "Lady Isabel and the Elf Knight," "Our Goodman," "The Farmer's Curst Wife."

studied result of the conscious artist, sitting alone with pen in hand, wondering what the world is going to think of his production. Let us examine some artistic stanzas. A Tennessee variant of "The Trooper and the Maid" (Child No. 299) has this stanza borrowed from "Jamie Douglas" (Child No. 204), and appearing in a variant of "Waly, Waly, Gin Love be Bonny":

> "O when will you come back, my love,
> Or when will we get married?"
> "When conk-shells turn to silver bells,
> O then, my love, we'll marry."

[Also one of its British archetypes:

> When cockle-shells turn silver bells,
> And mussels they bud on a tree
> When frost and snow turns fire to burn,
> Then I'll sit down and dine wi' thee.]

Some good stanzas from other songs follow:

> [There's many a star in the heavens above,
> And a green bunch of grass below;
> What a heavy, heavy cross will hang on a man
> That will treat a poor girl so.
> >   "The False Young Man" (North Carolina)

> [The blackest crow on yonder hill,
> Although she may turn white,
> If ever I prove false to you, my love,
> Bright day shall turn to night.
> >   "My Dearest Dear" (Kentucky)

> [When I see your babe a-laughing
> It makes me think of your sweet face;
> But when I see your babe a-crying
> It makes me think of my disgrace.
> >   "The Dear Companion"
> >   (North Carolina)]

> I wish I'd known before I courted,
> That love had been such a killing crime;
> I'd a locked my heart with a key of golden,
> And tied it down with a silver line.
> >   "Little Sparrow" (Kentucky)

[I never will believe what another boy says,
Let his eyes be dark or brown,
Unless he's upon a high gallows top,
Saying, "Love, I'd rather come down."
        "The False Young Man" (Kentucky)]

"Fly down, fly down, little birdie," she said,
"And 'light down on my right knee;
Your cage shall be decked with silver and gold,
And hung on a weeping-willow-tree."

"I could fly down, if I would fly down,
And 'light on your right knee;
But the way you've murdered your own true love,
You surely would murder me."

"Oh if I had my cedar bow,
My arrow and my string,
I'd shoot a diamond through your heart,
And you'd no longer sing."

"As you've not got your cedar bow,
Your arrow and your string,
I'll fly in the top of yonder's tree,
And there I'll sit and sing."
        "Young Hunting" (Kentucky)[14]

He loves me a little,
Like the dew-cup on the corn;
He puts it on at evening,
He takes it off at morn.
        "To Cheer the Heart"
            (Kentucky)

[Go dig my grave both wide and deep,
Place a marble stone at my head and feet,
And upon my breast a turtle-dove,
To show the world I died for love.
        "The Brisk Young Lover" (Kentucky)

["Don't you remember in yonder's town,
In yonder's town a-drinking,
You made the healths go round and round,
But slighted Barb'ry Allen?"

"Yes, I remember in yonder's town,
In yonder's town a-drinking,

[14] [This example, printed in the French version, is not in the English MS—
D. K. W.]

I drank a health to the ladies all around,
But my love to Barb'ry Allen."
"Bonny Barbara Allen" (Kentucky)

["What hills are those, my own true-love,
Those hills so black and blue?"
"It's the hills of hell, my own true-love,
Awaiting both me and you."

"What hills are those, my own true-love,
Those hills as white as snow?"
"It's the hills of heaven, my own true-love,
Where you and I can't go."
"James Harris" (West Virginia)]

It may be contended that some of the stanzas quoted above are not representative of the traditional folk-song. But the songs from which they are taken are traditional, and their origin is likewise vague, although not all of them are narrative. Kittredge's contention that "Waly, Waly, Gin Love be Bonny" is not a folk-song because it is not distinctly narrative is questionable.[15] But the point is that the above stanzas could hardly have been improvised by the communal throng on the spur of the moment, without deliberation; nor do they appear to be the work of medieval peasants, nor of the village throng dancing and singing around the returned fisherman of the Färöes. Such stanzas bear the unmistakable mark of individual authorship.[16]

The commonplace of the folk-song, that is, the recurrence of lines or stanzas, a process closely associated with incremental repetition, does not necessarily point back to communal composition. On the face of the matter, the process is one which appears natural enough, since the folk-song maker as an unconscious plagiarist is notorious. He borrows from other songs at will, and extensively. He is in this respect, then, certainly not the author of certain commonplace lines or stanzas, but the borrower of them. As a rule they form no integral part of the story, but are seized upon by the song maker to "fill in," because these

---

[15]Kittredge, Introduction to Sargent-Kittredge, p. xi. [Combs' misinterpretation of Kittredge's statements is rather typical of the often confusing uses of *ballad* and *folksong* during the dispute over "communal origins." Kittredge was pointing out that impersonality "distinguishes the ballad, strictly so called, from the purely lyrical poem. Such a song as 'Waly, waly, gin love be bony' . . . is, then, not a ballad, though it tells a story." One may, of course, question the treatment of "Waly, Waly" as a "purely lyrical poem" if it tells a story—D. K. W.]

[16] The better lyric songs certainly cannot be of popular origin; many of them, whose authorship is long since forgotten, are the work of skillful hands.

stanzas are so common in other songs which he knows. But their provenance? They appear to be no more mysterious than the average stanza of songs which are free from them. Many of them are artistic enough, and could easily be classed with the stanzas quoted above. The commonplace has a parallel in our habit of quoting certain lines or phrases from the written literature of the conscious artist, many of which have been used so much that we are not certain whether they be from Shakespeare, Milton, Gray, or from the Bible. In like manner may an aphorism in time lose all identity as to authorship, and become the property of everybody. "To hell with the Hapsburgs and Hohenzollerns" is the epithet hurled by the late Henry Watterson at Austria and Germany; within a generation or so, perhaps historians will be studiously seeking to ferret out its source.

From the viewpoint of structure, there is no logical reason for the assumption that the folk-song cannot be imitated.[17] That depends on the familiarity of the student with the folk-song, plus a certain amount of native ability at versifying. Percy and Walter Scott seem to have succeeded fairly well, for there is evidence that these two indefatigable folk-lorists added much to the lore of the "folk." And if Scott made "Kinmont Willie," the job was done so well that to all intents and purposes few people know the difference, if any there be. However, such a song thus made, once we know its source, as emanating from a literary artist, cannot be called a folk-song, unless it has been adopted by the folk. The point is that the folk-song can be imitated, and has been imitated. But this does not mean that all who have tried it have succeeded, nor that the attempts have been numerous. Sidgwick thinks that "You cannot write a popular ballad; in truth, you cannot even write it down."[18] However questionable the first part of this statement may or may not be, one wonders what interpretation should be given to the latter part. As wide as the divergence may be between the poetry of the folk and the poetry of art—and the chasm that separates the two is clear-cut—both are possible of imitation. The broadside, or stall-ballad, itself, offers partial proof for imitation, if we accept certain songs thus made as having no association or connection with previous originals. And some, as far as we know, seem to have no connection

[17] Sidgwick, *The Ballad*, pp. 7, 39; Pound, *Poetic Origins*; Frank E. Bryant, *A History of English Balladry*; Kittredge, Introduction to Sargent-Kittredge; and others.

[18] [Sidgwick, *The Ballad*, p. 39—D. K. W.]

with originals. The Child collection contains a number of broadsides, as do most other collections; they are freely accepted as folk-songs, although some of them doubtless never originated among the folk. On the other hand, some stall-ballads may point back to folk-originals, now lost beyond recall. That is a question which can never be settled. There is no absolute standard by which folk-song structure is to be measured, except that the song-story be told in the simple language of the folk; and this, like the language of the conscious artist, is subject to variation. Iteration, or incremental repetition, is not the chief mark of folk-song style, nor are we certain that such style was characteristic of the early folk-song.

Again, communal improvisation hardly seems possible for the finished folk-songs that have come down to us. No stretch of the imagination can lead us to believe that the communal throng had even the slightest connection with the making of "The Battle of Otterburn" and "The Hunting of the Cheviot" (Child Nos. 181, 162), which derive their material from the same source, the battle mentioned in the first title. They tell a story, and tell it well, with an imposing array of incidents and names of fallen warriors. We are not ready to believe that the hasty improvisations of the throng would have done the job so well, nor would the throng have carried the song to such length.

Communal improvisation is not a theory, but a fact, when applied to some other types of song. Our discussion has not been for the purpose of refuting its existence, even in modern times. Negro spirituals are largely the result of it; and one needs only to observe some of the old-time religious services among the Negroes of the South in the United States to be convinced. Such songs are as a rule simple and elemental, and seldom tell a story. Their singers often dance about until worn out by fatigue. A glance at such songs reveals a wide chasm between this type of song and the folk-song of the traditional type.[19] Even "The Maid Freed from the Gallows," the high-water mark of iterative composition, is far superior to the Negro spirituals. These simple, elemental Negro improvisations hold no hope for the study of folk-song origin. They are destined to throw little light on an already difficult question.

[19] I have seen many religious services in which a song is prolonged indefinitely by various members of the congregation until the singers almost fall from exhaustion, or until the "climax of relations" is exhausted. See, in this collection, "Jacob's Ladder," "We Have Fathers Gone to Heaven," "The Ship That Is Passing By," "I Got a Robe."

[The traditional British *rondes*[20] surviving in the United States are replete with iteration and incremental repetition, and are doubtless the result of a species of communal improvisation, not because such repetition is their chief mark, but because that seems to be the only explanation for them, owing to the manner in which they are played and sung, and to their undoubted antiquity. They, at least, point straight back to the singing, dancing throng, and the method of their composition is neither vague nor mysterious. In fact, they represent the throng "in action." There is evidence that many or most of them were once the property of grownups, who in time discarded them, leaving them to the children. But these *rondes*, like other primitive types, must not be too closely associated with the folk-song, whose genesis and development must be viewed from a different angle.[21]]

The method of composition of the folk-song has not changed, nor is it likely that it will change as long as it shall continue to be made among classes where the conditions for its composition and propagation are favorable. If communal improvisation produced the folk-song as we now have it, a similar process should be in vogue today; for we know that the art of ballad-making is not lost, numerous examples of it existing in different parts of the United States today. There appears to be no reason why the process of composition should change. In the Southern Highlands of the United States there dwells a class of society which is not far removed from its ancestors of the sixteenth and seventeenth centuries, in the British Isles, as far as its manners and customs are concerned, and its outlook on life in general. Three and four centuries ago song-making was at its zenith in the British Isles. Then in the eighteenth century balladry declined, undergoing a near débacle. A second phase of balladry may be said to have been entered upon, in the New World, when the people of isolated and remote sections in America brought about its renaissance, or rather continued what their

[20] [By *ronde* Combs means a ring play or game song, although the text quoted in the following note is usually classed as a fliting—D. K. W.]

[21] [A good type of the traditional *ronde* surviving in the Southern Highlands is "The Keys of Heaven" or "The Paper of Pins," which begins:

I'll give to you a paper of pins
If that's the way your love begins,
    If you'll be my true-lover.
I won't accept your paper of pins,
If that's the way your love begins,
    And I won't be your true-lover.]

ancestors had discarded. We venture to lay down as a postulate, then, that the method of composition among the Southern Highlanders today, if not exactly the same, must be very similar to that employed by the ancestors of the Highlanders. If the process is the same for both ages, the question of origin or authorship may not seem so mysterious, after all. Things equal to the same thing are equal to each other.

The folk-songs that the Highlander makes today should have a hearing whenever the question of origin or method of composition is the issue. In the Highlands the process is always that of individual composition. As far as is known, not one recent song of that section is the product of communal improvisation. The same thing can be said of other sections of America, wherever the folk-song is still made— chiefly among the lumbermen of Maine and the Northwest, the cowboys of the plains, railroad workingmen, rivermen, and others. We must accept these songs as folk-songs, for they are as much the property of the folk as ever were the songs of the British Isles four centuries ago. Most of them tell a story, their language is simple, and here and there their makers inject certain commonplace lines and stanzas, and words and phrases, from the traditional British folk-song. The making of folk-songs has been in progress since the era of colonization, although the songs surviving from that period are not numerous.

For a consideration of the genesis and development of the native American folk-song of the Southern Highlands, nine songs in the present collection are worthy of examination: "Floyd Frazier," "J. B. Marcum," "William Baker," "Talt Hall," "Hiram Hubbert," "The C. & O. Wreck," "Little Omie Wise," "Springfield Mountain," and "John Hardy." All of these but "Springfield Mountain" are native to the Highlands and are not yet hoary with age, none of them being older than the period of the Civil War. "Floyd Frazier" dates from 1907, the year in which the murderer in the song was hanged, in Letcher County, Kentucky. "J. B. Marcum" dates from the assassination of a prominent lawyer in Breathitt County, Kentucky, about twenty years ago. "William Baker" is about half a century old. "Talt Hall" dates from the early '90's when the "bad man of the mountains" was hanged, in Virginia, for the murder of a score of men. "Hiram Hubbert" dates from the Civil War. "The C. & O. Wreck" is not older than the year 1913. "John Hardy" is about a quarter of a century old. "Springfield Mountain" is about a hundred and fifty years old.

It will be noticed that none of the above songs, save "John Hardy," have stolen the thunder of the traditional folk-song, thus breaking away from the borrowing of stock stanzas, commonplaces, lines and phrases. "Floyd Frazier" was made by a Highland singer, Mrs. Mahala Day; "William Baker" is said to have been made by Baker himself, on his death-bed; the origin of "Little Omie Wise" is explained by Louise Pound.[22] "Bad Tom Smith" and "Jack Combs" were made by the two dying men themselves, both of whom were my close relations! These songs, along with many others, may easily mirror the process of ballad-making that was in vogue in the British Isles, and are beyond all question the work of individuals. All of them but "John Hardy," "Springfield Mountain" and "Little Omie Wise" have undergone little or no change [,only a single version of each being extant, as far as we know]. "John Hardy" was borrowed from the Negroes. The incremental repetition in this song is delightful. But it is not necessary to know the name of the maker of the folk-song; such a detail carries with it no interest. What is to the point is the negative fact: that communal composition has nothing to do with the making of any of these more recent songs.

I have seen none of the above songs "written down" among the Highlanders; they circulate orally. Although some of them are very recent, nobody seems to be interested in their composers, and cares less. In fact, whenever the Highlander makes a song, he seldom advertises it as his own. Seldom does he write it down when he makes it. Evidently the composer neither improvises nor falls into a trance for his song, as one Highlander frankly confesses, in "Floyd Frazier":

> This song came to me
> By day and by night,
> I think it is right to sing it
> In this vain world of *delight*.

Whenever the Highlander writes a song down, whether of his own making or not (and he seldom writes a song down), he usually writes at the top of the page, "Song Ballet," in lieu of a title. Sometimes he writes at the end, "Written by So-and-So" (with his name); which is often confusing, but is usually understood to mean that he merely has copied the song. Illiteracy of the song maker has been overemphasized by scholars.

---

[22] Pound, *American Ballads and Songs,* note to No. 51.

The folk-songs made by the Highlander are founded on fact, as are many of the traditional British songs of the narrative type. Wherever the song tells a story, its source is as a rule known. If we are to associate the folk-song with the metrical romance, and the two may be viewed from similar angles in certain respects, the method of folk-song composition in the Highlands of the United States may throw additional light on certain aspects of the metrical romance. The making of Highland songs is contemporary with the events which the songs describe, almost without exception. The Highlander, following a natural impulse, makes a song at about the time the incident described in his song transpires, usually only a few days after its occurrence. After years and years, or even after months or weeks, the incentive for composition is lost, since the incident ceases to be a topic of daily discussion as time passes. Of course, a distinction must be made between the simple lay of the Highlander and the "epic in grand style" of an age long past; the conditions favorable to the latter have passed, and we shall likely have no more folk-songs of "The Battle of Otterburn" type, nor any more "Chansons de Roland." But the principle involved in their making may be the same for both. However, the contrary may be argued with some force, since the epic usually reflected the sentiments of a whole people, or race, and was national in scope, long remembered by the nation as a whole, thus affording inspiration for makers of verse generations after the occurrence of the incident.

Minstrel composition for British folk-songs, the theory of Percy, Scott, and the early scholars, is no longer tenable. Joseph Ritson was the first English scholar to assail vigorously this theory.[23] But it is probable that the role of the minstrel in the propagation of folk-songs has not been given the prominence that it deserves. But for this mighty figure, balladry would perhaps never have arrived at the great currency and diffusion which it once enjoyed. Associated with song as he evidently was, the minstrel cannot be entirely ruled out of court, any more than can the *trouvere* or the *troubadour* in a discussion of French lyric poetry of the Middle Ages.[24] There is evidence of minstrel composition although not enough to induce us to conclude that the songs

---

[23] Joseph Ritson, *Ancient Songs* (1790).
[24] See Alfred Jeanroy, *Les origines de la poésie lyrique en France au moyen-âge*; Gaston Paris, "Les origenes de la poésie lyrique in France en moyen-âge," *Journal des Savants* (1891–1892); Joseph Bédier, *De Nicolao Museto* (Colin Muset), 1893.

of this kind are numerous.[25] James Rankin, the "blind beggar," made some of the songs of the Child collection, although they are of an inferior type.[26] The minstrel seems to have meddled with folk-song, because his business was to sing and entertain, and he freely adapted the songs of the folk to his own purposes. Probable evidence of this may be seen in personal touches here and there in the folk-song, such as the use of the first personal pronoun and the inclusion of certain moralizing stanzas at the close of songs. It is difficult to believe that the minstrel, who once catered to the demands of the high and noble, later met the demands of the common people by breaking up epics into smaller pieces (folk-songs).[27]

The social atmosphere of the folk-song of the traditional type is that of all classes—noble, middle, and lower—and from that no tangible evidence can be deduced as to the class of society that made the songs. Some of them may have been made for the delectation of the upper classes, and if they were, especially the longer ones of the epic type, they are the work either of minstrels or of members of the upper classes. Traditional songs as a whole, however, do not suggest noble origin. The opening lines of "Robin Hood Newly Revived" (Child No. 128 A) are not those of the folk-singer, nor is the song a typical folk-song, but rather that of a minstrel or poet:

> Come listen a while, you *gentlemen* all,
> That are in this *bower* within.

The concluding two lines of the poem,

> If you will have any more of bold Robin Hood,
> In his second part it will be,

---

[25] "The Boy and the Mantle" (Child No. 25) and "Crow and Pie" (Child No. 111) are minstrel compositions.

[26] [The authenticity of many of the ballads printed by Peter Buchan and the role played in their collection or composition by Buchan's assistant James Rankin are still in contention. See my *Anglo-American Folksong Scholarship Since 1898*, (New Brunswick, New Jersey, 1959) pp. 88, 102–103—D. K. W.]

[27] Child was of the opinion that our folk-songs are the work of a fraternity, whose business it was to provide tales and songs for the amusement of all ranks of society. He does not rule the minstrel out of court. [Combs apparently refers to Child's article in Johnson's *Universal Cyclopaedia* (1874). Although Child's discussion is none too clear, the section summarized by Combs seems to credit professional entertainers with disseminating the ballad *stories* among various nations, rather than specifically connecting minstrels with ballad authorship—D. K. W.]

suggest that the poem is one of the cycle, made by a minstrel or epic poet.[28]

The picture mirrored in the folk-song is not all that of chivalry, not all that of king, court, and palace; the middle class of society is well represented, and this is the class that probably gave us the bulk of our traditional songs. An examination of the Child songs, not to speak of many songs not in Child, is ample proof that the social atmosphere of the folk-song is not all that of the upper classes. Mere mention of lords, knights, ladies, princes, princesses, castles, and the like in songs does not argue their high descent; the simple song maker of the folk draws on incidents created by the upper classes, as the upper classes paint scenes from the lowly, or delineate that class in verse and story. The opening lines of one variant of "Young Beichan" appear to be noble in atmosphere, but not in composition:

> There was a man who lived in England,
> And he was of some high degree.

The poet of noble lineage would hardly commence a song in this way. "Thomas Potts," "The Kitchie Boy," "Lamkin," and "Richie Story" do not by any means exhaust the atmosphere of the lowly in the folk-song. "James Harris," which shares with "Barbara Allen" a very extensive currency over the United States, reflects no aristocratic atmosphere. Louise Pound's assumption that all literature (English?) up to the eighteenth century is aristocratic, is not well founded.[29] Certainly there is no aristocratic atmosphere in "Piers Plowman," not to mention other productions prior to the eighteenth century. And we know that not all *literati* up to that century were aristocrats.

From the preceding discussion the following summary presents itself:

1. *Communal composition* or *improvisation* for the traditional British folk-song, as for the native American folk-song, is untenable. It is

---

[28] One wonders what part the common people could have played in the making of the following stanza:

> When Phoebus had melted the sickles of ice,
> And likewise the mountains of snow,
> Bold Robin Hood he would ramble to see,
> To frolick abroad with his bow.
> —"Robin Hood and the Ranger" (Child No. 131).

[29] Pound, *Poetic Origins and the Ballad*, p. 105.

not certain that the folk-song *as we now have it* is even remotely connected with the singing, dancing throng.

2. *Popular origin* is a dangerous, uncertain phrase, and also untenable, if it be interpreted as meaning that the throng made the folksong, or that the folk built it up little by little, stanza by stanza.

3. *Individual authorship* plus *communal composition,* or *communal re-creation,* cannot be seriously considered, unless it mean that various individuals among the folk, lacking written copies, and often illiterate, changed minor details of the song from time to time, thus causing variants. Even in this case, the word *communal* is a misnomer.

4. The *minstrel* theory has spent its force, and is not formidable.

5. *Individual authorship* alone is hardly correct, since for the most part the songs of British origin have not come down to us as their authors first made them.

6. *Individual authorship* plus later *individual remaking,* or *re-creation,* which may or may not be termed *popular,* since the individual belongs to the folk, may be accepted. The method of remaking is of course unconscious and unstudied, the result of oral transmission. The author is not always, nor usually, illiterate. A few folk-songs are probably of aristocratic descent, but the number of these is too insignificant to affect the question of origin.

7. The bulk of traditional British balladry does not antedate the fifteenth, sixteenth, and seventeenth centuries.

CHAPTER IV

The Quest of the Folk-Song

"BY CORRESPONDENCE, and by an extensive diffusion of printed circulars, I have tried to stimulate collection from tradition in Scotland, Canada and the United States, and no becoming means has been left unemployed to obtain possession of unsunned treasures locked up in writing. . . . But what is still lacking is believed to bear no great proportion to what is in hand, and may soon come in, besides."[1] The monumental work of Child, the great Harvard scholar, represents the first serious attempt of an American to compile the great body of British folk-songs. His five massive volumes, in ten parts, are the result of half a century of labors. It will be noticed in the above quotation that Child employs the words "unsunned," and "locked up in writing," which may be interpreted as indicating that he was interested chiefly in manuscripts, and collections previously made or printed in the British Isles; and that he considered ballad-making and ballad-singing as a closed account. In preparation for the great work, he spent much time in England and Scotland, examining various manuscripts and collections, and occasionally jotting down a song from oral transmission.[2] A few songs reached Child from contributors in America. But there was no popular response to his call, owing to the fact that the folk-song

[1] Francis James Child, *The English and Scottish Popular Ballads*, Advertisement to Part I, p. vii.

[2] [Child's search for ballads was conducted largely on the west side of the Atlantic by correspondence and purchase of manuscripts. See Sigurd Bernhard Hustvedt, *Ballad Books and Ballad Men* (Cambridge, Massachusetts, 1930), pp. 213 ff.— D. K. W.]

is no longer extensively distributed over America, and that Americans in general have no interest in it.

Child was of course ignorant of the existence of a large mass of folk-songs, traditional and modern, in the Southern Highlands of the United States. His compilation was finished in 1898, at which time there was little interest in American folk-lore. However, William Wells Newell had published his *Games and Songs of American Children* (1883) and was thus the first American scholar to turn directly to the folk for his material. While the great mass of songs in the Highlands was lying untouched and uninvestigated (but not unsung), scholars of folk-songs, notably Francis B. Gummere, were busy writing books and studies based on British collections. In Professor Gummere's *The Popular Ballad* (1907), one of the most scholarly studies that have yet been made in the English-speaking world, not one song is mentioned as surviving in America. Then came Professor George Lyman Kittredge, of Harvard, and the *Journal of American Folk-Lore*, founded by William Wells Newell (1888), giving a new impetus to the recovery and study of the folk-song in America.

A genuine search for the folk-song began in America fifteen or twenty years ago, the following collectors showing the greatest activity: Professor H. M. Belden, University of Missouri; Professor H. G. Shearin and J. H. Combs, Transylvania University (Kentucky); Professor John A. Lomax, University of Texas; Professor S. Alphonso Smith, University of Virginia; Mr. Phillips Barry, of Massachusetts; Professor Louise Pound, University of Nebraska; Professor A. H. Tolman, University of Chicago; Professor J. H. Cox, West Virginia University; Cecil J. Sharp, of England; and Mrs. Olive Dame Campbell.

The quest in America is now in full swing, with the Southern Highlands and the plains of the West as the chief focus of attention. Many songs of the traditional type have been recovered in New England and other sections, but they appear to be no longer sung in those sections. New England has never been a fertile field for the folk-song. Foreigners are bringing songs over from year to year, but with the exception of the Irish songs, they are not having any noticeable influence on the singing of songs in English. Several years ago some erroneous impressions prevailed among scholars with respect to the making and singing of folk-songs. Professor Kittredge, in his introduction to the one-volume edition of Child's *English and Scottish Popular Ballads* (1904), remarks that ballad-making and ballad-singing are lost arts among the English-speaking nations. Later (1915) he modified his statement as to ballad-singing, but left unchanged his views as to ballad-making.[3] Gummere[4] states that ballad-making is a closed account. In a similar strain write C. S. Baldwin[5] and Professor F. E. Bryant.[6] Says Bryant: "Traditional balladry is a closed account, though personally I cannot see that that means much in defining the origin of the type. . . . Still, whatever the conditions were that brought forth the peculiarities of the traditional ballad, they are at least now passed and presumably beyond recall."

In the light of recent discoveries in the field of folk-lore, both in England and the United States, it is very evident that neither ballad-singing nor ballad-making are lost arts in the English-speaking world; consequently not at all a "closed account."[7] The songs of this collection, as well as those of other American collections, bear witness that the art is hale and hearty in more than one section of America, although beginning to lose ground. The following are some of the types which are in the process of making at all times, in various sections of America:

1. Songs more or less of the Child type, mostly in the Southern Highlands.

2. Songs of the plains, or cowboy songs.

3. Railroad songs, or songs of laboring men on the railroads.

4. River songs, or songs of men who transport "rafts" by stream.

5. Songs of lumbermen, chiefly in Maine and the northwest.

6. Songs of the Negroes, religious and secular.

7. Songs of or by criminals, of the confessional or "goodnight" type, generally distributed over the United States.

Discoveries made during the past two decades are destined to throw some additional light on the origin of the traditional type of folk-song. Scholars like Gummere, Bryant, and others evidently do not understand that the present-day type of folk-song (that is, songs made by the folk in recent times) may have some bearing on the method of composition in earlier times. The sudden renaissance of interest in the tra-

---

[3] [C. Alphonso Smith, "Ballads Surviving in the United States," *Musical Quarterly*, II (1916), 111.—D. K. W.]

[4] F. B. Gummere, *The Popular Ballad*, pp. 14, 313; *Cambridge History of English Literature*, II, 448; and elsewhere in his works.

[5] C. S. Baldwin, *Introduction to English Medieval Literature*, p. 243.

[6] F. E. Bryant, *A History of English Balladry*, p. 35.

[7] A North Carolina mountain woman sang sixty-four traditional songs to Sharp! Another sang thirty-five. A West Virginia mountaineer sang fourteen to Carey Woofter, an indefatigable folk-lorist of that state.

ditional folk-song, and those of other types, owes much to the discovery
of the Southern Highlanders, who are conservators of the folk-song,
ancient and modern. There is no particular reason for inferring that
"the wish to collect and preserve popular song may be viewed as ac-
companying or growing out of the trend toward democracy."[8] The
trend toward democracy is one thing, and the interest of a few scholars
in the folk-song is another, the two seeming to bear no relation whatsoever to each other. The quest and the question are old enough, having had their inception with such collectors as Bishop Percy[9] and Joseph Ritson,[10] followed by Walter Scott[11] and others. These collectors
seem to have had merely a scholarly interest in the matter, and do not
appear to have been consumed by any particular interest in democracy.
The quest of the folk-song is a matter of interest, ever old and ever
new, in "antiques."

For him who would embark on the quest of the folk-song, traditional
or modern, the Southern Highlands lie before him, scarcely touched
as yet. Here he will find himself breathing the atmosphere of the
"heroic" ballad age, when men were brave, when ladies mounted
"milk-white" steeds, the atmosphere of a people who not only fight,
but sing. For our Highlander goes to the field singing in the morning,
or as he drives his team of oxen or horses along the lonely mountain
road. The housewife, molested by myriad cares and a hard lot, sings as
she goes about her daily duties, be it in the "kitchen-house," garden,
at the "wash-block," at her knitting, or over the cradle. Young and old
alike sing, for the art flourishes among all classes and ages, as it did
among the English commons in the sixteenth century. In the words of
a well-known folk-song, the Highland singer

> Has rings on her fingers and bells on her toes,
> *And she carries music wherever she goes.*

Cecil J. Sharp has remarked that he was unable to find any songs in
Somerset worth recording from people under seventy.

The collector not on intimate terms with the Highlander may experience difficulty in his quest, for usually the singer is secretive, sen-
sitive, and keenly alive to any criticism of his songs, or of his language.
His intuition tells him that his songs are somehow "different" from

---

[8] Louise Pound, *American Ballads and Songs*, p. 30.
[9] Thomas Percy, *Reliques of Ancient English Poetry*.
[10] Joseph Ritson, *Ancient Songs* (1790).
[11] Sir Walter Scott, *Minstrelsy of the Scottish Border*.

those of other folks, whenever an outsider expresses a desire to hear him sing. The collector who comes into the Highlands posing as a collector will not succeed materially; such a one is likely to earn the soubriquet of "that furriner come to make fun of us," unless he learns to know the Highlander intimately, and can gain his confidence. If he sings a song himself to the Highlander, the latter will reply with a song, for he is a mighty singer, and does not like to be outdone. It reminds one somewhat of the singing contests among the cannibal islanders of the Pacific.

To understand the quest properly, one should know something of the social life of the Highlander. Social life, although not a marked characteristic of the people, because of isolation, manifests itself in many ways. Three forms of amusement, differing in different localities, seem to stand out prominently: the dance ("shin-dig," or "hoedown"), the "party," and the "social." The "party" consists of a gathering at a neighbor's, usually in the evening, at which apples may be peeled for preserves or drying, beans strung (in the pod) for winter, or quilts made. The "social" seems to be a more refined affair, where mountain folk of social pretensions gather for cards and other inside games. [The square-dance may or may not descend from Elizabethan England, but its origin is uncertain. The various movements, or "calls," are called in stentorian tones by someone present, who may or may not participate in the dancing. Sometimes the fiddler or banjo picker himself calls them, which is quite an accomplishment. At all times the tapping of a foot by the fiddler keeps time with the music. I once asked a Highlander in college to get his banjo and entertain a gathering of students. He flatly refused, on the ground that his right foot was sore! For the sake of those interested in the dance, a typical "set" in a square-dance is here reproduced:

Eight hands up, circle to the left! Half way back on a single line! Lady before and gent behind! First gent lead out and swing his partner! First to the right and then to the left! Don't forget the two-hand swing! Break to the left on the Wild Goose Chase, and around that lady! Back to the right, and around that gent! Take on four, and circle to the left! Half way and back on a single line! Lady before and gent behind! Swing your opposite partner, and promenade your own! Catch as you were, and circle to the left! Break to the left and around the next couple, and back to the beginning! (Then the second couple follows, and so on, till eight couples have finished. This makes sixty-four parts to the "set." Each movement is called a "figure.")

This "set" is called "The Wild Goose Chase." One young mountaineer said off to me eight of these "sets" in rapid succession, without hesitating—an accomplishment which would have done honor to the early scop, or troubadour.]

But it is in the lonely, isolated cabin that the traditional folk-song is most alive; in places that have not yet felt the impact of civilization, education, pianos, organs, phonographs, the "singing-school master," jazz, the turkey-trot, and ragtime music. I paid a visit to one such remote cabin, and found a middle-aged mountaineer with his large family living in two rooms. At first he was uncommunicative, because he had joined the Primitive Baptist Church, which is a sworn enemy of the folk-song, as well as of all other secular music. Finally, on learning that I was a mountaineer myself, he laid his Bible aside, refreshed himself with a fresh quid of chewing tobacco, stared vacantly into space, and began to sing. I left that cabin with "The Golden Vanity" (Child No. 286), one of the few real sea-songs surviving, "The Cherry-Tree Carol" (Child No. 54), "The Nightingale," and others bearing the earmarks of tradition.

I called at another cabin and talked with an old woman who was eighty-five-years old, and whose people had come from North Carolina. She said that the (Civil) war (1861–1865) had caused her to forget most of her songs. I succeeded in getting her into a singing, or rather a chanting, mood. If full and complete proof were needed of the oft-repeated assertion that the ballad singer is oblivious of his audience, that personality counts for nothing, this aged woman furnished it on this occasion. Placing her hands in her lap, and fixing her eyes steadily on the ground, she literally chanted "Vilikins and his Dinah" (a splendid variant of an English stall-ballad), "Kate and Her Horns," "Jack Williams," and "Come all ye jolly boatsman boys." Gummere says: ". . . it is to that chanting vigor of recitation, in a style very close to singing, that we owe the almost uniform perfection of rhythm in our old ballads, short or long."[12] It is not clear that most folk-songs were originally sung. The length of the Robin Hood songs, and the fact that almost none have been recovered in recent times, would seem to indicate that the ballads clustering around that legendary robber were not sung.

One old mountaineer was suspicious of my good intentions. When I was a boy he used to sing for me while he worked on his mill-race. He was a mighty singer of ballads, descending from a mighty singing

---

[12] Gummere, *The Popular Ballad*, p. 248.

family. Years later, when I approached him for some songs, he was adamant. Now, our Highlander is not one to be pushed where he does not care to go, nor does he respond submissively to a shaping process. My old mountaineer friend continued silent, until I resorted to strategy. I sent a cousin around to his home at night, armed with a stenographer's notebook and pencil. He liked my cousin, and sang loud and long on the porch of his house, in total darkness. On the following day my cousin turned over to me "The Banks of Sweet Dundee," and "Davy Crockett," a song of the Texas-Mexican War.

In the Highland country it is not necessary to confine oneself to any particular class of people in the quest of the folk-song. I asked a lawyer, who was from a singing family, for some songs. He at once sang many traditional and modern songs, including "Little Musgrave and Lady Barnard" (Child No. 81), "William Hall" (a song reminiscent of the French-English wars), "In Seaport Town," "The Frog and the Mouse" (one of the most ancient folk-songs), "Fair Nottiman Town," and "The Gosport Tragedy" (or "Pretty Polly"). Pulling out a desk drawer, he took from it a "ballet," saying, "I guess this one is no good, but you can have it." The "ballet" that was "no good" proved to be "The Den of Lions" (or "The Lady and the Fan"), based on an incident at the court of Francis I, of France. It was one of Child's favorite ballads, but somehow or other it failed to get into his collection. A "ballet," or "song-ballet," among the Highlanders is a song that has been written down, as opposed to orally transmitted. It is not a "ballet" if it has not been written down, and most of the traditional songs of the Highlands circulate by oral transmission, and are termed "old songs."[13]

I accosted a barber, who was reputed to have been once a singer of ballads. While he was shaving me, he hummed the air of an old song. I asked him if he knew the words of the song, and he immediately sang "There Was a Sea Captain" from beginning to end. The next day I returned (with a big plug of chewing tobacco), and he sang to me "The Three Ravens" (Child No. 26), and "The Farmer's Curst Wife" (Child No. 278). If tobacco and time (I left that town soon afterward) had held out, the barber's contribution might have been more considerable.

The "jail-bird," or prisoner, is a mighty singer of songs, of almost every type known to the Highlander, with the exception of Primitive Baptist Church hymns. The banjo is the musical instrument that ac-

---

[13] "Ballet," however, is no newcomer, having been used as early as 1575 by Lanham in his "Letter from Killingwoorth" as in "a bunch of *ballets*."

companies him, and he seldom picks it without singing. But as a rule, the traditional ballad is not in his repertory, because he prefers outlaw and railroad songs. One can hear his loud voice as it floats out from behind the prison bars to every quarter of the village. He does not consider that any stigma attaches itself to his incarceration, and sings the more merrily because of it. I once heard a Highland prisoner singing "John Hardy," a famous song of railroaders. At the same time a man was riding by the jail on a poor specimen of a horse. The singer paused long enough to cry out, "Say, pard, how would you like to swap your plug to my thirty days in jail?"

The pure feud- or clan-ballad is not common, although songs are made about clansmen, usually after their death "in action." In one section I chanced to talk with a mountaineer about a song which I wanted, a song which told of the murder of a lawyer who had vigorously prosecuted a clan leader. There was a small organ in the room. The singer looked about the room and said cautiously, "A feller might get shot around here for singing that song." I told him to sing anyway, and that he could shoot as well as he could sing. He then placed himself at the organ, and sang and played by ear "The Assassination of J. B. Marcum," a song modeled on "Jesse James," whose hero was the most notorious outlaw in the history of American banditry.

Many songs have been taken down from the singing of young people in communities into which the organ had been introduced. This instrument seems, for a time, to have given a new impetus to the singing of folk-songs. Of course, the players, nearly always girls, played by ear [, or "chorded" the airs], because there was no music for the songs. In this way I found many traditional love songs and some genuine folk-songs. From my observations, I have been unable to determine whether or not women and girls in the Highlands know more songs than men and boys. Including all types, traditional and otherwise, I am of the opinion that the women and girls know more. As to young and old, the old appear to know more traditional songs, although communicants of the Primitive Baptist Church won't sing them, while the young, already commencing to become ashamed of their traditions, lean rather toward the later songs and the love songs. In the Highlands the Primitive Baptist Church is made up almost entirely of people who have passed the stage of young manhood and young womanhood, and who have scruples against all secular music, and especially against the folk-song. At any rate, the singing of all classes, young and old alike, demonstrates the wide prevalence of folk-songs, and the fact that the Highlanders possess a music and ballad literature of their own, which would have been of unusual interest to the late Professor Child.

The collector in quest of the folk-song has been guilty of some mistakes. Child's great compilation blazed a trail from which the subsequent collector has been slow to depart, considering as unworthy of recording those songs which cannot be identified in Child. As we now well know, *three hundred and five songs* do not fix the limit to British folk-songs, as Professor Kittredge thinks.[14] Not all the folk-songs have been recovered, or discovered, nor will they ever be. Even in England, a field which the average student of folk-song believes to have been long ago exhausted, Sharp had discovered more than twelve hundred songs and airs up to the year 1907, and these largely from one shire! Scores of songs are as traditional and worthy of preservation as are the best ones in the Child compilation. Campbell and Sharp record from the Southern Highlands eighteen traditional British songs of which Child makes no mention.[15] Perhaps they failed to come under his observation, or perhaps, since he must have seen some of them, he had other reasons for omitting them. But Child was a compiler rather than a collector.

The collector should take down all songs that are the exclusive property of the folk, whether they be traditional or modern, of the Child type or not, whether they be play and dance songs, party songs, outlaw songs, railroad songs, cowboy songs, nursery songs, or not. The *modern* folk-song (I use the word boldly) may one day perhaps have the interest for the future student which the traditional song now enjoys. Besides, as has been mentioned above, it offers a partial solution for the origin of the traditional song.

Whenever a systematic search for the folk-song is made, the collector should observe certain other things, that his search may be as

---

[14] G. L. Kittredge, Introduction to the abridged edition of Child's *English and Scottish Popular Ballads*, p. xiii. [There is again confusion between *folksong* and *ballad*. When Kittredge wrote that Child's collection "comprises the whole extant mass of this material," he was referring to the "popular ballad." Nor did Child, as the succeeding passage seems to imply, equate his collection with the entire area of folksong—though some of his followers acted as if he did. And it is well to note that in attempting to discuss objectively the definition of "ballad" during the "Ballad War," Frank Egbert Bryant felt compelled to state that "narrative is still not a distinguishing characteristic of balladry. . . . It is not the narrative element, for not all ballads are narrative" (*A History of English Balladry*, pp. 32, 36).—D. K. W.]

[15] Olive Dame Campbell and Cecil J. Sharp, *English Folk-Songs from the Southern Appalachians*, Nos. 38–55.

92265

complete and scholarly as possible. He should ask the singer to *sing* the song to him, by all means. This would preserve the choruses or refrains of many songs, which are otherwise lost when the singer merely *says* the words. Realizing his shortcomings in language, the singer often changes the words when he repeats the song without singing it. When the song is sung, one may easily discover if it has a refrain, or if every other stanza (of four lines) is used as a sort of refrain or chorus. Sharp has been especially careful and accurate in preserving the tunes to almost all the songs he has found. The tune may occasionally throw light on the age or origin of the words. In this instance I recall the air of a Highland lullaby, "Go Tell Aunt Rhody," which happens also to be the air of "Rousseau's Cradle Hymn" (words by Isaac Watts). One wonders how and when the air came among the Highlanders, since the era of English colonization in America was practically over when Rousseau wrote the music. It probably came via England, at the time of the American Revolution. The air of "Jinny Get Your Hoecake Done" is a Hindu air.

The question of title is often puzzling among collectors and students. Much confusion would be avoided if the collector would record all local titles of songs, as well as traditional titles which appear in standard collections. This would aid greatly in the matter of identification, both of British and American versions. Professors Kittredge and Cox have not been neglectful in this respect. Sometimes the collector is guilty of "doctoring," or changing texts, in order to fill out certain missing lines, or of lengthening the text itself, whenever it appears fragmentary. This has been remarked in at least two American collections, otherwise splendid for the tunes which they contain. The language of the song should be recorded as it is sung, without any over-editing or Bowdlerization.

CHAPTER V

An Attempt at Classification of Folk-Songs

AT THIS TIME the word "ballad" appears to be one of the loosest terms employed in literature. It no longer has a precise and well-defined meaning, owing to the confusion of the folk-song with it. For the ballad lost its definite, literary character in the fifteenth century, and the term came, in time, to be loosely applied to that endless procession of short epic or narrative poems whose authorship and origin are unknown. What term, then, should one employ in a study of the songs of the folk today? "Ballad" is hardly correct, although it is convenient and usually understood to have reference to a song of the Child type. "Popular songs," or *chansons populaires*, is not exact enough, since neither term is definite. "Dixie," "Yankee Doodle," "My Old Kentucky Home," "La Marseillaise" and many others are popular songs, songs of the people, in a sense, but we cannot call them folk-songs. There seems no reason for applying the banal term "piece" to the folk-song, as some scholars have done.

The term "folk-song" appears to be the most definite, and the one which will probably prevail in subsequent studies of the songs of the people. One can use it without necessarily committing one's self to the "popular," or communal, theory of the origin of the folk-song, since the folk-song is the especial property of the folk, regardless of the method of composition or origin. There seems to have been some misunderstanding of Child's use of the term "popular" in the title of his great collection (*The English and Scottish Popular Ballads*). There is no record of Child's subscribing to the "popular" theory, and he doubtless meant by "popular" that the songs which he compiled were at one time (fifteenth, sixteenth, and seventeenth centuries) popular among the great masses of the British people. For purposes of convenience the term "folk-song" will be used in the collection herewith presented; but even with that a certain classification is necessary in order to distinguish the genuine folk-song of tradition from various other types.

At the outset such an attempt at classification is difficult, and one which could be continued indefinitely, entailing endless cross-divisions and cross-references. For example, one is tempted to make a division of the genuine narrative songs; of the love songs; of the English, Scottish, or Irish songs; of the native American songs. But such a classification is too general, besides carrying with it numberless pitfalls and difficulties. In the Southern Highlands one finds the traditional song rudely jostled by the extensively diffused, more modern type, each vying with the other for persistence; in the former, lords, kings, princes, "ladies of high degree," foot-pages, sea captains, foreign countries, French bullets, the "old salt sea," bonnie boats; in the latter, the forsaken lover, the murdered lover, the outlaw, the pioneer, the railroader, the adventurer, the soldier. The following more detailed classification of the Highlander's songs presents itself.

I. British, or English and Scottish survivals, identified in the Child collection.

II. British survivals which are not found in the Child collection, but which may or may not be identified in British collections. Their structure and subject matter class them as survivals of Old World originals.

III. Songs of Irish origin, traditional and more recent.

IV. Songs of uncertain origin, some of which may be British, others American.

V. Songs of the era of American colonization. Some of these may be adaptations of British archetypes, but if so, they have lost the distinguishing traits of their nativity, and are, in their present state, more or less closely associated with the colonial period in America.

VI. Songs of the American Civil War. Many songs of this type cannot be classed as folk-songs, since they are more or less closely associated with history and politics, and bear the signs of unmistakable authorship, having been written by partisans and soldiers of the North and South. As songs, they were short-lived, and of greatest currency while the war was in progress. Others, more local and personal in character, and bearing the distinctive marks of the folk-song, have survived and are more or less popular.

VII. Songs of the pioneer movement westward, and of the gold rush toward California. As contemporary with this period, songs of the Mexican War (1846–1848) might be mentioned in this class.

VIII. Outlaw or bandit songs.

IX. Songs of criminals, being their meditations or confessions while in prison awaiting trial, or while under sentence of death.

X. Railroad songs, or songs of laboring men on the railroads. Many of these are contributed by the Negroes.

XI. Other occupational songs, or labor songs. Here are included a wide variety of songs relating to various occupational pursuits, trades, etc. Railroad songs could of course be classed here, but they are so numerous and characteristic as to require a separate heading.

XII. Cowboy songs, or songs of the plains, not numerous in the Highlands and imported by Highlanders returning from the West after the Civil War. Most of these are indigenous songs.

XIII. Love songs. The representatives of this type could be classed under other headings, but they are numerous enough to fall under a classification of their own. Many, or most of them, are of British origin, but not of the epic or narrative type.

1. Songs of the lover murdered.

2. Songs of inconstant love.

3. Songs of constant love.

4. Songs of the lover baffled. These are largely from British archetypes, and similar to those in Child. Some of them, evidently of great age, are too obscene to be printed.

5. Songs of the returned lover disguised, usually bearing with him a token.

XIV. Humorous songs, many of which are of British origin. Some are survivals of stall-ballads, others are American, and still others are adaptations of vaudeville and minstrel show songs.

XV. Songs of sentiment and emotion. They represent no particular folk-song type, and are numerous. Most of them were written during the nineteenth century by authors once known, but such songs have circulated by oral transmission until the identity of the authors is now lost. The songs are therefore the property of the folk.

XVI. Songs of moral incident or reflection. Many of these could be classed under XV, since they are heavily charged with sentiment and feeling. The authorship of many of these songs was probably also once known.

XVII. Vulgar songs, largely British in origin.

XVIII. Songs of the Negroes. These cover a wide variety, and should not, perhaps, be discussed in this collection, but they have been adopted by the Highlanders. They include railroad songs, occupational songs, spirituals, love songs, outlaw songs, humorous songs, jigs, nonsense songs, etc. A few are modeled on traditional folk-songs.

XIX. Play and dance songs. Mostly the property of children, and survivals of Old World originals from England, Scotland, Germany, France, and other European countries.

XX. Sequence-, number-, or counting-out-songs. British and American in origin, with a few dating from Greek and Roman times.

XXI. Miscellaneous songs. These are so numerous and so varied as to baffle classification. Usually they are short, and are played to the accompaniment of the fiddle or banjo, often without words. Some are of American origin, others are British, and some are from the Negroes. They include ditties, lullabies, nonsense-rhymes, nursery-rhymes, jigs, animal songs, etc.

For purposes of convenience, and in order to avoid unnecessary cross-division, the songs of this work are classified as follows:

I. Songs of British (English, Scottish, Irish) origin, identified in the Child collection or otherwise.

II. Native American songs.

It is hoped that no songs not the exclusive property of the folk have been included in this collection. It is not enough that a song must persist in oral currency through a fair period of years in order to become a folk-song; all knowledge of authorship or origin must also be lost, or at least, the folk version or variant must differ essentially, either in words or story, from its archetype.

CHAPTER VI

Songs of British Origin

IT IS REASONABLE to conclude that the Highland songs of British origin were borne westward on the tide of emigration from the British Isles, mostly from England, in the seventeenth century. Very few exceptions could be noted, and these would be open to question. For more than a century the sequestered vales of the Southern Highlands in the United States have, by their sheer isolation, preserved, sometimes untouched and unchanged, those "canticles of love and woe" of a bygone age, of an age when men were heroic, and when knights gleamed in shining armor. Whatever may have been the conditions that produced British balladry, whatever may have been the method of composition, the serious student of folk-lore no longer doubts the existence in America of a considerable mass of survivals in song of that heroic age. The civilization of that period has been transformed, but the Highlanders, our "contemporary ancestors," have remained stationary, preserving much that is Elizabethan, both in speech and song.

A retrospection, with the folk-song as a basis, leads one to compare the Highlander's traditional songs with their British archetypes. Their subjects cover a wide range, just as they did in the ballad age, and their manifold variety of theme is suggested in: incidents of romance, tragic and comic, cavaliers shivering their lances for love of their ladies, ladies gaily caparisoned in all the "seven prismatic colors," ladies in waiting; foot-pages hastening to break bad news to their lords or masters, milk-white steeds, ancestral halls and castles; jolly boatmen on the Thames, London apprentices, silk merchants, heroes and lovers returning from the wars in France; naval encounters, court intrigues, kings and queens, voyages to the New World, condemned criminals making their confessions, lovers baffled in their overtures to the coy, rustic maid, the wronged housewife reforming her husband, or the husband flogging his housewife.

Now, the Highlander knows little or nothing of the epoch or people from whom he inherited his folk-songs. Much historical and geographical confusion has crept into his traditional songs. Each locality invents its own nomenclature for the folk-song, thus causing an unlimited number of variants with respect to all proper names. For example, Edinburgh becomes Eddingsburgh; Nottingham, Nottiman; Sheffield, Shearfield; Lady Isabel, Pretty Polly; Lady Margaret, Fair Ellender; Lord Douglas, Sweet William; Lord Randal becomes Johnny Randolph, Johnny Randal, Johnny Ramsey, Johnny Reeler, or Sweet Harry; Sir Lionel, Bangum; Young Beichan becomes Lord Bate(s)-man, or Lord Wetram; the Turkish lady, Susan Pious; Young Hunting becomes Lord Henry, Loving Henry, or Love Henry; Lord Lovel becomes Lord Lover, Lord Lovely, or Lord Leven; King Henry's throne becomes King McHennery's throne; Giles Collins becomes John, Johnny, or George Collins; Lady Alice, Fair Ellender (which name, like Pretty Polly, is common in balladry); Prince Robert, Harry Saunders; Sillertoun Town (or Sittingen's Rocks), Nicut Hill; the Gypsy Laddie, the gypsy (or Gypsen) Davy; John Blunt, John Jones; Scotland becomes Scotchee. It must be remembered also that similar confusion existed in the folk-song even before its transportation to America, for reasons similar to those which cause such confusion today.

A North Carolina variant of "Fair Annie" has these lines:

> It's King Henry he's my father dear,
> Queen *Chatry's* my own mother.

Queen "Chatry" does not appear to be "in the records." A Georgia variant of "Young Hunting" puts the heroine in Arkansas:

> For the girl that I left in the *Arkansas land*
> Will think long of my return.

In "Little Musgrave and Lady Barnard," according to a North Carolina variant,

> Lord Dannel's gone to *Kentucky*,
> King Georgie for to view.

In a Kentucky variant of the same song,

> Little *speedfoot* was standing by
> To see what he could hear.

"Speedfoot" is used for "foot-page," probably. In a variant of "Johnie Scot" it becomes *foot-spade!* Gypsies do not frequent the Highlands, and the term "Gypsy" means nothing to the Highlander. A Tennessee variant of "The Gypsy Laddie" uses "Gypsens." A North Carolina variant of "Geordie" calls the king's horses "staff," and has them sold in Virginia:

> He stole sixteen of the king's white *staff,*
> And sold them in Virginee.

A West Virginia variant of "Young Beichan" makes the "Turkish lady" sail *east* from Turkey to reach England. According to a North Carolina mountaineer, a man hanged on the gallows tells the story himself, in "The Sheffield Apprentice":

> Then I was executed
> And on the gallows hung.

A West Virginia singer, preserving the humor of an earlier variant, thus pays his respects to the medical profession in a stanza of "Lady Alice":

> Her mother made her some chicken broth
> From the fattest pullet and the best;
> Fair Ellender swallowed only one spoonful,
> And the doctor swallowed the rest.

As a rule, British survivals are shorter than their originals of three and four centuries ago. This is not to be wondered at, owing to the method of transmission, and to other causes. Shortening of texts is a gradual, natural process not only for the folk-song, but for other types of poetry and song which circulate orally. Such a process seems to have no connection with the present day tendency to shorten the drama, the essay, and prose fiction, as one American scholar thinks.[1] The tendency was already in process, for the folk-song, even in the sixteenth and seventeenth centuries, and many fragmentary and abbreviated texts have come down to us, along with the fuller texts. The statement that "American texts (of traditional songs) cannot be accepted without qualification"[2] means nothing. If we take as a basis the songs as

---

[1] Louise Pound, *American Ballads and Songs,* p. xxxiv.

[2] [Combs is apparently under the impression that he is quoting Louise Pound, who wrote (*ibid.,* p. xxviii) that "American texts *can* (my italics) be accepted with-

they must have stood originally, English and Scottish texts likewise are incomplete. That is a question which we cannot settle, because origins are surrounded with mystery, and the original singers and many of their songs are gone, beyond recall. A few survivals in America are superior even to early British texts. A number of songs in this collection appear to be fairly complete, while a few are fragmentary. A Kentucky variant of "Barbara Allen" has twenty stanzas, and is therefore more complete than the average British text, and in addition, contains two traditional stanzas which are not in British texts.[3]

In the main, the story told in the folk-song has not changed materially in Highland variants. Opening and closing stanzas are often missing, as is to be expected; for these are always, for all of us, the most difficult stanzas to remember. "If I could just remember how the song (or poem) begins, I could go ahead with it," is not an uncommon expression. The ballad maker or ballad singer, like the poet or musician of art, finds difficulty in beginning his composition. While the story does not change materially, incidents, names and places do, and, as has been remarked elsewhere, much historical and geographical confusion is common. Professor H. M. Belden offers a good example of this in "Jack Went A-Sailing" ("Jackie Row," "Jackie Frazier," or "Jack Monroe"), a song which seems to be generally distributed over most of the United States. Now, Jack is a British Tommy, who finds himself fighting in France, a long time ago. His sweetheart "dresses herself all in men's gray," hires out as a cabin "boy" on board a vessel, and goes to seek her lover on the battlefield. After "sailing all over the sea" (across the Channel!) she reaches the battlefield, where she "views them up and down," and finds her lover, wounded. She nurses Jack to health, they return to England, and the song ends:

---

out qualification" because native collectors have left them "as they were" instead of altering them as did Percy, Scott, and others in the Old World—D. K. W.]

[3] Other songs which compare favorably with their British prototypes are: "The Lass of Roch Royal," "Little Musgrave and Lady Barnard," "Mary Hamilton," "The Maid Freed from the Gallows," "Lamkin," "The Cruel Brother," "Lord Randal," "Edward" (better than British texts), "The Broomfield Hill," "Young Beichan," "The Cherry-Tree Carol," "Fair Margaret and Sweet William," "Lord Lovel," "Lady Alice" (better), "The Bailiff's Daughter of Islington," "The Gypsy Laddie," "Bonnie James Campbell," "Our Goodman," "Get Up and Bar the Door," "The Farmer's Curst Wife," "Jack Went A-Sailing," "Vilikins and His Dinah," "The Miller of Gosport," "Sweet Dundee," "In Seaport Town," "Shooting of His Dear," "The Frog and the Mouse," "My Boy Billy," and a number of lyric songs.

> Now here's a handsome couple,
> So quick-ly did agree;
> So stylish they got married—
> And it's why not you and me?

This stanza was evidently added by some Highland singer while making love to his sweetheart. Belden, commenting on the song, says: "In one (variant), Mollie's father is a 'wealthy London merchant'; Jack is drafted to 'the wars of Germany,' he goes to 'old England,' and the wedded pair return from Spain to 'French London,' wherever that may be. Another version has the merchant still in London, but (perhaps by association with the mention of Spain) has Jack, now become a farmer, drafted into the army 'for Santa Fe,' where he is cut down by 'a bullet from the Spaniards.' In still another version the transference to America, though vague, is complete. The wealthy merchant 'in Louisville did dwell'; Jack 'has landed in New Mexico, in the wars of Santa Fé'; whereupon Mollie 'harnessed up a mule-team, in a wagon she set sail (a prairie schooner, evidently), she landed in New Mexico on a swift and pleasant gale,' where presently 'the drums did loudly beat and the cannon's balls did fly,' and Mollie rescues her lover as before."[4]

The supernatural element—the world of ghosts, spirits, fairies, and sprites—has lost much of its old flavor in Highland traditional songs, but something of the weird and mysterious still survives in a goodly number of them. An old Norse (?) myth survives in "Mary o' the Dee," in which Mary's dead lover returns to her, but immediately departs on the crowing of the cock. The dead lover returns in "Fair Margaret and Sweet William," "Shooting of His Dear," and a few others. In "The Wife of Usher's Well" three dead babes return at Christmastide to see their mother. In "James Harris" the "hills of heaven" and the "hills of hell" are seen by two guilty lovers as the ship goes down. But the elfin knights in "Lady Isabel and the Elf Knight" and "The Elfin Knight" were too much for the Highlander, and he has taken them from the two songs, substituting flesh and blood in their stead. A West Virginia variant of the former substitutes a priest!

Old World emblems are quite common, and have been preserved almost intact by the Highlander. One of the most common ones, ap-

[4] Henry M. Belden, "Balladry in America," *Journal of American Folklore*, XXV, 8.

pearing in a large number of songs, is what might be termed the "two-shrub" emblem, consisting usually of a rose and a briar. It marks the closing stanza or two, and is found in: "Earl Brand," "Fair Margaret and Sweet William," "Lord Thomas and Fair Annet," "Barbara Allen," "Lord Lovel," and some others. This intertwining of two shrubs over the graves of lovers is common in European balladry. In a West Virginia variant of "Lord Lovel" the shrubs are a lily and a briar, the latter springing from the backbone of one of the lovers! One variant of "Earl Brand" has only a lily, which is split in twain by a storm.[5] The turtle-dove, emblematic of love, has survived in all its simplicity and beauty, and marks the close of numerous songs. A typical stanza, from "The Brisk Young Lover," follows:

> Go dig my grave both wide and deep,
> Place a marble stone at my head and feet,
> And upon my breast a turtle-dove,
> To show the world I died for love.

A Kentucky variant of "William Bluet," an unidentified song, has these lines:

> When he had hung till he was almost dead,
> There came a dove and hovered [over] his head.

If the turtle-dove is allegorical of love, the (weeping) willow often accompanies it as an emblem of grief or sorrow. A dying lover says, in "The Brisk Young Lover,"

> And at my feet a weeping-willow tree
> For many a year may wave over me.

One version of "Charles J. Guiteau" (or "James A. Garfield") has these two lines:

> I'll weep like a willow, I'll mourn like a dove,
> Mr. James A. Garfield is dead.

The Highlander's *veillées* are full of the supernatural, as are those of the French peasant, although it does not appear to characterize the French folk-song. Such differences in the folk-songs of the English and the French may be explained partly by racial differences, partly by education.

Colors and numbers play a prominent part in British survivals, also

---

[5] See Child, I, 96 ff.; *Melusine: Recueil de Mythologie*, IV, cols. 60, 85, 142; Constantino Nigra, *Canti popolari del Piemonte*, p. 133.

in native American songs. They are of course not usually an essential part of the narrative, being employed largely for the sake of rhyme, etc. We cannot escape such stock expressions as: "milk-white steed," "lily-white hands," "rose-red lips," "snow-white-cheeks," "raven-black hair." Sometimes members of a family enter into the story dressed, each one, in white, black, red, green, or blue, depending on the rhyme, until all the popular colors (or relations) run out. Glaring anachronisms in time relationships or conceptions occur commonly, also for the sake of rhyme:

> O now to me the time draws near
> That every day is *three*, my love,
> And every hour is *ten*.

The banjo picker has made inroads on the traditional folk-song text, as he has also on its music. Although the folk-song of this type is not usually a main feature of his repertory, yet he gets his fingers on it, and leaves it almost unrecognizable. Two or three examples will suffice. "William Bluet," a type of the "good-night" song, and perhaps once a fair example of what this sort of song ought to be, got in the path of the banjo picker, and this is how it begins:

> There was a woman lived in Hampshire,
> She had only one son, and him she loved most dear;
> She had no other child but he,
> She brought him up in pomp and vanitee.

And the close:

> When he had hung till he was almost dead
> There came a dove and hovered his head three times,
> Then ascended to the sky,
> Which put the people in a sad *disprise*.

"My Boy Billy" has suffered untold agonies at the hands of the banjo picker, who puts whiskers on Billy's sweetheart's chin, freckles on her ears, has her "milk the heifer calf, and not miss the bucket more than half," prepare Billy a dinner of "corn-pone with fat meat," "make good home brew," "feed a sucking pig," etc. Perhaps the banjo picker, or a wandering British fiddler of the seventeenth century, with a slouch hat on, wearing a celluloid rose in his coat lapel, and a high, blue, celluloid collar, with a banjo across his knees, and smelling of cinnamon oil, is the individual who makes the doctor drink the chicken broth in one of the songs mentioned above; also the one who adds the closing stanza of "Jack Went A-Sailing," as he was proposing to some man's daughter. No doubt about it, he leaves the traditional folk-song "in a sad *disprise.*"

Among British survivals it is the lyric or love song that now shows the greatest vitality, not only in the Highlands, but in other sections of the United States. Begun in the seventeenth century, the transition from the epic or narrative type to the lyric has continued, even among the Highlanders, the great majority of whose songs are now lyric, or at least epic-lyric. In many songs it is difficult to determine which of the two elements predominates, but the transition is there, which would indicate that such songs belong to the seventeenth century. It has been contended that the extensive currency of such songs as "James Harris," "Lord Thomas and Fair Annet," "Little Musgrave and Lady Barnard," "The Wife of Usher's Well," "The Gypsie Laddie," "Fair Margaret and Sweet William," "Jack Went A-Sailing," and some others, all story-songs, puts the epic type above the lyric type, as to persistence. That is because all the above mentioned songs but the last one happen to be songs of the Child collection, and have therefore been given more prominence than they would have received otherwise. Yet, there are certain native American lyric songs which show considerably more vitality than any of the above: "Florella," which is sung in every state of the Union; "Springfield Mountain"; and "The Dying Cowboy," which is an adaptation, but nevertheless an American ballad. "Young (Fair) Charlotte," although hardly a folk-song, has a currency over the country rivalling that of "Florella." "Barbara Allen," a traditional British song of the Child collection which is certainly more lyric than epic, has the most extensive currency of any British song in America. Nearly a hundred variants have been found to date.

Traditional vulgar and humorous songs have shown great vitality in the Highlands, although they are not so extensive in currency as the love songs, for obvious reasons. One of such songs, "Kind Betty," evidently of great age, is too obscene to be printed. "The Rich Old Lady," commonly known over America as "Johnny Sands," and sometimes as "The Old Woman of London," is a survival of the British "The Old Woman of Slapsadam," or "The Wife of Kelso," included in the Child manuscripts in the Harvard College Library. It is often attributed to John Sinclair (1842), but Sinclair wrote only the music used for variants of it that appear in some songbooks. Other vulgar and humorous survivals are: "The Tailor and the Chest," "There Was a Sea Captain," "Kate and Her Horns," "Come all ye jolly boatsman boys," "Fair

Nottiman Town," and "The Old Wife." ["Kate and Her Horns,"
known in the Highlands as "Kate and the Clothier," commences ab-
ruptly in the midst of the story, the first half of the song having been
lost. Professor Mackenzie has found a twenty-stanza variant of it in
Nova Scotia, which preserves the story intact.[6] This song is a good example of a traditional song derived from a literary source. In Mackenzie's variant, the opening stanza is certainly not that of a ballad
maker, nor does it have anything in common with the commonly accepted ballad text:

> You that in merriment delight,
> Pray listen now to what I write;
> So shall you satisfaction find
> Will cure a melancholy mind.

Another example of a song probably derived from some source other
than the folk is "Come all ye jolly boatsman boys." Its structure places
it away from folk origin, and it is *in toto* apparently complete. A certain mark of its literary or artistic origin is the *rime concatenée*, which
appears in eight of the ten stanzas, thus putting this song with respect
to structure, in a class of its own among the Highlanders. It was contributed by an old lady who was then (1909) in her eighties, and who
said that the song had been known for a long time in her family.]

Two vulgar songs of the Child collection survive in "Our Goodman" and "The Broomfield Hill." A number of variants of the former
have been found in the Highlands. A West Virginia variant, imported
from Michigan, surpasses all British texts in vulgarity.[7] "The Broomfield Hill" has not, to my knowledge, been hitherto recorded in
America. Distinctly humorous songs of the Child collection survive in
"The Wife Wrapt in Wether's Skin," "The Farmer's Curst Wife," and
"Get Up and Bar the Door."

Almost no distinctive songs of the sea have survived among the
Highlanders, a condition which may seem unusual, since the Highlanders are direct descendants of a race of seamen. The sea, ships,
sailors, "bonny boats," and sea captains are mentioned often enough
in the Highlander's songs, but they are incidental. For some reason or
other, Child includes only four sea-songs in his collection: Nos. 285,
286, 287, 288. No. 286, "The Golden Vanity," survives in the Highlands, in a fairly good variant.

[6] [W. Roy Mackenzie, *The Quest of the Ballad*, 146 ff.]
[7] [See Appendix, No. 11—D. K. W.]

Survivals of carols and ballads of sacred tradition are likewise rare. Child himself included but few songs of this type,[8] one of which is sung by the Highlanders, "The Cherry-Tree Carol." A peculiar variant of this song of sacred tradition comes from West Virginia. Two other survivals of the traditional carol are "The Little Family" and "Three Ships Came Sailing In." A song of later origin, probably dating from the eighteenth century, is "The Romish Lady," directed against Roman Catholicism. A century ago it was very popular among the settlers who were opening up the country west of the Alleghenies, and was one of Abraham Lincoln's favorites.[9]

Among the folk-songs of this collection appearing under the heading of "Songs of British Origin," one may class at least twenty-five of the more than fifty as worthy representatives of balladry. The majority of them are lyric. One of them, "The Lady and the Fan" (the ballad of the den of lions), failed to find its way into Child, although it was one of the great compiler's favorites. Up to date, it has been found only in Kentucky and Missouri, and is a rare song. With the poems of Browning, Leigh Hunt, and Schiller in mind ("The Glove," "The Glove and the Lions," "*Der Handschuh*"), Professor Kittredge thinks this famous ballad is derived from a literary source.[10] It is more probable that the two poems of Browning and Leigh Hunt are derived from the ballad of "The Lady and the Fan (Glove)," or at any rate, have as their source an incident celebrated in French history.[11] Of course, Schiller's poem is derived from the same source. Browning and Leigh Hunt may or may not have been familiar with the folk-song in question, but it is quite possible that they were since the song is a variant of an eighteenth-century broadside, "The Faithful Lover; or

[8] "St. Stephen and Herod" (No. 22), "Judas" (No. 23), "The Cherry-Tree Carol" (No. 54), "Dives and Lazarus" (No. 56).

[9] W. H. Herndon and J. W. Weik, *Abraham Lincoln*, I, 56. ["The Romish Lady" occurs in seventeenth-century broadside texts, and one line is quoted in the text of Fletcher's *The Knight of the Burning Pestle* (1613), V, iii. See G. Malcolm Laws, Jr., *American Balladry from British Broadsides* (Philadelphia, Pennsylvania, 1957) for basic references—D. K. W.]

[10] Letter to J. H. Combs. But Kittredge adds: "Of course the broadside may well be based upon a 'popular tale.'"

[11] The incident at the court of Francis I, in which an infantry captain, de Lorge, recovered a lady's glove which she had thrown into a den of lions. See Brantome, *Memoires*; de Saintfois, *Essais historiques sur Paris*. [In addition to the eighteenth-century English ballad cited by Combs, there is a print of the seventeenth century, "The Distressed Lady, or A Trial of Love. In Five Parts." The source of the English ballad tradition has been traced to sixteenth-century Spain. (See Helen Hartness Flanders *et al.*, *The New Green Mountain Songster* [New Haven, Connecticut, 1939] p. 69.)—D. K. W.]

The Hero Rewarded." And if the song belongs to the eighteenth century or earlier, certainly it is not derived from the poems of any of the above authors.

The refrain or chorus has been dropped from many British survivals in America, and preserved in a number. Some scholars, notably Sharp, think that the refrain is an unmistakable sign of the folk-song's antiquity.[12] There appears to be no absolute norm for the determination of the antiquity or age of a song from its refrain, nor does the refrain have any particular bearing on what should constitute a folk-song. Some of the earliest folk-songs that have come down to us have no refrains, while some of the more recent ones do have refrains. Such an element in balladry is a fleeting, uncertain thing, depending largely upon the whim of the maker or singer of the song. Adequate proof of this is not wanting in one of the oldest songs, "The Frog and the Mouse," commonly known in the United States as "The Frog Went A-Courting" or "The Frog's Courtship." This song is known in every state of the country, in various versions, and is the most universal of all traditional songs surviving in the English-speaking world. Some versions have the refrain in different forms, some have a repetend or a line or more repeated in each stanza, while others have no refrain at all. [For the sake of comparison, let us examine the refrains and inset burdens of six variants of this song, from Kentucky, Pennsylvania, West Virginia, and from the Negroes:

> A frog went a-courting and he did ride,
>> *Too a rig tum maddy middy kamo!*
> With a sword and a pistol by his side,
>> *Too a rig tum maddy middy kamo!*
> *Chorus*:
> *Kamo naro do see kamo kamo,*
> *Too my step stap stum a-diddle,*
> *Lar-y bony link tum,*
> *My bony maddy maddy middy kamo,*
> *Kamo gaido gaido kamo gaido linton gaido,*
> *Step stap stum a-stiddle lar-y bony linktum!*
>> —Pennsylvania

> A frog went a-courting he did ride, *uh huh,*
> A frog went a-courting he did ride,
> Sword and pistol by his side, *uh huh.*
>> —West Virginia

> There was a frog lived in a rill,
>> *Too roo loo rup ah loo rah lay,*

[12] Cecil J. Sharp, *English Folk-Song: Some Conclusions*, p. 93.

There was a frog lived in a rill,
 Too roo lay,
There was a frog lived in a rill,
While lady mouse lived in the mill,
 Too roo lay too roo lay.

     —West Virginia

A frog he went a-courting and he did ride,
 Too tiddle dee dum,
Sword and pistol by his side,
 Too tiddle dee dum,
Rode till he come to the miller's house,
Off come in and take a chair,
 Too tiddle dee dum.

     —Kentucky

A frog went a-courting and he did ride,
 Lickety splickety lickety lunk,
With a sword and pistol by his side,
 Lickety splickety lickety lunk.
Chorus:
Onrey orey ickery Ann,
Fillison follisen Nicholas John,
Neavey queavey English navy,
Strimm stramm buck.

     —West Virginia

Dar wuz uh frog what lived in uh spring,
 Sing song Polly cain't ye ki me-o,
He had sich uh cold dat he could not sing,
 Sing song Polly cain't ye ki me-o.
Chorus:
Kamo kimo daro war mee hi mee ho,
My rumpstipumstididdle,
Soot bag piddy winckem linck em nip cat,
Sing song Polly cain't ye ki me-o.

     —The Negroes

From such a medley, one may choose and take![13]] It will readily be seen that the refrain is often an unintelligible jumble of nonsense, devoid of all sense or meaning, and may appear in either serious or silly songs. There is no evidence that the original ballad maker employed it at all. Whenever a singer recites the words of a folk-song (which is always difficult for him), he usually omits the refrain, repetend, or

[13] [Two variants from New Hampshire have different refrains; out of three additional variants from Kentucky, two have different refrains, while one has none; out of two from North Carolina, one has it (a refrain?), one does not.]

both. If called upon to sing the song, he always includes the chorus, if the song has one. Of the Child ballads in this collection, only two have retained the refrain: "The Two Sisters" and "The Mermaid," and it is doubtful if the refrain of the former could be called a refrain.[14] Nonsensical lines and the repetition of certain lines are, however, quite common.

The nonsensical refrain is not dialect, and should be divorced or dissociated from the dialectal peculiarities of the folk-song. The ravaging hand of time has handled it more relentlessly than the song text itself. "Many refrains," says Streenstrup, "have become meaningless; by daily repetition their form has been marred and their substance rendered uncertain. Finally many ballads have lost their original refrains, and have been forced to borrow others, in many cases getting hold of one that did not fit. At length they have ended up with the modern nonsensical refrains, *nonnenino, didaderit*, and the like."[15] Perhaps the nonsensical refrains have always been meaningless, from their beginning, albeit their form has changed. Steenstrup supposedly speaks with reference to his native (Danish) ballads, in which the refrain is more universal than it is in British folk-songs. Certainly it is not necessary to refer to the nonsensical refrains as "modern." [A case of borrowing appears in a West Virginia variant of "Sir Lionel," which has taken over the refrain of "The Frog and the Mouse."]

The Language of the Folk-Song

In their centuries-old oral transmission, survivals of the traditional British folk-song in the Southern Highlands, thrown into the crucible of new environments in a new world, have undergone certain linguistical transformations and changes. Like the language spoken by their singers, they have been fitted more or less to new and changing conditions. In general it may be said that the language employed by the Highland singer in his folk-songs is superior to that employed in his everyday speech, both as to diction and to grammatical accuracy. When he sings a folk-song, the Highlander realizes that its language is something which is different, somehow, from that of his daily speech; this is true for the traditional song, and for that of his own making.

---

[14] [Combs evidently failed to revise this passage, as he did others, after being required to omit certain texts from the printed collection. The text of "The Mermaid" is lost—D. K. W.]

[15] J. C. H. R. Streenstrup, *The Medieval Popular Ballad*, trans. E. G. Cox, p. 81.

True, many sorts of irregularities, syntactical and grammatical, appear in both sorts of speech of the Highlander, but his daily speech is more loose and careless. Folk-song speech, then, does not hold close to everyday speech, at least with respect to the Southern Highlands.[16] Bujeaud has remarked this difference in French folk-song also, observing: "Le paysan qui parle patois à son ordinaire, le repousse quand il chante."[17] There is, however, a folk-song patois, if one considers certain mannerisms and stock expressions common to traditional balladry as such. Of this, Highland songs are replete, most of it inherited, and the rest indigenous.

An examination of such Child songs in this collection, and of such native American songs as "Floyd Frazier," "William Baker," "John Hardy," as well as many others, reveals a paucity of patois and grammatical inaccuracies. If the Highlander were asked to relate the story of these songs, his language would be full of both.

Aside from certain general ballad mannerisms, no general rules can be laid down for Highland folk-song diction, because the Highlander's speech differs over the South, as does that of the Negroes. Slurring of the *r*, a characteristic of Southern lowland speech, is almost unknown among the Highlanders, and consequently does not appear in their folk-songs. Even the Highland Negroes do not know it. Rhyme and meter may be mighty instruments in the hands of the ballad singer, and often bring about changes from his everyday speech. Pronouns may be freely omitted, and *have* is made to rhyme with *brave*. At the entrance to a lonely "grave-yard" on the summit of a Kentucky mountain these words appear: GOD BLESS THOSE SLEEPS HERE. The familiar ending -*ing* seldom becomes -*in'* in the Highlander's folk-songs, although the latter is common in his everyday speech. Even an auxiliary verb, or other part of speech, may be dispensed with if it gets in the way of rhyme or meter:

> I will tell you of a circumstance
> Which happened not very long (ago).
> —"Floyd Frazier"

> But the one who lingered near
> Was the man they all did fear
> Who had (done) the awful deed.
> —"J. B. Marcum"

---

[16] See J. H. Combs, "Dialect of the Folk-Song," *Dialect Notes*, IV (1916), 311 ff.
[17] Jerome Bujeaud, *Chants populaires des provinces de l'Ouest*, I, 7.

Ago and *done* are omitted. A Virginia variant of "The Holly Twig" has these two lines:

> But kisses and guineas I made them fly,
> I slipped on my beaver hat, and who was like I?

A stanza of "Come All You Fair and Tender Ladies" has these lines:

> The leaves they may wither, the flowers they may die,
> Some young man may fool you, as one has fooled I!

Many of these irregularities are of course due to the Highlander's tendency to use formal terms glibly, and the pronoun *I* is a good example of this, in song and speech. A Tennessee singer says, in "The Warfare is Raging,"

> O Johnny, O Johnny, I think it's you're unkind,
> When I love you better than all other *mankind*.

And this:

> I knew her mind was changing,
> By the *movements* of her eye.

Or this:

> Go on at your own *exposition*,
> And court whoever you please.

Or,

> With sad *limitation* I surely must die.

As has been remarked elsewhere, the Scottish vocabulary has practically vanished from Highland survivals, as it has in the same songs in England. But English and Scottish mannerisms have not vanished, by any means, as some American scholars think. They are even carried over to native American songs, which will be discussed later. One of the finest, as well as the most artistic stanzas in British balladry is stanza 5 of the Scottish song, "Waly, Waly, Gin Love be Bonny," four lines of which follow: [18]

> But had I wist before I kisst,
> That love had been sae ill to win,
> I had locked my heart in a case of gowd (gold),
> And pinned it with a siller pin.

[18] Thomas Percy, *Reliques of Ancient English Poetry*, 2d ed. (1767), III, 143 ff.

Compare this stanza with the following, from a Kentucky variant of
"Come All You Fair and Tender Ladies," or "Little Sparrow," which
may be a distant variant of the famous Scottish song:

> I wish I'd known before I courted,
> That love had been such a killing crime;
> I'd a-locked my heart with a key of golden,
> And tied it down with a silver line.

The conventional beginnings and endings of the folk-song, full of mannerisms, are well accounted for; the folk find it difficult to commence
or to close a song.

Stress on a final syllable of the final word of a line has been faithfully preserved in Highland song, for the most part. The most frequent
instance of this is the ending *-ly*, as in love-*lie*, quick-*lie*, hase-*lie*
(hastily), la-*dee*, etc. Present and past participial endings are also
stressed, the most common ones being *-ed*, *-en*, and *-ing*. However, the
final syllable of almost any part of speech may be thus stressed. Such
a tendency, for the sake of rhyme or meter, seems always to have been
common in British balladry. Percy's contention that this tendency is
a cast of style that belonged to the minstrels must be taken *cum grano
salis*; the minstrels merely adopted it, because they were no better
rhymesters than the folk. He gives as examples coun*trie*, la*dy*, harp*er*,
sing*er*, batt*el*, dam*sel*, morn*ing*, lov*ing*. Louise Pound is of the opinion
that the tendency to stress a final syllable represents ". . . traces of the
retention of French accent, the language of the upper classes and the
court, and there is frequent transference of it to native words like *lady,
water, thousand, Douglas, London*."[19] There is no proof that stressing
of final syllables was ever common among the upper classes and at
the court, and certainly these classes had little to do with ballad-
making! [The "French accent" is likewise foreign to the question, since
the folk were ignorant of that language in the ballad age; the pronunciation of the final syllable in French is not particularly stressed anyway.]

[19] Pound, *Poetic Origins and the Ballad*, p. 109.

CHAPTER VII

Native American Songs

IF ANY JUSTIFICATION for the above title is needed, it must of necessity be sought in the folk-songs that have come to be called American. In the beginning we venture the assertion that there is a native American balladry, however much or little it may owe to Old World types. Since the era of colonization, conditions in the New World have been ideal for the making and propagation of the folk-song. The spirit of British balladry did not die with the advent of the eighteenth century in England and Scotland; it continued to live here and there in the remote farmhouse, whose humble occupants even today give voice to what was once a mighty instrument for the amusement of the people. Some parts of America, far removed from the populous and industrial centers, have preserved the spirit of balladry in the New World, because the people of these parts are living under conditions similar in part to those which produced much British balladry; and because their way of living and their habits have not changed materially from those of their ancestors of the seventeenth and eighteenth centuries. If a hundred British folk-songs identified in the great Child collection have been discovered in America, if they still have considerable currency in certain sections, notably the Southern Highlands, it is quite reasonable to assume that the singers of these songs are making more songs. In other words, one may say that we are now witnessing the second phase of British balladry, transplanted to the New World. Of course, it is not on such a large scale as that of the British Isles, but its existence seems to be well established. What if a number of American songs are based on British archetypes, or are adaptations of them? That does not nullify the contention for a native American balladry. We say that certain folk-songs common to France are similar, in subject matter or incident, to songs of the other romance nations, but we call them French songs. But as we shall show later on, there is a native American balladry, quite distinct from British balladry.

It is incorrect to assume that those songs commonly called American songs are "imported," or that they are all "adaptations." Sharp is of the opinion that the United States has no folk-lore of its own, for all of that which at first seemed to have originated there could be traced back to some other country.[1] A considerable mass of Negro and Indian folk-lore, including songs, is not even questioned in America. It has been the subject of much study in America, including a number of books, brochures, and magazine articles.[2] Louise Pound likes to assume that too many American songs are adaptations, or are imported.[3] Yet she lists and includes in her collection twenty-four songs as "native." "Awake! Awake!" ("The Silver Dagger"), listed by Miss Pound as native, is, however, a British song, which is found in a number of British collections, such as Christie's *Traditional Ballad Airs* (I, 225), Greig's *Folk-Song of the North-East* (I, art. 54), and *Folk-Songs from Somerset*, by C. J. Sharp and C. L. Marson (No. 99). Among the best known adaptations are, as Pound points out, "The Lone Prairie" and "The Dying Cowboy," both of which have considerable currency over the United States. But their subject matter is such that they must be classed as American songs.[4]

It is a very natural thing for those scholars who hold to the theory of popular origin for the folk-song to deny the existence of a native American balladry. To admit that such balladry exists is to deny popular origin. For in these days, if the process of popular or communal composition were in vogue, we should certainly know something about it. Thus the silence of the champions of popular origin, with regard to native American songs, or songs of more recent origin. Says Phillips

[1] Cecil J. Sharp, lecture in Chicago, 1915.

[2] See Thomas W. Talley, *Negro Folk Rhymes*; W. F. Allen, C. P. Ware, L. McKim Garrison, *Slave Songs of the United States; Journal of American Folklore*, 1888–; and other publications and magazines.

[3] Louise Pound, *American Ballads and Songs; Poetic Origins and the Ballad*.

[4] It has not been seen fit to include "Young (Fair) Charlotte" in the present collection, a song widely discussed by American scholars. It does not have one ballad touch, and was written by W. L. Carter of Vermont, apparently in 1833. No variants of the song have been found, and it has little claim to the title of folk-song. [Authorship of the ballad has since been assigned to Seba Smith. See G. Malcolm Laws, Jr., *Native American Balladry* (Philadelphia, Pennsylvania, 1964), p. 221—D. K. W.]

Barry, an American folk-lorist of no mean repute: "Yet there is a certain proportion (of the abundance of folk-song now circulating in America) which is of our soil. The value of this small proportion, though of meagre worth when judged by literary standards and contrasted with 'Earl Brand' or 'King Estmere,'—beside which it may well seem but trivial stuff,—is great when approached from the viewpoint of the seeker after truth, by reason of the light it sheds on the process by which ballads come to be."[5] This was written in 1909, before the existence and currency of a large number of native American songs were generally known; hence the expression, "small proportion." Professor H. M. Belden, of the University of Missouri, holds a similar view with respect to the existence of a native American balladry. "Besides the representatives of Old World balladry so far considered, there is a considerable number of what may fairly be described as American ballads. Some of them, to be sure, are plainly derived or adapted from British vulgar ballads, but they have been so far made over as to have acquired a perceptibly American coloring."[6] Professor J. A. Lomax, of the University of Texas, is authority for the statement that there is a considerable body of indigenous popular song in the western United States, the states of Texas, Arizona, and New Mexico being the most fertile.[7] Lomax has collected numerous indigenous folk-songs belonging to the cowboys of the United States and Canada, railroad men, lumbermen, rivermen, miners, soldiers, seamen, and Negroes.[8]

There is, then, a native American balladry, although even its best representatives cannot be said to compare favorably with those of the "ballad age" in the British Isles. The conditions have not been favorable for such a comparison, or for the making of songs of the "heroic" type. The hero of Owen Wister's *The Virginian* sings sixty-three stanzas of "My Lulu Girl," in Montana! The distribution and currency of the native American folk-song vary according to the conditions of society, isolation, occupation, etc. Mention of some of the types of song in the process of making has been made in the chapter "The Quest of the Folk-Song." Supplementing the list there given, the following geographical distribution may be noted: The Southern High-

[5] Phillips Barry, "Native Balladry in America," *Journal of American Folklore*, XXII, 365.

[6] H. M. Belden, "Balladry in America," *ibid.*, XXV, 12.

[7] J. A. Lomax, "Cowboy Songs of the Mexican Border," *The Sewanee Review*, XIX, 1.

[8] See also Lomax, *Cowboy Songs and Other Frontier Ballads.*

lands; the plains of the West, Southwest, and Northwest, or wherever the open range is still found—including sections of the following states: Texas, Oklahoma, Arizona, New Mexico, Utah, Colorado, California, the two Dakotas, Montana, and elsewhere; the forests of Maine and the Northwest, and wherever the lumber industry thrives;[9] the water courses of the United States, wherever they are used for transporting rafts of logs to market, chiefly in the mountainous sections; the South, in general, wherever the Negro is found, especially outside the larger cities; the Ozark Mountains, in Arkansas and Missouri. The Ozarks still lie before the collector of the folk-song, as yet almost untouched. They represent a section of America similar in many respects to the Southern Highlands.

Grouped as to periods of American history, native American songs fall under two divisions: songs of the Colonial Period, and songs of the National Period. The first period is unimportant, having produced few songs that have come down to us as folk-songs. The period may have been prolific in the making of songs, but if so, they survived probably no longer than the generation that produced them. It is possible that the Indian wars, the French and Indian War (1754–1763), and the Revolution brought into prominence for a time a large body of American folk-songs; a few of these have survived, and are current here and there over the country. The two songs of widest diffusion that have come down from colonial times are "Springfield Mountain" and "The Pretty Maumee (Mohee)," the first dating from around 1761, and being one of the few native New England songs. The second relates a love affair between an Indian lass and a colonist evidently. Its history is vague, and nothing is known of its origin or age. Both of these songs are heard in almost every section of the United States. "Brave Wolfe" survives from the French and Indian War, and describes the Battle of Quebec, in which Generals Wolfe and Montcalm are both mortally wounded. In West Virginia, school children have been heard singing it to the tune of "Yankee Doodle." Professor Mackenzie says that every peasant in Canada has his version of this song.[10] But the song is not representative of the ballad spirit and style. [It may be a Canadian or an English product.] "Paul Jones," a song of the redoubtable naval hero, is a product of the Revolution, and, as Phillips Barry has pointed out, is also well known to British folk-singers.

---

[9] See Roland P. Gray, *Songs and Ballads of the Maine Lumberjacks.*
[10] W. Roy Mackenzie, *The Quest of the Ballad*, p. 3.

Native American folk-song assumes a more definite shape and character in the nineteenth century, because we are able to examine it from actual, current representatives of the folk. [A classification of the various types has been made in a previous chapter.] From this heterogeneous mass of song, at least two conclusions can be drawn: first, the United States can lay claim to a native balladry; second, songs whose history lies within the memories of those who sing them must help to clear up the mystery (if any there be) of the method of folk-song composition. As a result, some theories of bygone days are destined to become antiquated and untenable.

How do these native American songs differ in structure and content from British balladry of the past? And which among them are the most characteristically American? A glance at the narrative songs reveals at once a sweeping transition in theme, one that has been the result of a society which no longer knows kings, queens, royal and noble personages, elfs and sprites, and the supernatural. For all these there has been substituted a variety of themes which are close to the people and the conditions under which they live. Songs of outlaws, of murder and tragedy have considerable currency, as they had in the British Isles. The lyric or love song has not materially changed in theme, in the very nature of things. Structurally, indigenous American songs, with the exception of those of the Negroes and Indians, have undergone no perceptible change from British types. Here and there mannerisms and commonplace lines and stanzas have crept in, but they cannot be said to characterize indigenous songs. Two famous stanzas of "The Lass of Roch Royal" have been incorporated in "John Hardy," "The Brown-Eyed Boy," and a few others. A Highland singer has put into "I'm Going to Join the Army" two fine stanzas from "Jack Went A-Sailing" ("Jackie Row"). The familiar "Come all ye" beginning is common in a large number of songs. The excrescent *all*, so common to British balladry, characterizes many Highland songs, *e.g.*: "*All* in the merry month of May"; "A bottle of wine *all* in my hands"; "He picked her up *all* in his arms." The sea, so vividly reminiscent of the Highlander's ancestors, has crept into many songs, sometimes where it is ludicrously anachronistic or out of place. A variant of "John Hardy," whose hero is a Negro hanged for murder in West Virginia, has the criminal's father "cross the deep blue sea" to bail him out of jail!

In some respects, songs of the plains, or cowboy songs, are the most characteristically American of all. As a rule, they are free from the mannerisms of British songs, are intensely personal, have little romance or sentiment, reflect the solitary life of the plainsman, and afford a fairly complete analysis of the cowboy's state of mind. No early folk-song maker ever poured forth in "strains of unpremeditated art" a more personal note than does this holder of a government claim, in Oklahoma:

> Ernest Smith is my name, an old Bachelor I am,
> I'm keeping old batch on an immigrant plan;
> You'll find me out West on a highroad to fame,
> A-starving to death on a Government claim.
>
> How happy I am when I crawl into bed,
> The rattlesnakes rattling a tune at my head;
> The shy little centipede crew of all fears,
> Creeps over my shoulders and into my ears.
>
> —"The Government Claim"

The variety of theme in songs of the plains is suggested in the following: the hard lot of the cowpuncher—his solitary existence, his hardships and troubles, his daily routine of life, his mother, sister, or sweetheart; his differences with organized authority, with which he sometimes comes in conflict in the frontier towns, while under the influence of drink; his thoughts of death and the hereafter, caused by his loneliness; his burlesques on certain of the unfavorable topographical features, climate, animals, and insects of the Southwest; his thoughts as he follows the long trail, driving cattle to market, or to the range; the Texas Revolution, the Mexican War, and troubles of the Texas Rangers with the Mexicans along the Rio Grande.[11]

The few traditional folk-songs that have found their way into the cowboy's repertory were probably taken to the West by Southerners who became cowpunchers. It is not likely that such songs were imported by the scions of English nobility who have from time to time become cowboys temporarily. The cowboy song as a type, as characteristically American as it is, certainly does not stand up favorably in comparison with the British folk-song. Many or most of such songs have no distinctive style, and are very crude structurally. Lomax has referred to them as "raw collops slashed from the rump of nature."[12]

---

[11] Buffalo Bill, perhaps the most celebrated Indian scout, buffalo hunter, and frontiersman in American history, has miraculously escaped the folk-song maker. His reputation has been international; yet, as far as is known, no songs have been made about him.

[12] Professor Lomax's collection, *Cowboy Songs*, consists of a hundred and fifty-three songs, the majority of which are native American songs; some are adaptations of other songs and poems, while others are plainly the work of newspaper poets.

For the plainsman seems not to have inherited the folk-song traditions common to the Southern Highlander, and being thus despoiled of this inheritance, has usually only himself and his daily routine as subjects for song. No wonder his songs are self-centered and self-conscious. In a way, there is an abundance of incident and excitement in the life of the cowboy, that picturesque and romantic figure in American history. He is adventuresome, chivalrous, hospitable, calm, and of a taciturn character, facing the hot sands of the desert, heat, cold, rain (whenever he can get it!), always on the skirmish line of danger, living hard, shooting quick and sure, dying with his face to the foe. The fearless man on horseback has been the most potent factor in the opening up of the West and Southwest. Although bemoaning in song his hard lot, yet he is proud of his profession as a bull-whacker:

> Abraham emigrated in search of a range,
> And when water was scarce he wanted a change;
> Old Issac owned cattle in charge of Esau,
> And Jacob punched cows for his father-in-law.
> —"The Cowboy"

The period which was especially prolific for the song of the plains was the latter half of the last century, or the beginning of the great pioneer movement westward. But many cowboy songs must have been made as early as the Texas Revolution (1835–1845),[13] in which Texas became free from Mexico. A number of songs precede even this period, for pioneers and roving adventurers had begun to populate the country north of the Rio Grande not long after the Louisiana Purchase (1803).[14]

The Highlanders have adopted a considerable number of songs belonging to or originating among the Negroes. Some of these songs have long been current in the Highlands, from the days prior to the Civil War, and include banjo- and nonsense-songs, besides some spirituals and songs of the British type. Since the Civil War a number of Negro occupational songs have crept in, notably such well-known ones as "John Hardy," "John Henry," "The Yew-Pine Mountain," "Frankie," "Lynchburg Town," "The Kicking Mule," "Turkey in the Straw," and others. As a rule, the Negro folk-song, even at its best, has few of the real ballad touches. "John Hardy" is almost the sole

[13] [Combs seems to be dating the entire period of Texan-Mexican violence, rather than simply the Texas Revolution—D. K. W.]

[14] The true cowboy is not to be found in dime novels and cheap, sensational moving pictures, but rather in the stories of Emerson Hough and Zane Gray.

exception, and it is possible that the ballad touches in it are the result of re-creation by the whites. The Negro does not know the traditional folk-song, and rarely do its mannerisms come under his observation. The Negroes have adopted very few traditional songs of the whites; among them are: "The Maid Freed from the Gallows" (Virginia); "The Frog and the Mouse"; "Little Pink"; "Jesse James" and some outlaw and railroad songs; "Here Comes a Duke," a *ronde*. Neither "John Hardy" nor "John Henry" ("The Steel-Driving Man") originated among the whites, as most American balladists claim. Nor are they two variants of the same song. The court records of southern West Virginia show that Hardy was a Negro. The story in "John Henry" is entirely different—Henry, also a Negro, loses his life in an attempt to compete with a steam-drill on the railroad. Both songs happen to be similar in structure, and are undoubtedly products of the Negroes. "The Yew-Pine Mountain" is an offshoot of "John Henry." There is no proof that "Jesse James" was made by the Negroes; it belongs probably to the central West, the scene of most of the modern Robin Hood's "operations."

[The most characteristic of the Negro songs are the spirituals. Along with the songs of the Indian and the plainsman, they are a distinct contribution to native American song. It may be a mistake to include Negro spirituals in a collection such as this; but they differ so essentially in form and content from the songs of the whites that they merit consideration. Their emotional pitch is mentioned in the chapter dealing with the Highlander's music, and their relation to mode of composition, in the chapter dealing with the question of origin. Four of them are especially interesting because of their evident communal origin: "Jacob's Ladder," "We Have Fathers Gone to Heaven," "The Ship that Is Passing By," and "I Got a Robe." They are representatives of hundreds of their kind among the Negroes over the Southland.]

As valuable as are the songs of the Negroes in a study of folk-songs, not only with respect to origins, but also in regard to the light they throw on the Negro's character or mentality, they can hardly stand inspection alongside the songs of the whites. The Negro is certainly not a fair representative of what we like to call the ballad-making epoch in America. His mental processes are not adequate to the burden which some scholars have imposed upon him. His period of slavery to the whites in America lasted two and a half centuries, yet there has sprung up no cycle of songs or poems commemorating or protesting his long bondage; on the contrary, his songs seem to praise his masters!

The written verse and literature that does deal with such subjects was made by Northern abolitionists just prior to and during the Civil War.[15] Genuine Negro songs have often been confused with songs of black-face comedians and vaudeville, and have often been corrupted by them. After the Civil War, Negro music and song were seriously impaired by the compositions of cheap song-writers and publishers. The emancipation of the blacks (1863) interfered with and interrupted much Negro folk-lore. At that time a considerable body of slave songs were current, few of which are now heard. The section in and around New Orleans produced a strange species of song neither French nor Negro, but a medley of the two, in dialect.[16]

Of widest diffusion and currency of all indigenous American songs are those relating to bandits, outlaws, and criminals. This type appeals to a people still crude in many ways, a people which still pays homage to brute force and physical prowess. Such songs are very popular among all classes that sing and make folk-songs in America. The songs among the Highlanders, included in the present collection, testify to their popularity and vogue in that section. Others not included, but which are also heard in the Highlands are: "Jack Donohoo," "McAfee's Confession," "Sam Bass," "Bonny Black Bess," "Turpin and

[15] *Uncle Tom's Cabin*, a grossly inaccurate picture of pre-war slavery, by Harriet Beecher Stowe; the poems of Whittier; etc.

[16] ["Belle Layotte" and "Calinda," two of such songs, are as follows:

Belle Layotte

Mo roulé tout la côte,
Mo roulé tout la colonie;
Mo pancor ouar griffone la
Qua mo gout comme la belle Layotte.

Refrain:

Mo déjà roulé tout la côte
Pancor ouar pareil belle Layotte,
Mo déjà roulé tout la côte
Pancor ouar pareil belle Layotte.

Jean Babet, mon ami,
Si fou couri par en haut,
Vous mandé belle Layotte
Cadeau la li té promi mouin.

Domestique la maison
Ye tout fach avec mouin,
Paraporte chanson la
Mo compose pou la belle Layotte.

Calinda

Michié Preval li donnin gran bal,
Li fait naig payé pou sauté inpé.

Refrain:

Dansé calinda, boudoum, boudoum,
Dansé calinda, boudoum, boudoum

Michié Préval li té capitaine bal,
So cocher Louis té maite cérémonie.

Dans le quirie la yavé gran gala,
Mo cré choual layé té bien etonné.

Yavé des negresse belle passé maitresse,
Ye volé bebelle dans l'ormoire mamzelle.

Notice the frequent omission of prepositions, articles, auxiliary verbs; and the contractions: *mo*—me, *mon, je*; *li*—*lui, le, la*; *ya, yavé*—*il y avait*; *oura*—*voir* and its inflections; *pancor*—*pas encore*; *michié*—*monsieur*; *inpé*—*un peu*.]

the Lawyer." [In the central West and elsewhere "The Death of Young Bendall," "John T. Williams" and some others are common. "John T. Williams" may be a Canadian song.] "Captain Kidd," still heard here and there, is another of the few songs that have lived from colonial times; it tells of the arrest, trial, and conviction in London (1701) of the bold buccaneer.

It may seem strange that no cycle of song has grown up around Jesse James, the most remarkable outlaw since the days of Robin Hood. Some American scholars think that such a cycle exists, in North Carolina and elsewhere, but not enough material has come to hand to justify the contention. The songs that have been made about the bandit are all similar, relating the same incidents, and doubtless spring from some one original. They have little in common with the Robin Hood poems, as to folk-song style, etc., and usually glorify the notorious outlaw. "Jesse James" may be a product of the Negroes, but this cannot be established; besides, the leonine rhyme throughout the song is a little too artistic for Negro composition. James was born in North Carolina, and "operated" in the central West chiefly, after the Civil War, his specialties being railway trains and banks. He was fearless, a quick and sure shot, and had some of the qualities attributed to Robin Hood, those of chivalry, courtesy, and kindness toward all who were unfortunate, especially women. His career may aid in clearing up the question as to whether or not Robin Hood was a real or legendary character. Historians and chroniclers do not include bandits and outlaws in their works and observations, else Robin Hood might be a more tangible conception. The scope of his operations was too extensive to have been merely a product of folk imagination. "Jesse James" has been popular enough to cause other songs to be modeled upon it, chiefly "J. B. Marcum."

Among nearly all outlaw songs there runs a current of sympathy for the man that has infringed the rights or laws of his fellow men or of his country. It is noticeable even when the outlaw's depredations are of the worst sort—this sympathy for the transgressor, and for his wife or children. But this attitude is not to be interpreted as meaning that the song maker respects the laws of his country and the rights of his fellow citizens less, or that he respects the outlaw merely because the latter breaks the law and resists arrest. The attitude is one not new in society, not new in the history of feuds and folk-songs. The Corsican peasant sheltered the outlaw and feudist, and the Robin Hood poems show evidence that the bold bandit of Sherwood Forest had considerable sympathy among the people. The Southern Highlander, until recent years, freely offered shelter, and often protection, to the fugitive from justice. Such unusual sympathy, then, may be explained by the folk's admiration for the man in trouble, for his boldness and prowess, his resistance against great odds, although his acts of lawlessness are not condoned. In the Southern Highlands a man is rarely hanged or executed for murder; he usually gets off with a few years in prison. Robbery or theft is considered a crime equal to or greater than murder—another echo of the sixteenth century. Most outlaw and confessional songs, as well as others whose theme is tragedy, close with one or more stanzas of moral reflection, either on the part of the condemned or about him. Such stanzas are more characteristic of American songs than of British songs. They represent a transition from the purely impersonal to the personal touch of the folk-song.

The elements of grotesqueness and vulgarity are not lacking in American songs, and the same qualities are preserved in most of the British songs that have survived. Many indigenous songs are too obscene to be printed. Collectors usually miss them, because the folk-singer does not like to recite or sing such songs to outsiders. Violence is certainly as common to American songs as it is to the traditional British songs; for that is one thing that makes a folk-song, a tragic incident, and the more tragic, the more likelihood is there for the making of a song. The songs of the present collection demonstrate this.

Interspersed throughout the Highlander's repertory of song is an endless flotsam and jetsam of songs which defy classification, and which have been referred to here and there in this work. Among them is a large body made by or about gamblers and prisoners. They are highly personal, and some of them do not even tell a story, while others are narrative. "The Gambler" and "Wild Bill Jones" are examples. The "action" in "John Hardy" takes place at a gambling table, in a saloon. Most of such songs are made and sung to while away the time, and can hardly be classed as folk-songs. They belong to the banjo and fiddle. The business of moonshining is such a thriving one that we wonder why a body of songs characteristic of the "trade" has not sprung up in the Highlands and elsewhere. "Groun'-hog" is a banjo song that relates with charming naïveté the story of a spirited hunt for the woodchuck, or groundhog. The song is based on fact, and arrives at the fearful length of forty-four stanzas—certainly theme and material for a sweeping epic had the incident transpired in earlier times!

Of late years the simple lay of the Highlander is influencing some of the well-known novelists and poets of America. Mr. William A. Bradley has written some delightful verse in the spirit and style of Highland songs.[17] Miss Lucy Furman, in "Mothering on Perilous," has written a narrative poem in the ballad style, entitled "Blant's Revengement." "Sourwood Mountain," the fiddler's "national anthem of the Southern Highlands," and a song which Mr. Bradley so well imitates, figures in one of the stories of the celebrated novelist, John Fox, Jr.; in this story a group of Highland rivermen sing and fiddle the song as they pass under the bridge on a raft of logs at Frankfort, the capital of Kentucky. "Houn' Dog" is reminiscent of the presidential campaign of 1912, when the adherents of Champ Clark, of Missouri, took up the song and sang it over the country. It is native to the South.

[17] W. A. Bradley, *Singing Carr, and Other Song-Ballads of the Cumberlands,* (New York, 1918); *Old Christmas and Other Kentucky Tales in Verse,* (New York, 1917).

CHAPTER VIII

The Highlander's Music[1]

THE LEISURED CLASSES of America, as well as students of the folk-song, are only beginning to discover that the Southern Highlands in the United States possess not only a folk-literature of their own, but also a folk-music. The reason for delay is perhaps not difficult to find: trained musicians and lovers of artistic music have always turned up their noses at the simple music of the folk, as beautiful as it often is. There is nothing forced in this music, no conscious effort on the part of the singer to produce or render something artistic. No trained musician living could reproduce before an audience the airs and words of the Highlander's folk-songs as *he* sings them. Nor can they, or rather their music, be properly noted down on paper. Herein, then, lies the element, or secret of folk-music: it belongs to a race minus all previous training; it is highly impersonal in character; the singer is unconscious or oblivious as to what the listener or audience may think of it. As soon as the trained singer attempts to reproduce it orally, it ceases to be folk-music, and becomes in a way, the property of the artist—and the folk-singer is certainly no artist. One is here reminded of the artist who was singing before a Highland audience. When he had finished, a mountaineer walked up to him and said, "Well, Mister, the words of yer song was mighty pretty, but ye didn't *sing*."

The Highlanders make no effort to cultivate the art of singing. If a thing like that should happen, their folk-music would vanish. The art (to use the term guardedly) flourishes universally among them un-

[1] [This entire chapter was omitted from the French edition. See Foreword, pp. xiv f.—D. K. W.]

consciously. This was perhaps also true of the English commons during the ballad age. There is no reason why music should be cultivated by a few, clothed with the garments of art and rule, while the great majority listen, unable themselves to do something which every normal human being should do, sing. Music should not be the especial property of the few, but of all. In the Highlands it belongs to everybody, and everybody takes advantage of it.

No guess is hazarded as to the age or origin of Highland folk-music, for reasons already well known. Collectors in the British Isles, long ago, interested themselves in recording the words of folk-songs, without the airs, and largely from manuscript collections. Much was thus lost, beyond hope of recovery. However, had all the airs been preserved, it is probable that their age and origin would still be more or less a mystery. Certainly the tunes vie in interest with the words, and their origin is as uncertain. The two should never be dissociated by the collector. Many folk-airs are doubtless of greater antiquity than the words which accompany them, for, as a rule, an air may linger in the memory long after its words have been forgotten; it may later be used with the words of other songs. The number of folk-songs extant probably is in excess of the number of folk-tunes, since one tune often serves several songs. Another reason, apparently, for the lack of preservation of folk-airs in the British Isles three and four centuries ago is that the trained musician scorned them, since they were the property of the folk and of the minstrels, and therefore "artless."

The Highlander assimilates and adopts much outside music, particularly love songs and humorous songs. Commenting on a version of "John Hardy," Sharp says: "No better proof could be adduced of the way in which the mountain singers have assimilated and acquired the technique of balladry." It hardly seems an "acquisition," since the art has belonged to the Highlander for so long, descending directly from seventeenth-century England. However much the Highlander may assimilate and adopt, he invents little or nothing. Almost without exception, the airs of his traditional British songs, and more recent songs, are his merely by inheritance. In their collection[2] Mrs. Campbell and Mr. Sharp have noted down the airs of four hundred and fifty folk and love songs in the Southern Highlands. Seven Child songs, among others, are recorded, each with more than six airs: "Lord Thomas and Fair Annet," 11; "The Daemon Lover," 11; "Barbara

[2] Olive Dame Campbell and Cecil J. Sharp, *English Folk Songs from the Southern Appalachians.*

Allen," 10; "The Wife of Usher's Well," 8; "Little Musgrave and Lady Barnard," 8; "Fair Margaret and Sweet William," 7; "The Gypsy Laddie," 7. The average for the traditional ballad among the Highlanders is probably as high as four or five airs for each song.

No attempt is made here to offer a scientific discussion of the technique of Highland music. This is for the trained musician; besides, Sharp has done this so well (for the folk-song) that little remains to be said on that point.[3] The following classification suggests itself:

1. Folk-song airs, mostly of the traditional type.
2. Love-song airs, traditional and more recent.
3. Play-party-song airs, largely of the children.
4. Nursery and lullaby airs.
5. Nonsense airs.
6. Airs played on the fiddle, usually without words.
7. Airs played or picked on the banjo.
8. Primitive Baptist hymns.
9. Hymns adopted from the hymnals of other churches, sung in Highland towns and villages.
10. Miscellaneous tunes, picked up here and there by the Highlander outside the mountains, or coming from circuses, vaudeville, etc., including a wide range of love-song airs.

Our chief interest lies in the first two mentioned above. Briefly summarizing some of Sharp's conclusions, "Very nearly all these Appalachian [Southern Highland] tunes are cast in 'gapped' scales, that is to say, scales containing only five, or sometimes six notes to the octave, instead of the seven with which we are familiar, a 'hiatus,' or 'gap' occurring where a note is omitted."[4] These five or six notes to the octave may represent an early stage in the development of music, when the primitive singer was content almost to chant his song in a sort of monotone. Some of the songs given to me were chanted by the singer. The lack of the seven-note octave accounts for most of the strange music of Highland folk-songs. The love songs, which for the most part are heavily charged with sentiment and emotion, usually have the full octave, and are doubtless of later origin than the epic or narrative song.

The diatonic scale is used by the folk-singer in England today, which would seem to indicate that the Highlander's folk-music is of

---

[3] Sharp, *English Folk-Song: Some Conclusions.*
[4] Campbell and Sharp, *English Folk Songs*, p. xiv.

more remote origin. In a lecture in Chicago in 1915, Sharp said: "The majority of our English folk-tunes, say two-thirds, are in the major or ionian mode. The remaining third is fairly evenly distributed between the mixolydian, dorian, and aeolian modes, with perhaps a preponderance in favor of the mixolydian."

A description or explanation of the pentatonic modes could not well be given here without the airs of the folk-songs themselves. The discovery of folk-tunes cast in Greek modes should awaken an interest not to be despised by students and composers of music. The coming composer in America who seeks new fields may well turn to the simple, elemental folk-tunes of his humble brother, the Southern Highlander, for inspiration. Though simple and elemental, these folk-tunes cover a wide variety. Sharp makes the following significant statement: "It is my sober belief that if a young composer were to master the contents of this book, study and assimilate each tune with its variants, he would acquire just the kind of education that he needs, and one far better suited to his requirements than he would obtain from the ordinary conservatoire or other college of music."[5]

All Highland folk-tunes are not mediocre as music. Whether of great antiquity or not, some of the tunes of the following songs are of a beauty not to be overlooked: "The Nightingale," "Fair Margaret and Sweet William," "The Gosport Tragedy" ("Pretty Polly"), "Florella," "Slago Town," "William Hall," "The Dear Companion," "Little Pink," "Kitty Clyde," and "Barbara Allen." Sharp lists eleven as being very beautiful.[6] Sometimes a weird effect is produced when women singers pitch the air an octave too high. They are more likely to do this than men singers, especially in the singing of Primitive Baptist songs. The minor key is more prominent than the major key.

As to whether ballad airs are more faithfully preserved than ballad texts, I am unable to state.[7] I am of the opinion that the airs are more constant, owing to the large number of variants and versions of the words which are being found from time to time. The fact that more than a dozen airs each have been discovered for "The Daemon Lover" and "Lord Thomas and Fair Annet" is not convincing argument for the constancy of the texts, since one song often is accompanied by a number of airs, depending on the locality where it is found. Similarity

---

[5] *Ibid.*, p. xx.   [6] *Ibid.*, p. xiii.

[7] Sharp thinks that the singer (in England) attaches more importance to the words than to music, because he (the singer) is unable to hum the music. The Highlander can hum, and does hum the music.

of metrical structure in ballad texts makes this easily possible. The Highlander did not make these tunes, but inherited them, and adopted others. Another seeming reason for the preponderance of word-texts over tunes could be sought in the inroads made by the broadside, or stall-ballad, which omitted the music, in England, thus ever increasing variants and versions.[8] Folk-airs are sometimes indefinite, because of the length of the lines. This accounts for the uneven lines in many songs, the singer having shortened or lengthened them to fit them to his tune.

It would be hazardous to attempt to define the age of the traditional folk-airs. As has been noted above, many of them are cast in Greek modes; but this of course does not argue that they descend part and parcel from Greek times. At any rate, Highland folk-airs do descend from Elizabethan England, however ancient they may or may not have been at that time. One thing seems certain; a number of them are of greater antiquity than the dates usually ascribed to them, that is, the fifteenth and sixteenth centuries. These centuries mark the golden age of the folk-song in the British Isles, but the singing of folk-airs must have commenced at a date previous to this. Dr. Burney thinks that none of them are as ancient as the fourteenth century.[9] Sir John Hawkins thinks that they are not even as old as the fifteenth century.[10] Joseph Ritson is of the same opinion.[11] Hawkins says that the oldest country-dance tune in England now extant is that of "Sellengers (St. Leger's) Round," which may be traced back nearly to the reign of Henry VIII (1509–1547). Dance tunes are more ancient than folk-song tunes, since the antiquity of the folk-dance is not disputed. We know now that "The Frog and the Mouse," a nursery song, was sung in the first half of the sixteenth century, and was actually printed in 1549. It is one of a number of songs which were probably sung a century or two previous to this. The riddle-ballads, if they were sung at all, certainly antedate the fifteenth century, and probably the fourteenth; that is, some of them. Perhaps some of the Robin Hood ballads were in fragments; if they were, their airs may belong to the twelfth century, when the bold outlaw was making his sallies out of Sherwood Forest. The music of some songs of sacred tradition, such as "The

---

[8] Child's compilation contains the tunes of only forty-six songs (*The English and Scottish Popular Ballads*, V, 411–424).

[9] Charles Burney, *A General History of Music*, II, 381.

[10] Sir John Hawkins, *General History of the Science and Practice of Music*, II, 91.

[11] Joseph Ritson, *Ancient Songs and Ballads*.

Cherry-Tree Carol," "Judas," "St. Stephen and Herod," "The Carnal and the Crane," "Dives and Lazarus," and others, may even antedate the twelfth century, but these poems are hardly folk-songs. If the minstrels are not to be ruled out of court, folk-airs are of considerable antiquity.

The nonsense and fiddling airs appear to have been overlooked or disregarded by collectors and students. These airs can lay no claim to the interest which is attached to the music of the folk-song; but their music belongs also to the folk and deserves to be preserved. This music also belongs to a remote period, to "Merrie England," at an epoch when the English were doubtless of a more jovial disposition than they are now. The term "Merrie England," it would seem, never had reference to climate, but to the people. It is a mistake to assume that folk-songs, love songs, and play and play-party songs were the only music with which the common people at that time amused themselves. There was a considerable amount of "jig" music, known to the minstrels and performers on the fiddle, which is today almost the exclusive property of the old-time fiddler of the Highlands, and of which the trained musician is ignorant, as he was in England. Ritson[12] is almost the sole ballad scholar to give prominence to it, quoting numerous references in literature to show that it was once widely prevalent in England.

One of the characteristics of jig-music is its absence of words, necessitating its performance on some musical instrument. This is another reason for its lack of preservation. After all that has been said for and against the minstrel, it is perhaps with this jig-music, quick and spirited, that he made his greatest contribution for the amusement of the people. But he adopted this music from the folk, as he adopted their folk-songs. In his entertainments for the delectation of both the high and the lowly, the minstrel probably employed jig-music more frequently than he did the folk-song; this is all the more probable whenever he used the fiddle, since the jig is certainly better adapted to the fiddle than to the other instruments which the minstrel used. The folk-song was often long, longer then than now, and naturally became sometimes tedious for the audience. E. K. Chambers[13] thinks that nine-tenths of secular music had its origin in minstrelsy. This is plainly an exaggeration with reference even to the music of the folk, which was adopted and changed somewhat by the minstrels.

[12] *Ibid.*
[13] E. K. Chambers, *The Medieval Stage*, I, 58.

The Highland fiddler has preserved not scores of jigs, but hundreds. They are brief, and are played rapidly over and over. When the fiddler gets "tuned up," he asks, "What do you want?" Someone replies, "O, something quick and devilish," which is interpreted as meaning a jig. The fiddler has a peculiar habit of tuning the fiddle for every piece he plays, using the open strings as drones, whenever possible. When he "goes into action," the larger end of the instrument rests not under the chin, but further down, on the breast. However, I once observed some West Virginia Highland fiddlers who placed the larger end under the chin. The fiddler seldom stands while playing, preferring a chair. Sometimes the player, one of whose feet is continually tapping on the floor to keep time, is accompanied by someone who taps about midway up on the strings with two knitting needles, or pieces of wood whittled down fine. The fiddler is much in demand at dances, weddings, Christmas parties, etc. One who is "give up" (admitted) to be the "best fiddler in the county" is indeed no insignificant personage. Most of the Highland counties have what are called old fiddlers' contests, once or oftener each year. They are held usually in the courthouses, at the sessions of the quarterly circuit courts. At these meetings one may see as many as six to a dozen fiddlers, playing such favorites as "The Arkansas Traveler," "Sourwood Mountain," "Old Kentucky River," "Cluck Old Hen," "Give the Fiddler a Dram," "Old Joe Clark," "Sally Goodin," "Soldier's Joy"—surely an echo of the minstrel age, long past and forgotten. The young vie with the old for the prizes offered. The old fiddlers look with scorn upon the younger ones, which reminds one of the dignity of an old English minstrel in 1594:

> I have been a minstrell these thirtie yeares,
> And tickled more strings than thou haires.[14]

There is another parallel to be drawn between the English minstrel and the Highland fiddler. Like the former, the latter is usually welcomed in all communities, and takes pride in singing,

> I'll tune up my fiddle, I'll rosin my bow,
> I'll make myself welcome wherever I go.

This hearty welcome, however, is becoming less noticeable every year, for reasons which will be explained later. The simile "as thick as fiddlers in hell" is sometimes heard in the Highlands. A young Highlander initiated me into the mystery of its interpretation: "So thick

[14] John Lilly, *Mother Bombie* (1594).

that they can't move their bows back and forth." Another parallel, since the English minstrel finally fell into disrepute, and lost his former dignity—if he ever had any to lose.

The banjo airs may be dismissed briefly. They have much in common with the fiddle tunes, and are played or picked rapidly. One thing is beyond dispute: whenever the banjo picker gets his hands on a traditional folk-song, as he sometimes does, he hangs, draws, and quarters it, until it is hardly recognizable. The banjo does not often accompany the traditional folk-song, the music of which is too slow for that instrument. Unlike the fiddler, the banjo picker nearly always sings the song while he picks, and also sits while picking. "Follow the boy with the banjo" is the advice given by some American scholars to those who seek the folk-song. A comparison of the folk-song as sung by the typical ballad singer unaccompanied by any musical instrument with that sung by the "boy with the banjo," demonstrates the folly of this advice, both as to words and to music. One of the best examples of the harrowing of the folk-song in the hands of the banjo picker is "The Gosport Tragedy," commonly known as "Pretty Polly." The traditional airs of this song are strangely beautiful, but are hardly to be recognized when heard on the banjo. Other examples are numerous. The banjo picker, too, adopts and assimilates much. One is led to wonder what Will S. Hays would think, should he suddenly come to life and hear a Highland banjo picker metamorphosing that famous love song of his, "I'll Remember You, Love, in My Prayers."

As has been remarked elsewhere, the chief stock-in-trade of the banjo picker consists of railroad songs and outlaw songs. They are the balm in Gilead of the "jail-bird" or prisoner, who is the best conservator of them. The Highlander has adopted many banjo airs from the Negroes, although the Negro population of the Highlands has never been extensive. Such airs came into the Highlands prior to the Civil War, while the Negro railroad songs came in afterward, largely during the past twenty-five years.[15] The tunes of "Lynchburg Town," "Shortnin' Bread," "Raccoon," "Shady Grove," "Hook and Line," "Houn' Dog," "Ida Red," "Little Gray Mule," "Big Stone Gap," and numerous others, are from the Negroes. The origin of such tunes is therefore as mysterious as that of the folk-tunes. It must be remembered that the Negroes have contributed some splendid airs; among them are "Swing Low, Sweet Chariot" and "Roll, Jordan, Roll" (both

[15] I.e., since 1900.

of which are spirituals), and "Dixie." The classification of "Dixie" as
a Negro air will be disputed, but at any rate it was heard in the South
before the Civil War, and before Emmett and Hays "composed" it.[16]

The airs of the Negro spirituals deserve a study by themselves. In
brief, they are charged with feeling, with a sensuous joy in emotion
and rhythm, representing true types of popular origin. It is a mistake
to attempt a proper appraisal of true Negro songs from the splendid
compositions of Stephen Collins Foster and Will S. Hays, which are
the best contributions of Americans to music. The element of pathos
does not (excluding spirituals) characterize real Negro songs, but has
been put there by composers. The Negro's character, frivolous and
free from worry, may easily be discovered in his songs. He is more
musical than the whites.

The music of Primitive Baptist hymns, like that of the Negro spirituals, is marked by its appeal to the emotions. Although its origin is
vague, one may conclude that some of it came from the Negroes, since
a number of spirituals have been taken over by the Highlanders. At
a Primitive Baptist "meeting" (church service) one is struck by the
orgies of emotion that take place, and may notice that they, with their
atavistic resurrections, depend largely on the hypnotic power of the
hymns that are sung and the sermons that are chanted. As far as I
know, there is no record of any such strange music in the British Isles.

The Primitive, or Regular, Baptist Church had its origin in the latter
half of the eighteenth century. Its music, therefore, is not likely to be
so ancient as that of the folk-song, although it has much in common
with it. If the Highlander did invent any music, it is perhaps the airs
of his church hymns. The Negro spirituals so move the Negroes that
they dance while they sing. This is not true of Primitive Baptist singers, although certain communicants in the audience often become
hysterical. At these services printed song texts are rare, which necessi-
tates that someone "line off" the words of the songs, that is, chant them
line by line, after which the assembly sings them, and so on, till the
entire song is sung. The preachers do not "sing their sermons to well
defined melodies," as one scholar has asserted, nor do the shouters cry

[16] See J. H. Combs, *All That's Kentucky*, 1915, p. 44. The music of some popular
Negro songs has appeared in print with the names of "composers" baldly affixed,
although the airs were stolen from British folk-airs. "Turkey in the Straw" and
"Polly Wolly Doodle" were stolen, respectively, from "The Jolly Miller" and
"Needle's Eye," play songs. "Red Wing," an American "composition," is stolen
(minus the chorus) from Schumann's *Der Lustige Bauer*.

out in the "same rhythmic movement." The one who does the "lining-off" sometimes gives directions as to how the song is to be sung, saying "Long meter," or "Short meter"; that is for lengthening or shortening the music, to make it fit the lines.[17] The Highlander's code of morals does not permit his performing on any musical instrument after the death of one of his family or near relations. Whenever he becomes a member of the Primitive Baptist Church he likewise puts musical instruments aside, as the works of the devil. The violin especially is shunned. Many of the church hymns are possessed of a strange beauty, and hold enchanted the listener who is a stranger to them, as they echo in the deep recesses of the Highland valleys. Of such beauty are "Guide Me, O Thou Great Jehovah," "Oh, Come with Me," a burial hymn, and "Been a Long Time Traveling."

Some of the musical instruments used by the Highlander have made their appearance, but are not common. Our mountaineer does not *play* musical instruments, but "follers" playing or picking. One was asked if he played the piano, and replied, "I don't know; I never tried." Another, carrying a dulcimer, was asked if he could "pick her." He replied naïvely, "I wouldn't pack 'er if I couldn't pick 'er." The Primitive Baptists sing without any musical accompaniment. The singer of the traditional folk-song is not usually accompanied. The guitar is rare, also the mandolin. The fiddle and banjo are the instruments mostly in vogue, but both are outlawed by the Primitive Baptists.

The "dulcimore" (dulcimer) is an instrument formerly much used, but now rapidly falling into decay. This strange instrument, probably indigenous to the Southern Highlands, has a slight resemblance to the violin, with a narrow and elongated body and a very short neck. It is usually made of walnut or maple wood, and is strung with three strings, plucked by a crow-quill held in the right hand. One of the three strings, the one nearest the body as the instrument lies on the lap, is tuned an octave higher than the third one, and in unison with the second. The melody is produced on the first string by moving a bit of smooth reed back and forth over it, pressing it down between the frets and strumming all three strings with the quill; the second and third strings are used as tonic-drones, thus causing a strange *bour-*

---

[17] [The terms "long meter," "short meter," and "common meter" refer normally to the metrical length of the stanzas of texts—and consequently to tunes to which they may be sung. On the other hand, the Negro folk now use the terms differently. "Long meter," for example refers to the older songs in slower tempo (also called "Dr. Watts")—D. K. W.]

donnement. Four heart-shaped sound-holes appear on the top side. The instrument is about thirty-four inches in length, with a width at its greatest of about six inches. The octaves included by the frets number about two and a quarter. The "dulcimore" is adapted to simple, one-part tunes, and to slow tunes rather than fast ones. Because of its simplicity many folk-airs even cannot be played upon it. It is not played with the fingers, as some scholars have claimed, and could not be thus played, because of its construction. Nor is it probable that it descends from Elizabethan England, as Miss Pound and others claim.[18] Histories of music give no description of the Highland dulcimer, nor of any instrument similar to it. It must not be confused with the classical or traditional dulcimer, to which it bears no resemblance.[19]

In an old metrical romance entitled "The Squyr of Lowe Degre," an imposing array of early English musical instruments are mentioned, among them the "dowcemere." In "The Schole House of Women," mid-sixteenth century, these lines appear:

> Or as the minstrel dooth intend
> With help of lute, finger, or *quill.*[20]

It is not probable that these references have any bearing on the Highland dulcimer. Ritson may be in error in supposing that the cistole and traditional dulcimer are the same, since the metrical romance mentioned above makes reference to both instruments, in the same poem. There is a Highland dulcimer on display in the New York Metropolitan Museum of Art, labeled as a German "zither" of the eighteenth century. Upon inquiry it was learned that the authority for the label was the Rev. F. W. Galpin, of England, who catalogued the Crosby-Brown Collection of the Museum in 1901.[21]

[18] Louise Pound, *American Ballads and Songs*, p. xvi.

[19] I am now (1932) of the opinion that it was brought over by the Pennsylvania "Dutch" and thence to the Southern Highlands. [Recent research has tended to support Combs' later opinion in postulating the derivation of the Appalachian dulcimer from the Pennsylvania German *zitter* (see Charles Seeger, "The Appalachian Dulcimer," *Journal of American Folklore*, LXXI [1958], 40 ff.). I have found in Cumberland County, Kentucky, instruments called "dulcimores" which closely resemble the *zitter*. That these instruments apparently represent an early stage in the development from *zitter* to Appalachian dulcimer is quite interesting in relation to the local legends that settlement in the area now Monroe and Cumberland Counties was the earliest in Kentucky—D. K. W.]

[20] The ballad singer in England appears to have sung unaccompanied, but the minstrel used musical instruments, his music being wild, irregular, and the notes often chanted. (Cf. Ritson, *Ancient Songs and Ballads*, p. xxix.)

[21] Letter from the Museum, 26 March, 1924.

CHAPTER IX

The Passing of the Folk-Song

HUMAN SOCIETY, in the very nature of things, does not remain stationary and impassive. We may easily apply this dictum to the civilized races of the world. The folk, the subject of much controversy touching on ballad origins, is to a greater or less degree subject to a sort of development theory of social conditions, as well as of ethics. Even its lore, at a certain period flourishing and in the full bloom of popular and oral currency, must pass into oblivion, to make way for newer beliefs, ideas, customs, songs, for a newer culture. It has been said that from the art, traditions, and etiquette that it knows, the folk never wavers.[1] The folk wavered in the British Isles, as to some of its traditions, when the ballad age passed. It wavered when it discarded the majority of its superstitious beliefs and customs. The folk changes, as certainly as do styles, and will continue to be subject to the rule of flux and change whenever and wherever the conditions require it. The strongest rampart of the folk is but a feeble defense against the battering-ram of civilization, an instrument which, only too often, is a poor respecter of the folk and its traditions.

But it is not to be understood that ballad-making and ballad-singing are lost arts among the English-speaking people. Rather are the makers and singers slowly in the process of preparing their swan-song, which must certainly be sung in a few generations, at any rate among the Southern Highlanders of the United States. Whether or not the culture of the folk in this section is a thing more to be desired than

---

[1] Louise Pound, *American Ballads and Songs*, p. xvi.

civilization, it is a fact that the advance guard of civilization is slowly pushing back the outposts of folk-culture. The spirit of balladry is not dead, but slowly dying. The instincts, sentiments, and feelings which it represents are indeed as immortal as romance itself, but their mode of expression, the folk-song, is fighting with its back to the wall, with the odds against it in our introspective age. Science, with all the ramifications which that term may comprehend, is preying like a vulture upon the preserves of the folk, dragging its Diana from her car, driving its Hamadryad from the wood, tearing its Naiad from her flood, and its elfin from the green grass.

We are to examine here some of the reasons which seem to be most potent for the passing of the folk-song in the Southern Highlands of the United States. Other sections of the country have already seen the folk-song of the traditional type pass, beyond recall. True, from time to time survivals from sections other than the Highlands find their way into print, notably in the *Journal of American Folk-Lore*; but they are thin echoes of an age that was, songs which are remembered by individuals here and there, and certainly neither known nor sung by the people in general of those sections. The traditional song of the Child type has almost passed out of the central West, and is hardly known in the Far West. Wherever it is found in those sections, it is but a miserable excuse of its former self. The cowboy does not sing it extensively, and whenever he does, he makes it run the gauntlet of untold injury and insult.[2]

The reasons for the passing of the folk-song are numerous, and cannot be accounted for by a single, simple statement, such as "The people are forgetting their traditions," and the like. That is a generalization which must be given more detailed explanation. "The ballad was guilty of the unpardonable sin of lacking in literary merit."[3] Such a statement has no bearing on the persistence or lack of persistence of the folk-song. "The art of printing tolled the death knell of balladry." That all depends upon the conditions, the age, and the locality.

In general, the reasons for the passing of the folk-song at this time

---

[2] See John A. Lomax, *Cowboy Songs*. In this collection of one hundred and fifty-three songs only one of the Child songs appears, "The Farmer's Curst Wife," under the title of "The Old Man Under the Hill" (p. 110), which is only a shadow of its former self.

[3] F. E. Bryant, *A History of English Balladry*. [I am unable to find this statement in Bryant's book—D. K. W.]

may be said to be similar to those which caused its passing in the British Isles: the impact of civilization and commerce. In proportion as the Highlander is exposed to education, he becomes ashamed of his folk-songs, considering them "old-fashioned," along with many others of his traditions. Whenever the young Highlander enters the door of the college or university, he leaves his "batch of ballads" on the outside, and never takes it up again on leaving. Mr. Carey Woofter, a tireless folk-song hunter of West Virginia, tells of a student who remarked that his grandfather knew "heaps of those old things, and he makes us ashamed by wanting to sing them when we have company." That is the attitude of the young college man toward his traditions, all over the Highlands. Finding himself in the atmosphere of a more sophisticated society, he straightway begins to listen to newer music, newer songs, and wonders why he or any of his relations ever sang a folk-song.

But the college and university are not the sole educational institutions which unconsciously militate against the propagation of the folk-song.[4] The Highland schools themselves, whether they be colleges, academies, preparatory schools, church schools, or public schools, are almost without exception sworn enemies of the folk-song. The sole reason seems to be that the songs of the people are not "culture," because they do not appear in the pedagogical *curricula* of a time-worn educational system. Every toll of the isolated country school bell, even, removes the Highland youth, boy or girl, that much further away from the traditions of his people, in spite of all that may be said in favor of education. I now recall a number of communities in which there were formerly no schools. In recent years schools have been established in them. Today not one folk-song can be heard in these communities![5] The rural schoolmaster of the Highlands will have none of the folk-song. Viewed from his austere dignity, it is sacrilege.

Commerce and industries are not only dispossessing the simple, unsuspecting Highlander of his worldly goods and belongings, but are also driving the folk-song from its once secure habitation. One of the curses of the civilization which is now invading this simple, pure-

[4] In fact, some of these institutions, in recent years, are making a serious attempt to preserve the lore of the folk.

[5] [Three notable exceptions are the Hindman Settlement School, Hindman, Kentucky; the Pine Mountain Settlement School, Pine Mountain, Kentucky; and the Mount Berry School in Georgia.]

minded folk is that its vanguard is made up of a type of men who have little or no interest in the welfare of the folk they are despoiling and dispossessing. These jackals of civilization are abusing the confidence of the hillsmen, even debauching them in many instances, and possessing their lumber, coal, and mineral wealth, without according to them the right to share in the development of the resources of their own native hills. Many a community of once simple folk, formerly enjoying the simple pleasures afforded by their songs, has several years since heard the clank of the colliery on the hillsides, the shrill notes of the factory whistle, the roaring of the furnace, and the rattle of the locomotive reverberating through the Highland valleys. These things can have only one interpretation for the folk-song: *destruction*. It retreats at their advance, and never returns, save in songs of a greatly inferior type, Negro songs and railroad songs. But the vast reaches of the Southern Highlands are not by any means in the clutches of commerce—not yet. Whenever they shall be, within a generation or two, the destruction of Highland balladry will be complete.

The Primitive Baptist Church, one of the most primitive religious institutions in the United States, is the most deadly enemy of the folksong. This institution admits no secular literature, oral or written, and long ago excommunicated the folk-song. Its antipathy has been mentioned in two previous chapters, "The Quest of the Folk-Song," and "The Highlander's Music." The most celebrated singer of the folksong often becomes the most loyal and observant member of the church, and the greater his loyalty to it, the greater his antipathy to his former *penates*. Why? he does not know precisely, but "those old things must be the very works of the devil" along with the fiddle and the fiddler. Thus the transition from "The Daemon Lover" and "Bonny Barbara Allen," highly respectable inheritances from his ancestors, to the sombre, rheumatic-jointed, "lined-off" Jeremiads of his church hymns. Once a Highlander who was mighty in the realm of fiddling and ballad-singing decided to align himself with the church. He had been especially proficient at performing on the fiddle that famous air of all the Highlands, "Sourwood Mountain." At his baptism (by immersion) a local wit sat on the bank of the stream and cried out, just as the new communicant disappeared under the water, "Good-bye, Sourwood Mountain!" The wit spoke Gospel truth, for the once celebrated fiddler emerged from the flood with a familiar hymn on his lips, "Been a Long Time Traveling Below"! An old woman "had prayed to the Lord to take them fool songs out of her mind." Still another said, "I ain't got no time to be studyin' 'bout them old songs, an' don't know none of 'em nohow."[6]

It is significant that this church in the Highlands has proscribed the folk-song, while freely allowing the traditional play or party songs of the children. The children may sing, dance, and indulge in movement games and songs at will. But grown-ups, once members of the church, must leave off singing of the folk-song, and dancing. By way of mockery at this proscription, one stanza of a Highland dance song goes:

> Take a lady by her hand,
> Lead her like a pigeon,
> Make her dance the "Weevily Wheat,"[7]
> She loses her religion.

In the Highlands the children do not belong to the church. Its membership is made up almost entirely of those who have reached or passed the middle stages of life. The Primitive Baptist Church is the church of the Highlander, although all Highlanders do not by any means belong to it.[8]

Closely associated with the anathemas hurled by the church against the folk-song is the Highland "minstrel" himself, that itinerant, wandering, shiftless fiddler, or banjo picker, who makes a specialty of seeking out all "parties" and dances. The attitude of the church, as well as of other classes toward this worthy scion of a past age, has already been expressed in the figure of speech mentioned elsewhere, "As thick as fiddlers in hell!" But like his British prototype, this picturesque figure was not always thus held in disrepute. Time was when he was highly respected, before he discarded the traditional folk-song for the "quick and devilish" tunes and various other types of songs, frivolous, vulgar, etc. For the traditional song is no longer an essential part of his repertory. Not that most of his repertory is indecent, but rather that the average Highlander takes into account the personal equation as he muses: "I can't hear what that feller is playing for thinking about what he *is*." One Highlander put it this way: "Every time one of them fellers comes into the community, I go straight home to my daughter!"[9]

---

[6] [The two preceding sentences are not in the English MS—D. K. W.]

[7] The famous Scottish play-song, "Charlie."

[8] For a detailed description of the tenets and practices of this church, see John C. Campbell, *The Southern Highlander and His Homeland.*

[9] [The inclusion in this edition of the previously rejected chapter "The Highlander's Music" has made repetitious six sentences Combs included in the French edition. They have been omitted from the preceding two paragraphs—D. K. W.]

The Highland minstrel has also fallen from the graces of the courts in that section. An eccentric mountain judge once instructed his grand jury as follows: "Gentlemen! whenever you see a great big overgrown buck [young man] sitting at the mouth of some holler, or at the forks of some road, with a big slouch hat on, a blue, celluloid collar, a celluloid, artificial, red rose in his coat lapel, a banjo strung across his breast, and a-pickin' of 'Sourwood Mountain,' fine that man, gentlemen! fine him! For if he hasn't already done something, he's a-goin' to!"[10] The banjo picker, rather than the fiddler, has thus brought down the enmity of the law upon his head; for often he gets into its clutches and finds himself incarcerated for various misdemeanors and infringements of the law. His predilection for singing and making music has been mentioned in the chapter, "The Quest of the Folk-Song." No "royal edict" has yet been enacted against the Highland minstrels, as in the spacious days of "good Queen Bess," but he is surely and certainly aiding in the destruction of his own household gods. Now, as has been also mentioned elsewhere, the fiddler and banjo picker are not the sole conservators of traditional song; fortunately all classes of Highlanders sing, but the minstrel is bringing Highland song into disrepute among the better classes. All Highland fiddlers and banjo pickers are not shiftless characters, however.

Certainly one may draw a striking parallel between the average mountain minstrel and his British ancestor of the long ago, from the fifteenth-century epitaph of a ballad man:

> Here lyeth under this marbyll Ston
> Riche Alane, the ballid man;
> Whethar he be safe or noght,
> I reche never, for he ne roght.

In addition to registering what was perhaps becoming the popular attitude toward the wandering minstrel of that age, the above lines also throw some light on the period at which the minstrel began to fall into disrepute, and when the word *ballad* began to connote a song of the folk or Child type. Of course, there could be some question as to the precise meaning of a "ballad man" of the fifteenth century. Presumably the term connoted a player, maker, or singer of the song which we now call a ballad or folk-song; it is even possible that the term as used above could refer to a printer of ballads, but this is improbable, since the printing of cheap, stall-ballads had not commenced in the fifteenth

[10] J. H. Combs, *The Kentucky Highlanders*, p. 23.

century, as far as we know. At any rate the term "ballid" seems to refer to the folk-song as we now know it, and not to the former, literary type. Gummere thinks that "Riche" is an indication of the "ballid man's" fortune, and that such men were often men of means. This is hardly probable, since the minstrel is proverbially "stranded," and since "Rich" is among the folk a common abbreviation for "Richard." The Highland minstrel, fiddler, or banjo picker is almost without exception a shiftless character, "making himself welcome wherever he goes." Mr. Rich(ard) Allen may have been no exception. The term "ballad" had doubtless come to mean a folk-song, also, in Shakespeare's time, and earlier, as the above lines indicate. The custom of pasting ballads on the walls of homes was common in the seventeenth century:

> We in the country do not scorn
> Our walls with *ballads* to adorn
> Of *Patient* Grissel and the *Lord* of *Lorn*.

The "singing-school" master, or "perfessor," has put in his appearance in the Southern Highlands, as well as elsewhere over the rural sections of America. Upon his arrival he carried no brief for the folk-song, but instead, a huge tuning-fork. Another inveterate antagonist of the folk-song. This pompous individual is held in high esteem by the Highlanders, and occupies a place in their respect equal to that enjoyed by the rural schoolmaster. He may be a native Highlander or an outsider; in either case he turns up his nose at Highland music, which is "old-fashioned," out of date, and "not in books." He would "be laughed at" if he attempted to instruct his audience in the technique of any of the fine old folk-airs. But he could not do this if he tried, since his stock-in-trade usually consists of the simplest tunes, those of the hymn books used by churches in the lowlands and in Highland towns. Once the young Highlander comes under the spell of the singing-school "perfessor," his folk-songs cease to be a part of his culture.

Musical instruments themselves, which are difficult to be dissociated from music in general, are aiding in the destruction of the folk-song in the Highlands, and elsewhere over America, in the rural sections. Such are the organ, piano, and especially the phonograph. They are importing *printed* music, which the Highlander is learning; something far removed from the *unwritten, oral* music of his ancestors. At first the organ and piano aided in the propagation of folk-music, since the Highlander knew nothing of technical, artistic music when they came in, and "chorded" or played by "ear" the music of his folk-songs. But gradually these instruments are overshadowing the folk-song. The phonograph has exerted a bad influence on Highland music, as it has over America in general, among all classes. Whenever an instrument makes all the music itself, "canned music" as the Highlander sometimes calls it, one acquires quickly the habit of listening to it, thus losing personal initiative to learn the art himself. The Highlander is learning to "listen," and to listen to cheap, undignified jazz music and ragtime, and to silly, mushy, sentimental love songs and vaudeville music, along with the good music which the phonograph offers. These things come in the wake of civilization. Due partially to similar influences, the American people is forgetting its old songs, becoming ashamed of them. Few Americans today, with the exception of school children, can sing their national anthem through to the end; the people no longer sing the fine old plantation songs of Stephen Collins Foster and others. Gone also is the old "parlor," once the near sanctum of the American home, where parties were wont to gather to sing the old songs. It has given place to the phonograph, the dance, jazz, and the fox-trot.

The art of printing, so often advanced as a reason for the decline of British balladry, has had little influence on the status of the folk-song in the Southern Highlands. Elsewhere it has perhaps actually aided in the persistence of the folk-song, as Professor Belden and Louise Pound have pointed out, notably in the central West. The Highlander reads little, and the stall-ballad or broadside is unknown to him. However, stall-sheets of sentimental songs and poetry, usually composed by some local bard or cripple, are seen here and there, as they may be seen in almost any part of the English-speaking world. Weekly county newspapers in the Highlands sometimes print an old song which has been called for by some subscriber, but the dissemination of the folk-song by such a method is rare. Other rural sections of America, however, avail themselves of a number of monthly rural publications, published largely in Augusta, Maine, which print old ballads and songs when called for; the songs are requested by readers, and are sent in by readers. Professor Mackenzie reports that printed ballads from Scotland have played an important part in the perpetuation of the folk-song in Nova Scotia. Even some of the greater American newspapers now print ballads called for, in their "Notes and Queries" columns.

Here and there in the "archives" of some remote Highland home one finds a book of "song-ballets" in manuscript form. One of such books was given to me years ago, and contained a number of native American songs, but no Child songs. The songs thus preserved are usually those of the sentimental type, or those recounting some local incident, written by a local bard. The weekly newspaper, one of which is published in almost every Highland county, at the county seat, often prints songs of this character.

But print and manuscript seem to bear little relation to the perpetuation of the traditional folk-song in the Highlands. Other and later types thus reduced find their way into some Highland homes. The oft-repeated assertion that the art of printing sounded the death knell of traditional balladry has much truth in it, even in the twentieth century. The complaint of the old Scotch woman, more than a hundred years ago, that the "spell was broken" when her native songs were reduced to print,[11] was prophetic, for it is applicable to folk-song everywhere, at all times. Oral transmission is the medium of perpetuation, for print interferes with and interrupts tradition; whenever the songs, superstitions, and other property of the folk circulate among the folk in printed form, they soon cease to be traditions actually in vogue. Naturally enough, whenever the printed copy of a song finds its way into the hands of a singer, that singer makes less effort to memorize the words of the song, depending on his copy whenever necessary. Then the fear of forgetting vanishes from his mind, for does he not have a *copy* of the song? Then when the copy is misplaced or lost the song is lost, the *tradition* is lost. The basis of appeal for perpetuation (among the folk) is not through the press. Such an agency may easily destroy what it sets out to accomplish.

The empire of the man on horseback, the great plains of the West and Southwest, is also threatened. That picturesque figure, the cowboy, or cowpuncher, silent singer of his personal woes on a vast, silent plain, is passing, and with him his songs. His profession is becoming a lost art, for the West is becoming like the East, and civilization, the relentless star of empire, is continually moving westward. Within another generation the rancho, rodeo, and lasso will have become only memories of the days that were. Already the vast ranches are being cut up into smaller farms. The buffalo and the Indian war whoop have already passed. The romantic West, the West of the early days, lives now only in story and song, and in the sensational motion picture

---

[11] [An elderly Scotswoman to Sir Walter Scott: "They were made for singing and no for reading, but ye hae broken the charm now and they'll never be sung mair" (James Hogg, *The Domestic Manners and Life of Sir Walter Scott*, p. 61).]

shows. Like the "schooner" of the old American barroom, the "prairie schooner" of pioneer days has slipped into oblivion. Of course, wherever the open range still exists, wherever the cowboy rules the plains, wherever the famed Texas "longhorn" steer roams the wild reaches of the mesquite and chaparral thickets of the Southwest, the clear voice of the cowpuncher is still heard:

> My foot's in the stirrup, my hand's on the horn,
> The best damned cowpuncher that ever was born.

Since the seventeenth century, the period in which the transition from the epic to the lyric type of folk-song may be said to have had its inception in the British Isles, the narrative song has been rudely jostled by the lyric song. The latter type has continued to gain momentum, and folk-song in America is no exception to this process of transition. In the struggle for the "survival of the fittest" in song, the lyric is gradually pushing out the narrative song. And there is no question as to the priority in years of the story-song over the lyric song. The number of the newer songs is legion. These newer songs are perhaps not destined to arrive at the antiquity of the traditional epic songs; that is, the majority of them. At any rate, the fact remains that the Southern Highlanders, as well as singers elsewhere over America, are slowly but surely discarding the old for the new songs. The mere fact that "The Daemon Lover" or "Jack Went A-Sailing" has held its own for so long is no reason that it is going to persist indefinitely, however superior either of these songs may be to the newer songs. Whenever the conditions for the propagation of the folk-song cease to exist, the folk-song itself ceases to exist. [No one can at this time make a safe prediction as to which of the newer songs among the folk are destined to live as long as some of the older ones, if any. That is one of the mysteries surrounding folk-lore—why some songs should persist while others perish.]

Louise Pound thinks that the older song will outlive the newer. "Much in modern song is unsingable (*sic*) and unrememberable (*sic*); no one can expect it to make a deep impression on the popular mind."[12] That is no reason that the traditional folk-song is going to continue to persist. As universal as song seems to have been in the British Isles in the sixteenth century, much of it was likewise "unsingable and unrememberable." Such has been true of all ages. Singable or unsingable, the newer song has arrived, and with its arrival the traditional song

---

[12] Pound, *Poetic Origins and the Ballad*, p. 233.

is retreating—at least in America. Some American scholars are so optimistic about the status of the folk-song in America that they maintain that almost any sort of song can be found in any section of the country; that there is no reason why ballad-making and ballad-singing should not continue indefinitely.[13] The student of the folk in a country where conditions change so rapidly cannot accept such an optimistic attitude.

The charge that the folk-song (of the British Isles) was lacking in literary merit, which brought it into disrepute, needs little discussion, since this phase of the folk-song is incidental as far as both the literary world and the folk are concerned. It matters little to the folk whether its songs have literary merit or not; such a question has no interest for the simple singer and his simple lay. Perhaps if its songs had been heavily laden with artistic or literary merit their vogue would have been short-lived, or else they never would have existed—for the folk, as *their* especial property. However these things may be, the oft-repeated assertion that the folk-song is artless is not any too well founded. There appears to be considerable art in a number of folk-songs, unconscious art, of course, but art nevertheless. Viewed even from the high conning tower of literary criticism, the stanzas quoted in the chapter on folk-song origin or authorship might well do credit to any poet who writes with "spirit-level and square." [After all, much art is unconscious. Does inspiration dwell only on Mount Parnassus?] The poetry of the folk, like the poetry of art, has its limitations, and there is no *Laocoön* as a standard of perfection—in the eyes of the folk.

As far as the Southern Highlands and the rest of America are concerned, the songs of the folk as such are passing; [not gone, but viewing in the distance the Promised Land—Immortality—which they shall never reach]. The thin tones of the Highland "dulcimore" have all but vanished, like the wailing of the banshee over the ancient Scottish moor. For the damsel with the "dulcimore" is retreating before the boy with the banjo, and the second phase, perhaps the last one, of traditional balladry is beginning to close its account among the English-speaking peoples.

[13] H. M. Belden, "Balladry in America," *Journal of American Folklore*, XXV, 1 ff.

BIBLIOGRAPHY

Allen, William Francis, Charles Pickard Ware, and Lucy McKim Garrison. *Slave Songs of the United States.* New York, 1867.

Baldwin, Charles S. *Introduction to English Medieval Literature.* New York, 1914.

Barry, Phillips. "Native Balladry in America," *Journal of American Folklore,* XXII (1909), 365 ff.

Bédier, Joseph. *Chansons de Colin Muset.* Paris, 1912.

——. *De Nicolao Museto.* Paris, 1893.

Belden, Henry Marvin. "Balladry in America," *Journal of American Folklore,* XXV (1912), 1 ff.

——. "Boccaccio, Hans Sachs, and the Bramble Briar," *Publications of the Modern Language Association,* XXXIII (1918), 327 ff.

——. "Popular Song in Missouri—The Returned Lover," *Archiv für das Studium der nueren Sprachen und Literaturen (Herrig's Archiv),* CXX (1908), 62 ff.

——. "The Vulgar Ballad," *The Sewanee Review,* XIX (1911), 213 ff.

Bradley, William A. "Song Ballets and Devil's Ditties," *Harper's Monthly Magazine,* CXXX (1915), 901 ff.

(Brantôme) *Memoires de Messire Pierre du Bourdeille, seigneur de Brantôme, contenans les vies des dames illustres en France de son temps.* 1666.

Brigham, Albert Perry. *Geographic Influences in American History.* Boston, 1903.

Bryant, Frank Egbert. *A History of Balladry and Other Studies.* Boston, 1913.

Bujead, Jerome. *Chants populaires des provinces de l'Ouest.* Noirt, 1895.

Burney, Charles. *A General History of Music.* 4 vols. London, 1792–1799.

Cambridge History of American Literature, Vol. IV. New York, 1921.

Cambridge History of English Literature, Vol. II. Cambridge, 1908.

Campbell, John C. *The Southern Highlander and His Homeland.* New York, 1921.

Campbell, Olive Dame, and Cecil J. Sharp. *English Folk Songs from the Southern Appalachians.* New York and London, 1917.

Campbell, Robert F. *Classification of Mountain Whites.* Hampton, Virginia, 1901.

Chambers, E. K. *The Medieval Stage.* 2 vols. London, 1903.

Child, Francis James. *The English and Scottish Popular Ballads.* 5 vols. Boston and New York, 1882–1898.

Combs, Josiah H. *All That's Kentucky*. Louisville, Kentucky, 1915.

———. "Dialect of the Folk-Song," *Dialect Notes*, IV (1916), 311 ff.

———. "Early English Slang Survivals," *Dialect Notes*, V (1921), 115 ff.

———. *The Kentucky Highlanders*. Lexington, Kentucky, 1913.

———. "Old, Early and Elizabethan English," *Dialect Notes*, IV (1916), 283 ff.

Cox, John Harrington, *Folk-Songs of the South*. Cambridge, Massachusetts, 1925.

Fiske, John. *Old Virginia and Her Neighbors*. Boston, 1897.

Gannet, Henry. *Physiographic Types*. Washington, D.C., 1898.

Gray, Roland P. *Songs and Ballads of the Maine Lumberjacks*. Cambridge, Massachusetts, 1924.

Greig, Gavin. *Folk-Songs of the North-East*. 2 vols. Peterhead, 1914.

Grundtvig, Svend. *Danmarks Gamle Folkeviser*. Vols. I–V. Copenhagen, 1853–1890. Continued by Axel Olrik, *Danske Ridderviser*. Vols. VI–VIII. Continued after 1917 by H. Grüner Nielsen.

Gummere, Francis B. "The Ballad and Communal Poetry," *Harvard Studies and Notes in Philology and Literature*, V (1896), 41 ff.

———. "Ballads," *Cambridge History of English Literature*, II (1908), 449 ff.

———. *The Beginnings of Poetry*. New York and London, 1901.

———. *Democracy and Poetry*. Boston and New York, 1911.

———. *Old English Ballads*. Boston and New York, 1894.

———. *The Popular Ballad*. Boston and New York, 1907.

Haney, W. H. *The Mountain People of Kentucky*. Cincinnati, 1906.

Hawkins, Sir John. *General History of the Science and Practice of Music*. London, 1776; new ed., 1853.

Herndon, William Henry, and Jesse W. Weik. *Abraham Lincoln: The True Story of a Great Life*. 3 vols. New York, 1892.

Hogg, James. *The Domestic Manners and Private Life of Sir Walter Scott*. Glasgow, 1834.

Jeanroy, Alfred. *Les origines de la poésie lyrique en France au moyen-âge*. Paris, 1889.

Kephart, Horace. *Our Southern Highlanders*. New York, 1913.

Lomax, John. *Cowboy Songs and Other Frontier Ballads*. New York, 1910; with additions, 1916.

———. "Cowboy Songs of the Mexican Border," *The Sewanee Review*, XIX (1911), 1 ff.

Mackenzie, W. Roy. *The Quest of the Ballad*. Princeton, New Jersey, 1919.

Mélusine: Recueil de Mythologie. 11 vols. Paris, 1878–1911.

Miller, E. E. *Physiography of the United States*. New York, 1896.

Mutzenburg, Charles G. *Kentucky's Famous Feuds and Tragedies*. New York, 1917.

Newell, William Wells. *Games and Songs of American Children*. 2d. ed. New York, 1903.

Nigra, Constantino. *Canti popolari del Piemonte*. Turin, 1888.

Paris, Gaston. "Les origenes de la poésie lyrique en France en moyen-âge," *Journal des Savants*, 1891, pp. 674 ff., 729 ff.; 1892, 155 ff., 497 ff.

Percy, Thomas. *Reliques of Ancient English Poetry*. 3 vols. London, 1765.

Perrow, E. C. "Songs and Rhymes from the South," *Journal of American Folklore*, XXV (1912), 137 ff.

Pound, Louise. *American Ballads and Songs*. New York, 1922.

———. "Oral Literature," *Cambridge History of American Literature*, IV (1921), 502 ff.

———. *Poetic Origins and the Ballad*. New York, 1921.

Ritson, Joseph. *Ancient Songs and Ballads*. London, 1877.

Roosevelt, Theodore. *The Winning of the West*. New York, 1900.

Saint Foix, Germain-François Pollain de. *Essais historiques sur Paris*. 5 vols. Paris, 1754–1757.

Scott, Sir Walter. *Minstrelsy of the Scottish Border*. 3 vols. Kelso and Edinburgh, 1802–1803.

Sargent, Helen Child, and George Lyman Kittredge, eds. *English and Scottish Popular Ballads*. Boston, 1904.

Semple, Ellen C. *American History and Its Geographic Conditions*. New York, 1903.

———. "The Anglo-Saxons of the Kentucky Mountains," *Bulletin of the American Geographic Society*, XLII (1910), 561 ff.

Sharp, Cecil J. *The Country Dance Book*. London, 1909.

———. *English Folk-Song: Some Conclusions*. London, 1907.

Shearin, Hubert G. "British Ballads in the Cumberland Mountains," *The Sewanee Review*, XIX (1911), 313 ff.

Sidgwick, Frank. *The Ballad*. London, 1914.

Smith, C. Alphonso. "Ballads Surviving in the United States," *Musical Quarterly*, II (1916), 109 ff.

Steenstrup, J. C. H. R. *The Medieval Popular Ballad*. Trans. E. G. Cox. Boston, 1914.

Talley, Thomas W. *Negro Folk Rhymes*. New York, 1922.

Tolman, Albert H., and Mary O. Eddy. "Traditional Tunes and Texts," *Journal of American Folklore*, XXXV (1922), 335 ff.

Wentworth, Archdeacon [Frank Benjamin]. *A Strange People. Weird Customs and Curious Habits of the Kentucky Mountaineers*. [Winchester, Kentucky, 1911.]

Wilson, Samuel T. *The Southern Mountaineers*. New York, 1914.

PART II

Songs of British Origin

The Broomfield Hill [11]
(Child No. 43)

Known by the title "Green Broom." It is difficult to relate this to the "Brume, brume on hil" cited in *Complaynt of Scotland*, 1549, or to a song which appears in W. Wager's comedy *The Longer Thou Livest, the More Fool Thou Art*, 1568. The subject of the ballad is the flouted lover. The second line of the seventh stanza has been supplied. Contributed by Carey Woofter, Gilmer Co., West Virginia [1924].

I'll lay you five hundred pounds,
Five hundred pounds to ten,
That a maid can't go to the green-broomfield
And come back a maid again.

Then up spoke a sweet young girl,
Her age was not sixteen:
"A maid I'll go to the green-broomfield,
And a maid I'll come back again."

And when she went to the green-broomfield,
Where her lover was sound asleep,
With a gay goshork[1] and a green laurel twig,
And a green broom under his feet,

She pulled a bunch of the green-broom
And smelled of it so sweet;
She scattered a handful over his head,
And another around his feet.

And when she had done what she wagered to do,
She turned herself about,

---

[1] *Goshork*—goshawk.

She hid herself behind a clump of green-broom
To hear what her lover should say.

And when he awoke from out his sleep
A fearsome man was he;
He looked to the east and he looked to the west,
And he wept for his sweetheart to see.

"And where were you, my gay goshork
(That once I loved so dear),
That you wakened me not out of my sleep
When my sweetheart was so near?

"If my hork[2] had wakened me while I slept,
Of her I would have had my will,
Or the buzzards that fly high over the sky
Of her flesh should have had their fill.

"Come saddle me my milk-white steed,
Come saddle me my brown;
Come saddle me the speediest horse
That ever rode through town."

"You need not saddle your milk-white steed,
You need not saddle your brown,
For a doe never ran through the street so fast
As the maid ran through the town."

[2] *Hork*—hawk.

Fair Annie [16]

(Child No. 62)

Known by the title of "The Sister's Husband." The presence of
Indians in the first stanza seems to indicate that this variant arose dur-
ing the colonial period. Stanzas 1 and 2 are not found in British vari-
ants. A fragment has been published in the collection of Campbell and
Sharp (No. 14). Contributed by J. R. Umstead, Mt. Zion, Calhoun Co.,
West Virginia.

The Indians stole fair Annie
As she walked by the sea,

But Lord Harry for her a ransom paid,
In gold and silver money.

She lived far away with him,
And none knew whence she came;
She lived in a mansion-house with her love,
But never told her name.

"Now make your bed all narrow,
And learn to lie alone;
For I'm going far away, Annie,
To bring my sweet bride home.

"I'm going far over the river
To bring my sweet bride home;
For she brings me land and slaves,
And with you I can get none.

"But who will spread the wedding feast,
And pour the red red wine?
And who will welcome my sweet bride,
My bonny bride so fine?"

"O I will spread the wedding feast,
And I will pour the red red wine,
And I will welcome your sweet bride,
Your bonny bride so fine."

"But she who welcomes my sweet bride
Must look like a maiden fair,
With lace on her robe so narrow,
And flowers among her hair.

"Do up, do up your yellow hair,
And knot it on your neck,
And see you look as maiden-like
As when I met you first."

"How can I look so maiden-like,
When maiden I am none?
Have I not had six sons by thee,
And am with child again?"

Four months were past and gone,
And the word to fair Annie came

That the boat was back from the river
With the sweet bonny bride at home.

She took her young son on her hip,
A second by the hand,
And she went out on the upper porch
To see if the boat did land.

"Come down, come down, O mother dear,
Come down from the porch so tall;
For I fear if longer you stand there,
You will make yourself fall."

She took her young son on her arm,
A second by the hand,
And with the keys about her waist
Out to the gate has gone.

"O welcome home, my good Lord,
To your mansion and your farm;
O welcome home, my good Lord,
And you are safe from harm.

"O welcome home, my fair lady,
For all that's here is yours;
O welcome home, my fair lady,
And you are safe with yours."

"Who is that lady, my Lord,
That welcomes you and me?
Before I'm long about the place,
Her friend I mean to me."

Fair Annie served the wedding feast,
And smiled upon them all;
But before the healths went round
Her tears began to fall.

When night was late and dance was done,
All the guests were off for bed;
After the groom and the bonny bride
In one bed they had laid,

Fair Annie took a banjo in her hand
To play the two to sleep;

But ever as she played and sang,
O sorely she did weep.

"But if my sons were seven rats
Running over the milk-house wall,
And I were a great gray cat,
How I would worry them all!

"But if my sons were seven grey foxes
Running over those brushy hills,
And I myself a good fox hound,
I soon would chase their fill.

"But if my sons were seven buck deer
Drinking at the old salt-lick,
And I myself a good hunting dog,
I soon would see them kick."

Then up did speak the bonny bride
From the bride-bed where she lay:
"That's like my sister Annie," said she;
"Who is it that sings and plays?

"I'll slip on my dress," said the new come bride,
"And draw my shoes over my feet;
I will see who so sadly sings,
And what it is that makes her grief.

"O what is it ails my housekeeper,
That you make such a to-do?
Have you lost the keys from your belt,
Or is all your wedding feast gone?"

"It isn't because my keys are lost,
Or because my feast is gone;
But I have lost my own true-love,
And he has wedded another one."

"Who was your father, tell me,
And who then was your mother?
And had you any sister?" she says,
"And had you any brother?"

"The Lord of Salter was my father,
The Lady of Salter was my mother;

Young Susan was my dear sister,
And Lord James was my brother."

"If the Lord of Salter was your father,
I'm sure he so was mine;
And you're O, my sister, Annie,
And my true-love is thine.

"Take your husband, my sister dear;
You were never wronged by me,
More than a kiss from his dear mouth,
As we came up the bay.

"Seven ships were loaded
Brought all my dowry with me;
And one of them will carry me home,
And six I will give to thee."

The Lass of Roch Royal [21]
(Child No. 76)

Known by the title "Sweet Annie of Roch Royal." Lines 2 and 3 of stanza twenty have been supplied.[1] [From Dora, West Virginia.] Contributed by Carey Woofter, Gilmer Co., West Virginia [1924].

"O who will shoe my little feet,
And who will glove my hands?
And who will tie my waist so neat,
With the new made London bands?

"O who will comb my yellow hair
With the bright new silver comb?
O who will be daddy to my boy
Till my lover George comes home?"

Her father shoed her little feet,
Her mother gloved her hands;
Her sister tied on her waist so neat
The new made London bands.

[1] [But line 2 only is enclosed in parenthesis—D.K.W.]

Her cousin combed her yellow hair
With the new made silver comb;
But heaven knew the daddy of her boy
Till her lover George came home.

Her father gave her a new ship,
And led her to the sand;
She took her boy up in her arms
And sailed away from the land.

On the sea she sailed and sailed,
For over a month and more,
Till she landed her new ship
Near to her lover's door.

Long she stood at her lover's door,
And long pulled at the string,
Till up got his false mother,
Saying, "Who pulls at the string?"

"O it is Annie of Rock Royal,
Your own, come over the sea
With your own dear son in her arms;
So open the door to me."

"Be off! be off! you bold woman,
You come not here for good;
You're only a strumpet, or a bold witch,
Or else a mermaid from the sea."

"I'm not a witch nor a strumpet bold,
Nor a mermaid from the sea;
But I am Annie of Rock Royal;
So open the door to me.

"So open the door now, dear George,
And open it with speed,
Or your young son here in my arms
With the cold will soon be dead."

"If you be Annie of Rock Royal,
Though I know you may not be,
What pledge can you give that I
Have ever kept you company?"

"O don't you mind, dear George," she said,
When we were a-drinking wine,
How we gave the rings from our fingers,
And how the best was mine?

"Though yours was good enough for me,
It was not so good as mine;
Yours was made of bright red gold,
While mine had a diamond fine.

"So open the door, now, dear George,
And open it with speed,
Or your young son here in my arms
With the cold will soon be dead."

"Away, away, you bold woman,
Take from my door your shame;
For I have gotten another true-love,
And you may hasten home."

"And if you have gotten another true-love,
After all the oaths that you swore,
O here is farewell, false George,
For you will never see me more."

Slow-ly, slow-ly went she back
As the day began to dawn;
She set her foot on the new ship,
And bitterly did she mourn.

George started up all in his sleep,
And quick to his mother he said:
"O I dreamed a dream tonight, mother,
That made my heart so sad.

"I dreamed that Annie of Rock Royal,
(The flower of all her kin),
Was standing mourning at my door,
But none would let her in."

"O a bold woman stood there at the door
With a child all in her arms;
But I wouldn't let her come in the house,
For fear she would work you a charm."

Quick-ly, quick-ly got he up,
And fast he ran to the sand,
And there he saw his dear Annie
A-sailing from the land.

"And hey, Annie, and hee, Annie,
O Annie, listen to me!"
But the louder he cried, "Annie!"
The louder roared the sea.

The wind blew high, the sea grew rough,
The ship was broken in two,
And soon he saw his sweet Annie
Come floating over the waves.

He saw his young son in her arms,
Both tossed about by the tide;
He pulled his hair, and he ran fast,
And he plunged in the sea so wild.

He caught her by the yellow hair
And drew her out on the sand;
But cold and stiff were her snowy limbs
Before he reached the land.

O he has mourned over sweet Annie
Till the sun was going down;
Then with a sigh his heart did burst,
And his soul to heaven has flown.

Prince Robert [26]
(Child No. 87)

Known by the title "Harry Saunders." Contributed by F. C. Gainer, Tanner, Gilmer Co., West Virginia.

And it's forty miles to Nicut Hill,
The nearest way you may go;
But Harry Saunders has taken a wife
That he dares not to bring home.

His mother called to her hired girl,
"Sally, draw me a cup of tea,
For I see my son Harry is coming
To eat a meal with me."

His mother lifted the cup of tea
And touched her lips to the drink;
But never a drop of the poison cup
Of drinking did she think.

Harry took that cup of tea
And put it to his mouth;
He opened his bright red lips,
And the poison went quickly down.

His wife set at Nicut Hill
Waiting for Harry to come;
She called to her own sister dear,
"Has my husband now come home?"

She went up to her room
And put on a riding-skirt;
She went out to the stable old
And saddled her roan steed.

But when she came to Harry's home
The guests were in the hall;
The hearse was standing by the yard,
And the friends were mourning all.

"I've come for none of his gold," she cried,
"Nor for none of his lands so wide;
But his watch and his chain, they ought to go
To his own sweet bride."

"You will get none of his gold," his mother said,
"Nor none of his lands so wide;
His watch and his chain I threw in the well,
From his own sweet bride to hide."

And then she kissed his cold white cheeks,
And then she kissed his chin,
And then she kissed his bright red lips,
Where there was no breath come in.

And then she fell upon the floor,
Her head beside the bier;
Her heart did break, it was so sore,
But she shed not any tear.

Willie o Winsbury [29]
(Child No. 100)

The missing stanzas reconcile the father (the king) with the seducer of his daughter, because of the remarkable beauty of the youth, and the couple are married. In Child's H and I versions the father of the girl is the king of France:

It fell upon a time when the proud king of France
Went a-hunting for five months and more,
That his dochter fell in love with Thomas of Winesberrie,
From Scotland newly come oer.

Contributed by L. P. Williams, De Kalb, Gilmer Co., West Virginia.

There was a lass in the north countrie,
And her clothing it was all green;
She's look-ed over her father's castle wall
For to see her father's ships sail in, sail in,
For to see her father's ships sail in.

"What aileth thee, dear daughter?" he said,
"What makes thee so pale and wan?
I'm a-feared you've got some sore sickness,
Or have lain with some young man," etc.

"O I have got no sore sickness,
Nor I've lain with no young man;
But the true thing that grieves me to the heart
Is, my true-love is staying too long."

"O is he a lad or a duke or a Knight,
Or a man of birth and fame?
Or is he one of my own serving-men
That is lately come from Spain?"

"He is neither a lad nor a duke nor a knight,
Nor a man of birth and fame;
But he is one of your serving-men
That is lately come from Spain."

"O call him down, the Spanish dog,
O call him down to me;
Before eight o'clock tomorrow morning
Hang-ed he shall be."

"No, that forbid, dear father," she said,
"That such a thing there should be;
For if you hang my Johnny Benbow,
You'll get no more good of me."

Mary Hamilton [32]
(Child No. 173)

This narrative is based on an incident at the court of Mary, Queen of Scots, in 1563; it concerns the murder of a child, for which the mother and father (the Queen's apothecary) were hanged. The king (Darnley) is the lover of Mary Hamilton in some versions such as the following, "the highest Stuart of all." Historians relate the curious fact that there were four Marys as maids of honor at the court of Queen Mary, and Child's A version alludes to the fact:

> Last nicht there was four Maries,
> The nicht there'll be but three;
> There was Marie Seton, and Marie Beton,
> And Marie Carmichael, and me.

The four Marys, according to the legend, accompanied the Queen to France when she was sent there at the age of five and returned with her to Scotland thirteen years later. Contributed by Carey Woofter, Gilmer Co., West Virginia [1924]. [Originally from George Burris, Grantsville. See Appendix.]

> Word has gone to the kitchen,
> And word has gone to the hall
> That Mary Hamilton has borne a child
> To the highest Stuart of all.

She's tied it in her apron,
And she's thrown it in the sea;
She says, "Sink you, swim you, bonnie babe,
You'll never get more from me."

Then down came the old queen,
Gold ribbons tied her hair:
"O Mary, where is the wee, wee babe
That I heard greet so long?"

"There was never a babe into my room,
There never designs to he [be?];
It was but a pain in my sore side
Came over my fair body.

"I will not put on my robes of black,
Nor yet my robes of brown,
But I'll put on my robe of white,
To go through Edinbro town."

When she went up to the parliament stairs,
The heel came from her shoe;
And before she came down again,
She was condemned to die.

When she came down from Cannon Gate,
The Cannon Gate so fair,
Many a lady looked from her window
To weep for this lady.

"Make never a moan for me," she says,
"Make not a moan for me;
Seek never grace for a graceless face,
For that you will never see.

"Bring me a bottle of liquor," she says,
"The best that ever you have,
That I may drink to my well-wishers,
And they may drink with me.

"And here's to the jolly sailor lad
That sails upon the sea;
And let not my father nor my mother know
That I shall not come again.

"O little did my mother think,
The day she cradled me,
What lands I was to travel o'er,
What death I was to die.

"O little did my father think,
The day he held me up,
What lands I was to travel o'er,
What death I was to die.

"Last night I washed the queen's feet
And gently lay her down,
And all the thanks I've got this night
Is to be hanged in Edinbro town."

Bonnie James Campbell [34]
(Child No. 210)

Known by the title "Bonnie Johnnie Campbell." (A) contributed
by Lloyd Miller, Letter Gap [Gilmer Co.], West Virginia; (B) contributed by Mrs. Nora Edman, Big Springs, Calhoun Co., West Virginia.

A

High on the mountains and down in the cove,
Bonnie Johnnie Campbell day after day did rove.

Saddled and bridled and daring rode he;
Home came horse and saddle, but never home came he.

Down came his three sisters moaning so sore,
And down came his sweet wife pulling her hair.

"My house is not shingled, my barn is not raised,
My crops are not gathered and my babe has not come."

B

Booted and saddled and bridled rode he,
The saddle came home empty, but never came he.

His old mother came down weeping the more;
His lovely wife came down tearing her hair.

Booted and saddled and bridled rode he,
The saddle came home empty, but never came he.

The Rantin Laddie [35]
(Child No. 240)

Contributed by Mrs. Nora Edman, Big Springs, Calhoun Co., West
Virginia.

Oft have I played at cards and dice,
Because they were so enticing;
But this is a sad and sorrowful day
To see my apron rising.

My father he does but slight me,
And my mother she does but scorn me,
And all my friends they do make light of me,
And all the servants they do sneer at me.

Oft have I played at cards and dice,
For the love of my laddie;
But now I must sit at my father's fireboard,
And rock my bastard baby.

But had I one of my father's servants,
For he has so many,
That will go to the eastern shore
With a letter to the rantin laddie.

"Here is one of your father's servants,
For he has so many,
That will go to the eastern shore
With a letter to the rantin laddie."

"When you get there to the house,
To the eastern shore so bonnie,
With your hat in your hand, bow down to the ground,
Before the company of the rantin laddie."

When he got there to the house,
To the eastern shore so bonnie,
With his hat in his hand he bowed down to the ground,
Before the company of the rantin laddie.

When he looked the letter over
So loud he burst out laughing;
But before he read it to the end,
The tears they were down dropping.

"O who is this, O who is that,
Who has been so ill to my Maggie?
O who is this dares be so bold,
So cruel to treat my lassie?

"Her father he will not know her,
And her mother she does but scorn her;
And all her friends they do make light of her,
And all the servants they do sneer at her.

"Four and twenty milk-white steeds,
Go quick and make them ready;
As many gay lads to ride on them,
To go and bring home my Maggie.

"Four and twenty bright-brown steeds,
Go quick and make them ready;
As many bold men to ride on them,
To go and bring home my Maggie."

Ye lassies all, where'er ye be,
And ye lie with an east-shore laddie,
Ye'll happy be and ye'll happy be,
For they are frank and free.

Get Up and Bar the Door [38]
(Child No. 275)

Known by the title "Old John Jones." Contributed by David Chenoweth, Gip, Calhoun Co., West Virginia. [See Appendix for contra-
dictory documentation.]

The wind it blew from east to west,
And blew all over the floor;
Said old John Jones to Jane, his wife,
"Get up and shut the door."

"My hands are in the sausage meat,
So I cannot get them free;
If you do not shut the door yourself,
It will never be shut by me."

They agreed between the two,
And pledged their word on it,
That whoever spoke a word the first
Was to rise and shut the door.

There were two travelers journeying late,
A-journeying across the hill,
And they came to old John Jones's
By the light from the open door.

"Does this house to a rich man belong,
Or does it belong to a poor?"
But never a word would the stubborn two say,
On account of the shutting of the door.

The travelers said good evening to them,
And then they said good morning,
But never a word would the stubborn two say,
On account of the shutting of the door.

And so they drank of the liquor strong,
And then they drank of the ale;
"For since we have got a house of our own,
I'm sure we can take our fill."

And then they ate of the sausage meat,
And sopped the bread in the fat;
And at every bite old Jane she thought,
"May the devil slip down with that!"

Then says the one to the other,
"There, man, take out my knife,
And while you shave the old man's chin,
I will be kissing his wife."

"You have eat my meat and drinked my ale,
And would you make my old wife a whore?"
"John Jones, you have spoke the first word;
Now get up and shut the door."

The Crafty Farmer [89]
(Child No. 283)
[Laws L 1]

Known by the title "Selling the Cow," a secondary form of the Child ballad. In the New World the farmer or miller is replaced by a young South Carolina Negro, and the rent of the farm by a cow. The action takes place in Staunton, Virginia. Contributed by F. C. Gainer, Gilmer Co., West Virginia.

In Staunton there did dwell
A merchant by trade;
He had two niggers,
A man and a maid.

A South Carolina boy
He had for his man,
And for to do his business,
His name it was Fran.

He said to Fran early one morning,
"Franny, take the cow and drive her to
    the fair;
For she is in good order
And all we have to spare."

Fran took the cow
And drove her to the fair;
And on the way he met three men,
And sold the cow for three pounds ten.

They went into the tavern
All for to take a drink;
And there the farmers
Paid him all the chink.[1]

Franny said to the landlady,
This did he say:
"What shall I do
With all this money, pray?"

"I will sew it in your
Coat lining," said she;

[1] *Chink*—money.

"For on the highway
You robbed may be."

The highwayman sat behind,
Drinking of his wine;
Says he to himself,
"This money is all mine."

Fran got on his horse to go,
The highwayman also.

They rode till they came
To a long dark land;
"And now, black boy,
I will tell you plain,

"You must hand over your money
Without fear or strife,
Or I shall surely
Take your dear life."

Franny jumped off his horse
Without fear or doubt,
And from his coat lining
He pulled the money out,
And in the tall grass
He strewed it about.

The highwayman came
Down from his horse;
Little did he think
It was for his loss.

For a while he was picking
The money that was strewed;
Franny jumped on his horse
And away he rode.

The maid seeing Fran
Returning home,
Went to call her master
In another room.

"Why, Fran, has my cow
Turned into a horse?"
"O no, my good master,

I well sold your cow
But was robbed of the money
By a highwayman bold.

"And while he was putting
The money in his purse,
To make you amends
I came off with his horse."

The saddle-bags were taken off,
And out of them were told
Five thousand pounds
In silver and in gold.

"I swear, my good master,
I well sold your cow."

"As for a boy
You've done very rare;
One part of this money
You shall have for your share.

"But as for the villain,
You served him just right;
For you have put upon him
A South Carolina bite."

The Jovial Tinker [166]
(Joan's Ale Is Good)

Possibly a variant of a song known by the above titles. In the *Tale of a Tub*, Ben Jonson mentions this song at the point where the old father Rosin, chief minstrel of Highgate, and his two sons, all playing violins, enter near the end of the piece and perform: "Tom Tiler," "The Jolly Joiner," and "The Jolly Tinker." It also appears in D'Urfey's *Pills to Purge Melancholy* (1712), III, 133 [V, 61 ff, in 1719–1720 ed.]. It is quite likely that the song has been adapted to events of the American Civil War, as the last stanza seems to indicate. Contributed by Carey Woofter, Gilmer Co., West Virginia [1924].

[From a ballet by John Wolverton, Hardman, West Virginia. See Appendix.]

When I was a little boy I walked up and down,
And chanced to stop in a seaport town;
The drums they beat and the cannons did roar,
And the people there told me the war weren't o'er.

In come a soldier so very neat and fine,
"Come, landlady, draw me a pint of wine,
And we'll charge it to the barrow[1] along with the old score,
And I'll pay you for your liquors when the wars are o'er."

In come the barber wishing little harm,
With a great long beard as long as your arm,
Saying, "If I don't get a kiss from the girl I adore,
I don't intend to shave till the wars are all o'er."

In come the tailor and loud he did say,
"The way I make my living is by four and six a day,
Mending up old clothes all ragged and tore,
And they will never get new ones till the wars are all o'er."

In come the blacksmith, greatest trade of all,
Sold his bed and blankets for iron and coal,
And took up his lodgings on the cold floor,
He may lay there and freeze till the wars are all o'er.

In come the beggar with a coon on his back,
Picked up a hoe-cake and slipped it in a sack;
He cut me off a quarter and swore I'd get no more,
And I don't intend to eat it till the wars are all o'er.

In come the devil with a nigger on his back,
Picked up a Yankee to balance his knapsack;
The Yankee rode behind and the nigger rode before,
And away they went a-jogging till the wars are all o'er.

---

[1] *Barrow*—borrow?

The Spanish Maid [87]
[Laws K 16]

Contributed by Berlin B. Chapman, Webster Co., West Virginia [1924].

A gay Spanish maid at the age of sixteen
Through the meadows did stray far away,
And beneath a green tree she sat down to rest
With a gay handsome youth by her side.

"My ship sails tonight, my darling Lanette,
And with you I may nevermore roam;
When your friends in the cottage have settled to rest,
Meet me, darling Lanette, on the shore."

When her friends in the cottage had retired to their rest,
Young Lanette stole through the hall door;
With her hat in her hand she ran down the dry sand
And sat down on a rock by the shore.

The moon had just risen far over the deep,
Where the sky and the water seemed to meet,
And the murmuring of the waves as they rolled o'er the deep
Broke over the sand at her feet.

Her white hand she clasped to her wild throbbing heart,
Her sorrow there's no tongue can tell;
I kissed her again as we stood on the beach,
And bid her an affectionate farewell.

The night passed away with a wild crashing storm,
The rain in great torrents did fall;
There was no one left of that sad fated crew,
For the ship she was lost in the storm.

There as she lay on the wild troubled sea,
Proudly riding on wave after wave,
I jumped on a plank and escaped from the wreck,
While the rest met a watery grave.

That night found me floating far out on the deep,
Morning found me praying to my God;
I thought of the maid I had left on the beach,
And I wished, how I wished I was there!

Early next morning a sail I espied,
And for safety I prayed to my God;
My signal they see, and run down to me,
And most joyfully took me on board.

My attention I turned to the maid on the beach,
When she heard of her boy in the storm;
She died like a rose that was bitten by the frost,
And has left me in sorrow to mourn.

The Old Wife [128]

Contributed by Mrs. Mag Perkins, Cedarville, Gilmer Co., West
Virginia. [Communicated by Carey Woofter, 1924.]

There was a wife lived in a glen,
And she had daughters nine or ten,
That sought the house both but and ben[1]
    To find their mam a-spruncin.[2]

Her man into his grave had gone;
"Ho hum," said she, "let him begone,
For I must have me a stout young man
    To furnish me with spruncin."

Her eldest daughter said right bold,
"Fie, mother, mind, that now you're old;
And if you with a youngster would,
    He'll waste away his spruncin."

The youngest daughter gave a shout,
"Oh, mother dear, your teeth's all out;
Besides half blind you have the gout;
    Your legs can stand no spruncin."

"You lie, you limmers,"[3] cried old mump,[4]
"For I have both a tooth and stump,

---

[1] *But and ben*—inside and outside.
[2] *Spruncin*—holding sexual intercourse.
[3] *Limmer*—a jade, wretch.
[4] *Mump*—mama, mother.

And will no longer live in dump,[5]
  Because I want my spruncin."

"But look," said Peg, that cunning slut,
"Mother, if you can crack a nut,
Then we will all consent to it
  That you shall have your spruncin."

The old one did agree to that,
And they a pistol bullet got;
She powerfully did begin to crack,
  To win herself some spruncin.

Great sport it was to see her chaw it,
And 'tween her gums to squeeze and roll it,
While from her jaws the slaver flowed,
And how she cursed poor stumpy!

At last she gave a desperate squeeze,
And broke her long tooth near her nose;
And so poor stumpy was at ease,
  But oh, she lost hopes of spruncin.

She from her task began to tire,
And from her daughters did retire;
She laid her down before the fire,
  And died from want of spruncin.

You old wives, notice well this truth:
As soon as you're past tooth in mouth
Never do what is only fit for youth,
  And leave off thoughts of spruncin.

Else, like the old wife by the fire,
Your daughters against you will conspire;
Nor will you get, unless you hire,
  A young man to do your spruncin.

[5] *In dump*—in discard.

Kate and the Clothier *[101]*
[Laws N 22]

An incomplete variant of "Kate and Her Horns." Contributed by Mrs. Martha Smith, Smithsboro, Knott Co., Kentucky.

. . . .
. . . .
Kate knew when every night he came
From his new love, Nancy by name,

Sometimes at ten o'clock or more.
Kate to a tanner went therefore,
And borrowed there an old cow-hide,
With crooked horns both large and wide.

When she wrapped herself within,
Her new intrigue it did begin;
Kate to a lonesome field did stray,
At length the clothier came that way.

And he was surely scared at her,
She looked so like old Lucifer,
With hairy hide, horns on her head,
With near three feet asunder spread.

With that he saw a long black tail;
He strove to run, but his feet they failed;
Then with a groan, a doleful note,
Kate quickly seized him by the throat,

And says, "You've left poor Kate, I hear,
And wooed the lawyer's daughter dear;
Since you have been so vile with her,
You shall, whether you will or no,
Into my gloomy regions go."

Says, "Master devil, spare me now,
And I'll perform my firming[1] vow;
I'll make young Kate my lawful bride."
"See that you do," the devil cried.

[1] *Firming*—former.

Kate's friends and parents thought it strange
That there was such a sudden change.

.   .   .   .

.   .   .   .

Kate never let her parents know,
Nor any other friend or foe,
Till they a year had married been,
And told it at her lying-in.

It pleased the women to their heart,
Said Kate had fairly played her part;
Her husband laughed as well as they,
And it was a joyful, merry day.

There Was a Sea Captain [121]
[Law Q 12]

Contributed by George O. Humphrey, Morgantown, West Virginia.

There was a sea captain who was married of late,
He courted a lady to gain her estate;
He was a sea captain, and bound for the sea,
And before he was bedded he was call-ed away,
  With his fol dee die addy, fol dee die addy die ay.

Now there was a young squire who liv-ed hard by,
And he was resolv-ed this lady to try;
So early one morning the squire arose,
And dressed himself up in the best of his clothes,
  With his fol dee die addy, fol dee die addy die ay.

He called for his coach and his footman behind,
He met this young lady and bade her be kind;
She said, "Ye young squire, ye talk like a man that was poor,
And my husband captain would call me a whore,"
  With his fol dee die addy, fol dee die addy die ay.

So he took her in his arms and gave her a kiss,
Saying, "A slice from a cut loaf would never be missed."

.   .   .   .

.   .   .   .

With your fol dee die addy, fol dee die addy die ay.

Now when six months was over, and nine months had come,
That very same night this young captain came home;
He took her in his arms and gave her a kiss,
Said he, "My dear jewel, you are thick 'round the waist,"
    With your fol dee die addy, fol dee die addy die ay.

"It is nothing but fatness," this lady she cried

.   .   .   .

.   .   .   .

"Would you have me as slim as when I was a maid?"
    With my fol dee die addy, fol dee die addy die ay.

Now when supper was ended she went to the hall;
She opened her mouth and gave a loud call:
"The colic, the colic, the colic!" she cried;
"I am so bad with the colic I fear I shall die!"
    And my fol dee die addy, fol dee die addy die ay.

The cook she made answer out of the next room:

.   .   .   .

.   .   .   .

"I am so bad with the colic I can not come down,"
    With my fol dee die addy, fol dee die addy die ay.

The doctor was sent for, her pulse for to feel;
He said she was bad from her head to her heel;
He felt of her pulse, and shaking his head,
"She will get better, once she is brought to bed,"
    With her fol dee die addy, fol dee die addy die ay.

The midwife was sent for, and when she came there,
Herself was delivered of a young son and heir.
The cook and the housemaid all brought forth the same,
And then it was poor Jenny, she ended the game,
    With their fol dee die addy, fol dee die addy die ay.

He said, "My dear jewel, you have had a fine year,
And for the joke's sake I will forgive you, my dear;
But one thing I would ask you, tell me if you can:
Does all these four babies belong to one man?"
    With his fol dee die addy, fol dee die addy die ay.

"Sir, it is for myself that I can say;
It was the young squire that did me betray;
It was the young squire that did me beguile,
And the rest of his servants got my maids with child,"
  With their fol dee die addy, fol dee die addy die ay.

Now come all you sea captains, take warning from this,
And do not blame your wife for doing amiss;
For their husbands' long absence they can not well want,
Since the mistress and maids took the blanket carent (*sic*)[1]
  With their fol dee die addy, fol dee die addy die ay.

[1] *Take the blanket carent*—bear a child.

The Jolly Boatsman [114]
[Laws P 17]

Contributed by Mrs. Martha Smith, Smithsboro, Knott Co., Kentucky.

Come all ye jolly boatsman boys
That go to see your dear;
The moon is shining bright,
And the stars a-twinkling clear.

I dropped at my love's window
To ease her of her pain;
So quickly she rose and let me in,
And went to bed again.

"Come strip you quite naked,
Your mother will not know;
Come strip you quite naked,
And let the candle go.

"And let the candle go, my dear,
Without a fear or doubt,
And we'll have a little pleasure,
When you blow the candle out.

"Your father and your mother
In yonder's room both lie,

Abracing of each other,
And why not you and I?

"And why not you and I, my dear,
Without a fear or doubt?
We'll have a little pleasure,
When we blow the candle out."

Nine months and better,
Nine months being past,
This beautiful damsel
Brought forth a child at last.

Brought forth a child at last, my dear,
Without a fear or doubt,
And she damned the very hour
That she blowed the candle out.

Come all ye young ladies,
Wherever ye may be:
Do not trust a young man
One inch above your knee.

An inch above your knee, my dear,
Without a fear or doubt—
They are seeking out a way
For to blow the candle out.

Three Ships Came Sailing In [315]

A Christmas carol of religious tradition, heard among young school-boys; the grandfather of one of them came to America from England. Contributed by A. E. Harris, Little Birch, Braxton Co., West Virginia.

I saw three ships come sailing in,
On Christmas day, on Christmas day;
I saw three ships come sailing in,
On Christmas day in the morning.

And what was in those ships all three? etc.

Our Saviour, Christ, and His Lady.

Pray, whither sailed those ships all three?

O, they sailed into Bethlehem.

And all the bells on earth did ring.

And all the angels in heaven did sing.

Then let us all rejoice again.

The Gowans Are Gay [140]

Contributed by Charles McIntosh, Walkersville, Lewis Co., West Virginia.

There gowans are gay, oh joy,
    There gowans are gay;
They cause me to wake instead of sleep,
    The first morning of May.

Over the fields as I did pass, etc.
I chanced to meet a proper lass, etc.

Quite busy was that bonny maid,
I asked her, quick to her I said,

"O lady fair, what do you here?"
"Gathering the dew; what need you ask?"

"The dew?" said I, "what do you mean?"
Quoth she, "To wash my mistress clean."

I asked of her farther then,
If to my wife she would incline.

She said her errand was not so,
Her maidenhead on me to bestow.

Then as an arrow from the bow
She skipped away across the knoll,

And left me there to hold my peace,
And in my heart a twinge of pain.

The little birds sang full sweet,
But to my comfort it was not meet.

And thereabouts I passed my time,
Until it was the hour of prime.

And then returned home unseen,
Wondering what maiden that had been.

Ryner Dyne [113]
[Laws P 15]

Contributed by H. F. Watson, Marion Co., West Virginia.

One morning as I rambled,
Two miles below Palm Roy,
I met a farmer's daughter
All on the mountain high.

Said I, "My pretty fair maid,
Your beauty shines most clear;
Upon this lonely mountain
I'm glad to meet you here."

These words were scarcely spoken
When the maid fell in a maze,
With her eyes as bright as diamonds,
Upon me she did gaze.

Her cherry cheek and ruby lips
They cast their former hue,
And then she flew into my arms,
Upon the mountain high.

I had but kissed her once or twice
When she came to again,
When modestly she says to me,
"Pray, Sir, what is your name?"

"Go look in yonder forest,
My castle you will find;
'Tis wrote in ancient history,
My name is Ryner Dyne.

"And now, my pretty fair maid,
Don't let your parents know,

For they may prove my ruin,
Perhaps my overthrow.

"If you come to this forest,
Perhaps you will not me find;
But I'll be in my castle,
And call for Ryner Dyne."

Pretty Polly [133]

Contributed by Berlin B. Chapman, Marion Co., West Virginia
[1924].

I've traveled this country both early and late,
And having no fortune, my troubles were great;
I courted a damsel, Pretty Polly by name,
She has ofttimes denied me, but I'll try her again.

"Oh, Polly, oh, Polly, your parents are rich,
And me having no fortune, which troubles me much;
Come leave your old father, and mother also,
And through this wide world with your darling boy go."

"Oh, Jimmy, oh, Jimmy, that never would do,
To leave my old parents and go along with you;
My friends and relations would mourn for my sake,
For to think I would leave them and follow a rake."

"Some say I am rakey, some say I am wild,
Some say I am guilty fair maidens to beguile;
But I'll prove them all liars by the powers above,
That I'm guilty of nothing but innocent love.

"I'll go down to New Orleans, my boat there I'll steer,
And marry a Spanish beauty on the banks will appear;
But now I'm at Orleans, my heart ain't at rest,
For the thoughts of Pretty Polly roll soft through my breast.

"I'll go back to Kentucky, see Polly again,
And I'll never go leave her to follow the Main.
Her eyes are like charcoal, her hair is a brown,
And she lives in Kentucky, near Cynthiana town."

Slago Town [180]

Contributed by Mrs. John W. Combs, Hindman, Knott Co., Kentucky.

O once I knew a pretty little girl,
When pretty girls were but few;
Ofttimes I've rolled her in my arms,
All over the fog and dew.

Chorus:

I wish I was ten thousand mile,
And on some ship or shore,
Or in some howling wilderness,
Where I'd never be seen any more.

O once I courted a pretty little girl,
She didn't known [*sic*] what to do;
Ofttimes I've rolled her in my arms,
All in the fog and dew.

O once I courted a pretty little girl,
Way down in Waterloo;
Ofttimes I've rolled her in my arms,
All in the fog and dew.

Go hand to me my pen and ink,
And let me write a line;
I'll ask that girl to marry me,
Just say, "Will you be mine?"

I am sitting here so lone-ly,
My thoughts are all on you;
I'm waiting for an answer, dear,
Saying, "I will marry you."

I wish I was in Slago[1] town,
A-following up my trade,
A bottle of wine all in my hand,
And on my knee a maid.

[1] *Slago*—County Sligo, Ireland.

To Cheer the Heart [179]

Contributed by Mrs. John W. Combs, Hindman, Knott Co.,
Kentucky. [Text corrected from the Combs MS.]

Many, many winters since,
My beau has gone away;
I ought to be as happy
As a nightingale in May.
Then cheer up, my heart,
Be happy and gay;
For I have another beau,
Since he is far away.

Chorus:
Let him go, let him stay,
Let him sink or let him swim;
If he don't care for me,
I don't care for him.
I hope he will gain a fortune,
Make of himself a better man;
I hope he gains a fortune
In that far and distant land.

He is little, he is pretty,
And he dresses up so neat;
O isn't that a pity
He is so full of his deceit!
O he is little and he is pretty,
But why need I care?
For I have another beau,
Since he is not here.

He is the son of a rich merchant,
I the daughter of a laboring man;
Money in his pocket,
Let him jingle it while he can.
He has plenty in his pocket,
But little in his heart;
He loves me a little,
And he puts the rest apart.

He loves me a little,
Like the dew-cup on the corn:
He puts it on at evening,
And he takes it off at morn.
He loves me a little,
Like the dew-cup on the corn:
He puts it on at evening,
And he takes it off at morn.

Come All Ye False Lovers [135]

Contributed by Mrs. John W. Combs, Hindman, Knott Co., Kentucky.

"Come all ye false lovers
That love all alike;
Give love-ly attention,
And my counsel take.

"Beware of false lovers;
Never place your affections on them,
For it's hard to recall it
When they're gone away.

"My loves they come to me,
Likewise they go from me;
They swear that they love me,
But that's all in vain.

"For the best of an-y
I love my own Johnny;
I never will marry
Till my John comes again.

"I wish I were with him,
In all kinds of weather;
If there's any misfortune,
Let it all come together.

"God bless the salt sea
That my John sails upon;

Likewise the little boat
That carries him along.

"O keep him secured
From the wind and cold rain;
I never will marry
Till my John comes again."

When he came home
And she knew it not,
Unto her old parents
She then cast her lot.

As he entered the door
He heard her complain:
"I never will marry
Till my John comes again."

Then into her arms
Like lightning he flew,
Says, "O my dear jewel,
Since you've proved so true,

"Since you've proved so laurel (loyal),
Unto me you'll remain";
Says, "O my dear jewel,
I'll never leave you again."

He took her by the hand,
And straightway they went
Unto her old parents
To get their consent.

And now they are married
And a-living content;
What the heavens created,
No man can prevent.

Ranting Roving Lad [144]

One of the rare songs which have retained the Scots dialect in the Southern Highlands. "The Old Wife" (p. 135) also contains traces of it. [From George Burris, Grantsville, West Virginia.] Contributed by Carey Woofter, Gilmer Co., West Virginia [1924].

My love was born in Aberdeen,
The bonniest lad that ever was seen;
But now he makes our hearts full sad—
He's taken the field with his white cockade.

Chorus:

O he's a ranting, roving blade!
O he's a brisk and bonny lad!
Betide what will, my heart is glad
To see my lad with his white cockade!

O leeze me on the philabeg,[1]
The hairy bough[2] and gartered leg!
But aye the sight that glads my ee
Is the white cockade above the bree.

I'll sell my rock,[3] I'll sell my reel,
My rippling kame and spinning wheel
To buy my lad a tartan plaid,
A braidsword, dirk and a white cockade.

I'll sell my rokelay[4] and my tow,
My gude gray mare and hawkit cow,
That every loyal Buchan lad
May take the field with his white cockade.

[1] [*Leeze me on the philabeg*—dear to be is the kilt.]
[2] *Bough*—hough, hock.
[3] [*Rock*—distaff.]
[4] [*Rokelay*—cloak.]

The Soldier Bride's Lament [132]

Contributed by Mrs. John W. Combs, Hindman, Knott Co., Kentucky.

> The night that I were married,
> And on my new-married bed,
> Up stepped the old sea captain,
> And stood at my bed head.

> Saying, "Arise you up, my new married man,
> And go along with me
> To the lowlands of Holland,
> To fight your enemy."

> Old Holland is a pretty place,
> And in there grows no green;
> Oh, isn't that a pretty place
> For soldiers to obtain?

> The sugar grapes are plenty,
> And wine drops from the tree,
> But the lowland of Holland
> Has parted my love and me.

> Says mother to her daughter,
> "What makes you so lament?
> Aren't there men enough in this country
> To give your heart content?"

> "There is men enough in this country
> But none of them suits me;
> He shall not go to old Holland—
> No, that never can be.

> "No rings upon my fingers,
> No comb within my hair;
> No handkerchief upon my neck,
> To show my beauty fair."

> "A bride, a bride, a bride," she cried,
> Most glorious to behold;
> Her hair hung around her shoulders,
> Like lovely links of gold.

William Bluet [125]

Contributed by Bill Cornett, Hindman, Knott Co., Kentucky.

There was a woman lived in Hampshire,
She had one only son, and him she loved most dear;
She had no other child but he,
She brought him up in pomp and vanitee.

When this youth grew up in his estate,
He run through with it all, although it was very great;
There was nothing left undone that he could do the worst,
Of sin, theft, and murder too.

When he was bound in prison so strong,
His mother came there to see her son;
But her poor soul was not permitted to go in,
So she walked up to the bars and spoke to him.

She said, "Dear son, if you my counsel took,
And the Lord, heaven and His book forsook,
You might a-lived some pleasure for to see;
But to your dear old mother you are a miseree."

He said, "Dear mother, go leave off your pitiful cries,
Your weeps and mourns brings soft tears to my eyes;
Forget, dear mother, such a child you ever bore—
Kiss my lips once, dear mother, if no more."

She kissed his lips ten thousand times or more,
Her hands in her hair with sorrow tore;
Saying, "Dear child, you'll not forgotten be,
Although your body hangs a wonder for to see."

"I know my body hangs on chains so high,
I am doomed to see eterni-ty;
My race is run, my case is done,
My life goes down this evening with the sun."

When the officer from Brayon did appear,
Straightway to William Bluet he drew near,
Saying, "William, prepare yourself in speed,
For this almost makes my very heart bleed."

When he was on the gallows so high,
He prayed to the Lord for mer-cy,
Saying, "Pity, Lord, the only son,
Or my soul is forever left undone."

When he had hung till he was almost dead,
There came a dove and hovered his head three times;
Then ascended to the sky,
Which put the people in a sad disprise.[1]

[1] *Disprise*—surprise.

Native American Songs

Brave Wolfe [43]
[Laws A 1]

This song is a survival of the colonial period and describes the Battle of Quebec, in which Generals Wolfe and Montcalm were mortally wounded. The meeting of Montcalm and Wolfe in the thirteenth stanza is particularly striking. Contributed by Carey Woofter, Gilmer Co., West Virginia [1924, who heard school children on Bear Fork of the right hand fork of Steer Creek, West Virginia, singing it to the tune of "Yankee Doodle"].

Cheer up, my young men all,
Let nothing fright you;
Though oft objection rise,
Let it delight you.

Let not your fancy move
Whene'er it comes to trial,
Nor let your courage fail
At the first denial.

I sat down by my love,
Thinking that I wooed her;
I sat down by my love,
But sure not to delude her.

But when I go to speak,
My tongue it doth so quiver
I dare not speak my mind
Whenever I am with her.

Love, here's a ring of gold,
'Tis long that I have kept it;
My dear, now for my sake
I pray you to accept it.

When you the posy[1] read,
Pray, think upon the giver;
My dear, remember me,
Or I'm undone forever.

Then Wolfe he took his leave
Of his most lovely jewel,
Although it seemed to be
To him an act most cruel.

Although it's for a space
I'm forced to leave my love,
My dear, where'er I rove
I'll ne'er forget my dove.

So then this valiant youth
Embark-ed on the ocean,
To free America
From faction's dire commotion.

He landed in Quebec,
Being all brave and hearty,
The city to attack
With his most valiant party.

Then Wolfe drew up his men,
In rank and file so pretty,
On Abraham's lofty heights
Before this noble city.

A distance from the town
The noble French did meet them
In double numbers there,
Resolv-ed for to beat them.

Montcalm and this brave youth
Together they are walking;
So well do they agree,
Like brothers they are talking.

Then each one to his post
As they do now retire;
O then their numerous hosts
Began their dreadful fire.

---

[1] [*Posy*—the inscription within the ring.]

Then instant from his horse
Fell this so noble hero;
May we lament his loss
In words of deepest sorrow.

The French are seen to break,
Their columns are all flying;
Then Wolfe he seems to wake,
Though in the act of dying.

And lifted up his head,
The drum did sound and rattle,
And to his army said,
"I pray, how goes the battle?"

His adecomp [*sic*] replied,
"Brave Ginral, 'tis in our favor,
Quebec and all her pride—
'Tis nothing now can save her.

"She falls into our hands
With all her wealth and treasure."
"O then," brave Wolfe replies,
"I quit the world with pleasure."

Floyd Frazier [68]
[Laws F 19]

Contributed by Mrs. Margaret Green, Smithsboro, Knott Co., Kentucky.

Come you people of every nation,
And listen to my mournful song;
I will tell you of a circumstance,
Which happened not very long.

Floyd Frazier is now in prison,
And ought to hang-ed be,
For the killing of an innocent woman,
This world may plainly see.

He killed poor Ellen Flannery,
And hid her in the woods,
And made a quick return
To wash away the blood.

He crept into his cabin,
And lay there all night,
Believing his crime was hidden
From everybody's sight.

She had five little children,
From door to door they run,
To look for their poor mother,
But yet no mother come.

Their little hearts grew hungry,
At last they fell asleep,
To rise up in the morning
To cry and mourn and weep.

The night it passed away,
And the morning it did come;
Her neighbors all did gather,
To see what there was done.

They searched all round her cabin,
Went wandering up and down;
At last Joseph Williams found her,
And she was deadly wound'.

They found her poor body lying
Mouldering on the ground;
The rocks piled upon her,
They weighed sixty pound.

They took her to her house,
And there not long to stay,
And then unto the graveyard,
Until the Judgment Day.

The people all did gather
To see her dreadful wounds;
The sight it was the greatest
That ever has been found.

She suffered in great mis'ry,
In trouble and in pain;
I hope her soul is in heaven,
Forever there to reign.

This young man was arrested,
And rushed into the jail;
The jury pronounced him guilty,
They did not allow him bail.

He owned that he did kill her,
And all that he had done;
I think his case is dangerous,
He has all the risk to run.

They carried him to Pineville,
And there awhile to dwell;
I'm afraid the crime he's committed
Will send his soul to hell.

This song came to me
By day and by night;
I think it is right to sing it
In this vain world of delight.

Talt Hall [62]
[Laws dE 42]

Talt Hall, native of Kentucky, "the bandit of the mountains," was hanged in Virginia toward the end of the nineteenth century; he had on his conscience more than twenty assassinations. He furnished the basic outline for the character of "Bad" Rufe Tolliver in one of the Highland tales of John Fox, Jr. [*The Trail of the Lonesome Pine*]. Contributed by Rob. Morgan, Emmalena, Knott Co., Kentucky.

Come all you fathers and mothers,
And brothers and sisters all,
I'll relate to you the history
Concerning old Talt Hall.

He shot and killed Frank Salyers,
The starter of it all;
He's breaking up our country,
He's trying to kill us all.

They arrested him in Tennessee,
And placed him in Gladeville jail;
He had no friends nor relations,
No one to go his bail.

He heard the train a-coming,
Got up and put on his boots;
They're taking him to Richmond
To wear the striped suits.

He heard the train a-coming,
He heard those Negroes' yells;
They're taking him to Richmond,
To hear the Richmond bells.

He wrote his brother a letter,
To his own home country,
Say, "See your satisfaction, brother,
Wherever you may be."

He wrote another letter,
Saying, "Brother, now farewell";
Says, "See your satisfaction, brother,
Or send your soul to hell."

He got upon the platform,
He wrung his hands and cried,
Says, "If I had not a-killed Frank Salyers,
I would not have had to died."

J. B. Marcum [60]
[Laws E 19]

An adaptation of "Jesse James" which recounts the assassination of a noted lawyer during his actions against certain "partisans" of Kentucky. Ballads devoted solely to clan feuds are not found in the Highlands; however, some songs have been composed on the death of famous clan leaders. Contributed by Mr. Noble, Jackson, Breathitt Co., Kentucky.

It was on the fourth of May, half past eight o'clock that day,
J. B. Marcum then was standing in the door
Of the court house of his town, where Curt Jett was lurking round,
Just to get a chance to lay him on the floor.

Chorus:

Marcum leaves a wife to mourn all her life,
And his little children stand it well and brave;
But that little Curtis Jett, Thomas White and others yet,
Are the men who laid poor Marcum in his grave.

Thomas White, a friend of Jett, no worse man was ever met,
Then came walking boldly through the court house hall;
And as he was walking by, he looked Marcum in the eye,
Knowing truly that poor Marcum soon would fall.

White then walked out on the street, stopped to see it all complete.
He expected soon to hear the fatal shot.
Jett advances through the hall with a pistol leaden ball,
And he killed poor J. B. Marcum on the spot.

Judge Jim Hargis and his man, Edward Callahan,
Were across the street in Hargis Brothers Store;
Some believed they knew the plot, hence were listening for the
    shot,
And saw Jett's victim fall there in the door.

Captain Ewen, standing by, saw him fall and heard the cry:
"O Lord, O Lord, they have killed me now at last."
Ewen saw the man and gun, and then he hastily did run,
And then he heard the second loud and awful blast.

B. J. Ewen, wise and true, knowing well it would not do
To expose the man who held the weapon bare,

Had to keep the secret well, for he was afraid to tell,
Since he feared the judge would kill him then and there.

Thus he came to Marcum's aid, though at first they were afraid;
Hargis, Callahan, and White they never met.
But the one who lingered near was a man they all did fear—
Who had the awful deed was Curtis Jett.

They arrested White and Jett, and the court in Jackson met;
There the prosecution labored with its might,
And when Breathitt's court was o'er, Judge Redwine could do no
    more,
So he left it with the jury for the night.

And the jury disagreed; just one man began to plead
That he thought Curt Jett and White should both go free.
He contended to the last, his vote he would not cast,
And it is believed Judge Hargis paid the man a fee.

Then they tried the men once more, not in Jackson as before,
For they could not get justice in that town;
So the court in Harrison met, and condemned both White and
    Jett—
A verdict of their guiltiness they found.

Now the final trial is past, Jett and White are doomed at last
To the prison house where they will have to stay;
And with those of other crime they must labor all the time
Until death shall come and take them both away.

Their poor mothers grieve today o'er their boys while they're
    away,
For there's nothing that can sever a mother's love;
They will think of them each breath, and will cleave to them till
    death,
Then they will hope to meet them in the courts above.

Now 'tis true, but sad to note, there are others who had to go,
And be locked up in the Fayette County jail,
Awaiting trial for the crime they had covered for a time,
That was so great the court refused to give them bail.

The Tolliver Song [61]
[Law E 20]

This song is closely related to one of the most famous of Kentucky feuds, the Rowan County "War." It should be pointed out that the code of honor of the Highlander does not require that he give his opponent a fair chance to defend himself; any means, fair or foul, are suitable, and his behavior is in striking contrast to the chivalric spirit of the plainsman of the West. In Kentucky this ballad is known as "The Rowan County War." Contributed by Hattie Rowland, Cliff Top, Fayette Co., West Virginia.

It was in the month of August, all on election day,
Lent Martin, he was wounded, some say by Johnny Day.
But Martin could not believe it, or could not think it so;
He thought it was Bud Tolliver that struck the fatal blow.

They wounded young Ad Simon, although his life was saved;
He seems to shun grog shops since he stood near the grave.
They shot and killed Sol Bradley, a sober, innocent man;
Left his wife and children to do the best they can.

Martin did recover, some months had come and past;
All in the town of Morehead these men did meet at last.
Tolliver and a friend or two about the street did walk;
They seemed to be uneasy, with no one wished to talk.

They walked into Judge Carey's grocery[1] and stepped up to
    the bar;
But little did he think, dear friends, he had met his fatal hour.
The sting of death was near him; Martin rushed in at the
    door.
A few words passed between them concerning a row before.

People soon got frightened, began to rush out of the room,
When a ball from Martin's pistol laid Tolliver in the tomb.
His friends then gathered round him, his wife to weep and
    wail;
And Martin was arrested and placed in the county jail.

He was put in jail at Roand,[2] there to remain a while,

---

[1] *Grocery*—saloon.
[2] [*Roand*—Rowan.]

In the hands of law and justice, to bravely stand his trial.
The people talked of lynching him, at present though they
    failed;
The prisoner's friends removed him to Winchester jail.

Some persons forged an order, their names I do not know;
The plan was soon agreed upon, for Martin they did go.
Martin seemed to be discouraged, he seemed to be in dread.
"They have sought a plan to kill me," to the jailer Martin
    said.

They put the handcuffs on him, his heart was in distress.
They hurried to the station, got on the night express.
Along the line she lumbered, just at her usual speed.
There were only two in numbers to commit the awful deed.

Martin was in the smoking car, accompanied by his wife.
They did not want her present when they took her husband's
    life.
And when they arrived at Farmer, they had no time to lose.
A band approached the engineer and bade him not to move.

They stepped up to the prisoner with pistols in their hands;
In death he soon was sinking, he died in iron bands.
His wife overheard the noise, being in the smoking car.
She cried, "O Lord! they've killed my husband," when she
    heard the pistols fire.

The death of these two men has caused trouble in our land,
Caused men to leave their families and take the parting band.
It has caused continual war, which may never, never cease.
I would to God that I could see our land once more in peace.

They killed our deputy sheriff, Baumgartner was his name.
They shot him from the bushes, after taking deliberate aim.
The death of him was dreadful, it may never be forgot;
His body was pierced and torn with thirty-two buckshot.

I composed this song as a warning. Oh, beware young men!
Your pistols will cause you trouble, on this you may depend.
In the bottom of a whiskey glass a lurking devil dwells,
Burns the breath of those who drink it, and sends their souls
    to hell.

The Vance Song [67]

[Laws F 17]

If the first three stanzas of this song are the work of a Highland composer, they do him great honor, for they transcend the usual standards of Highland songs. Contributed by Hattie Towland, Cliff Top, Fayette Co., West Virginia.

Green are the woods where Sandy flows,
The wild beasts dwelleth there;
The bear is secure in the laurel groves,
And the red buck roves the hill.

Bright shines the sun on Clinde's Hill,
And soft the west wind blows;
The woods are covered with bloom so fair,
Perfumed by the wild rose.

But Vance no more shall Sandy behold,
Or drink of its crystal waves;
The partial judge pronounced his doom,
And the hunter has found his grave.

"I hope that pardon is found; Daniel Horton,
    Bob and Bill
A lie against me swore,
In order to take my life away,
That I may be no more.

"But they and I together must meet
When Immanuel's trumpet blows;
Perhaps when I'm at rest on Abraham's breast,
They will rove the gulfs below.

"Farewell, my friends, my children dear,
I bid you all farewell;
The love I have for your precious souls
No mortal tongue can tell.

"Since heaven has spoke kind peace to my soul,
This body will soon decay;
The blood that was shed on Calvary's hill
Washed all my sins away.

"Farewell, my true and loving wife,
To you I bid adieu;
And if I gain fair Canaan's land,
I'll wait and watch for you.

"I come, I come, ye angels of God,
To the realms of joy I come;
A Christian hope cheers my hours of death,
Dear Jesus, receive me home."

John Henry [81]
(The Steel-Driving Man)
[Laws I 1]

This song has been borrowed from the Negroes. John Henry, a steel driver, lost his life in a contest with a modern steam drill. The ballad is based on an actual incident, which occurred during the construction of the C & O Railroad line in southern West Virginia. "Babe" is a clear indication of Negro origin or adaptation; this generally unnecessary expression is one of affection. Contributed by Jesse Green, Smithsboro, Knott Co., Kentucky.

When John Henry was a little babe,
A-holding to his mama's hand,
Says, "If I live till I'm twenty-one,
I'm going to make a steel-driving man, my babe,
I'm going to make a steel-driving man."

When Johnny was a little boy,
A-sitting on his father's knee,
Says, "The Big Bend Tunnel on the C and O Road
Is going to be the death of me," my babe (*bis*).

John, he made a steel-driving man,
They took him to the tunnel to drive;
He drove so hard he broke his heart,
He laid down his hammer and he died, my babe.

O now John Henry is a steel-driving man,
He belongs to the steel-driving crew;

And every time his hammer comes down,
You can see that steel walking through, my babe.

The steam-drill standing on the right-hand side,
John Henry standing on the left;
He says, "I'll beat that steam-drill down,
Or I'll die with my hammer in my breast," my babe.

He placed his drill on the top of the rock,
The steam-drill standing close at hand;
He beat it down one inch and a half,
And laid down his hammer like a man, my babe.

Johnny looked up to his boss-man and said,
"O boss-man, how can it be!
For the rock is so hard, and the steel is so tough,
I can feel my muscles giving way," my babe.

Johnny looked down to his turner[1] and said,
"O turner, how can it be!
The rock is so hard, and the steel is so tough,
That everybody's turning after me," my babe.

They took poor Johnny on the steep hillside,
He looked to his heavens above;
He says, "Take my hammer and wrap it in gold,
And give it to the girl that I love," my babe.

They took his hammer and wrapped it in gold,
And give it to Julia Ann;
And the last words Johnny said to her
Was, "Julia, do the best you can," my babe.

"If I die a railroad man,
Go bury me under the tie,
So I can hear old number four
As she goes rolling by," my babe.

"If I die a railroad man,
Go bury me under the sand,
With a pick and shovel at my head and feet,
And a nine-pound hammer in my hand," my babe.

---

[1] *Turner*—the holder of the drill.

The Yew-Pine Mountains *[256]*

This song is obviously an offshoot of the preceding, "John Henry." It is not a narrative, but rather a banjo song of the Negroes, adopted by the whites. [From Harley Townsend, Dusk, West Virginia, "whose brother heard it years ago in the coal camps near Fairmont."] Contributed by Mr. [Carey] Woofter, Glenville, West Virginia [1924].

> This old hammer rings like silver (3).
> It shines like gold, babe, it shines like gold.
>
> I'm going back to the Yew-Pine Mountains
> For that's my home, babe, for that's my home.
>
> This old hammer killed my buddy,
> But it'll not kill me, babe, it'll not kill me.
>
> This old hammer killed John Hardy,
> But it'll not kill me, babe, but it'll not kill me.
>
> The people round here they don't like me,
> But I don't care, babe, I don't care.
>
> Forty-four days makes forty-four dollars,
> All in gold, babe, all in gold.
>
> I can hear my true-love calling,
> "O come back home, babe, O come back home."
>
> I can see my true-love coming,
> All dressed in red, babe, all dressed in red.
>
> When I meet her I will greet her,
> And she'll greet me, babe, she'll greet me.

The Irish Peddler *[70]*
[Laws F 24]

Contributed by Jesse Green, Smithsboro, Knott Co., Kentucky.

> Just as the sun was rising high,
> One day in merry June,
> The birds were singing in the trees,
> All nature seemed in chune (tune).

The peddler and his wife were traveling along
Upon the lonely way,
A-sharing each other's toils and cares,
They both were old and gray.

These men were hidden by the way,
With hearts like murderous Cain;
Their voices hushed, their pistols came,
To kill this weary twain.

Just as the wagons came in view,
Shots rang upon their hair;[1]
But little did they think, dear friends,
They'd met their fatal hour.

His wife fell out upon the ground
To toise (poise) her dying head;
The men rushed up and took her gold;
Poor lady, she were dead.

The horses rushed on with the dying man,
Till kind friends checked their speed;
Alas! alas, it was too late
To stop this horrible deed.

They both are sleeping in the tomb,
Their souls have gone above,
Where they cannot be disturbed any more;
It's all in peace and love.

[1] *Their hair*—the air.

Poor Goens [69]
[Laws F 22]

Contributed by Rob. Morgan, Emmalena, Knott Co., Kentucky.

Come all ye people who live far and near,
I'll tell you of a murder done on the Black Spur;
They surrounded poor Goens, but Goens got away
And went to Eli Boggs's, and there did he stay.

Old Eli's son, Huey, his life did betray,
By telling him he'd go with him to show him the nigh way;
When they saw him coming, they lay very still,
Saying, "It's money we're after, and Goens we'll kill."

They fired on poor Goens, which made his horse run;
The shot failed to kill him, George struck him with a gun;
"Sweet heaven! sweet heaven!" poor Goens did cry,
"To think of my companion when I have to die."

And when they had killed him, with him they wouldn't stay,
They drank up his whiskey and then rode away;
They sent for Miss[1] Goens, she made no delay,
And when she was coming, she saw his grave on the way.

I wish you could have been there and a-heard her poor moans,
Saying, "Here lays his poor body, but where's his poor soul?"

    .   .   .   .

    .   .   .   .

[1] *Miss*—Mrs. Common in the Highlands.

Rosanna [96]
[Laws M 30]

Contributed by Rob. Morgan, Emmalena, Knott Co., Kentucky.

Farewell, dear Rosanna, when shall I evermore
Behold that pretty fair face I've seen here before?

I bid you from my window away in great speed;
Rosanna is married to the squiro[1] indeed.

If Rosanna is married, the girl I adore,
I'll turn to the seashore and come here no more.

So early next morning the ship she set sail,
So early next morning she drew her fresh gale.

She sailed down the ocean until she struck a rock,
And in the ocean those sailors were lost.

[1] *Squiro*—squire.

Except one sailor, on a hogshead was tossed,
Blew away to old England, a many miles square.

Silimentary's body is drowned, Rosanna's own dear;

.   .   .   .

When Rosanna came to hear this she tore down her hair,
Saying, "Curst be the cruel parents who sent him there!"

.   .   .   .

For the sake of Silimentary Rosanna must die.

She drew her silver dagger, she pressed her body through;
Her blood came trinkling[2] like a morning of dew.

2 *Trinkling*—trickling.

William Baker [71]
[Laws dF 48]

Contributed by Mrs. John W. Combs, Hindman, Knott Co., Kentucky.

Come ye people of every nation,
And listen to what I say;
I'll tell you of a circumstance
Which happened here in Clay.

William Baker's now in prison,
And shortly hang-ed be,
For killing of one Prewitt,
The world may plainly see.

He went to Prewitt's dwelling,
These words to him did say:
"Come bear me your company."
He said it night and day.

But O the cruel evil
That dwell in Baker's heart;
He took the life of Prewitt
Before the day did part.

Poor Prewitt was a-sitting
Most perfectly at ease,
When Baker fell upon him,
And knocked him to his knees.

He killed him in an instant,
And carried him to the woods;
He ha-si-ly[1] return-ed,
To wash away his blood.

He went to Prewitt's lady,
These words to her did say:
"Your husband he has left you,
He sure has run away.

"I told you that he'd leave you,
Some days or weeks ago,
And you'd no right to doubt it,
But what I said was so."

Her mind was filled with trouble,
Her heart was broke with woe;
She left her land and dwelling,
And to her father go.

"A word or two, Mrs. Prewitt,
A word or two with you;
You've been robbed of your companion,
By William Baker, too.

"You've been robbed of your companion,
It is a cruel thing;
Go seek the Lord for mercy,
And he will heal the sting."

(Go kill a man for riches,
Or any such a thing,
Go seek the Lord for mercy,
And then you'll feel the sting.)[2]

The life of William Baker
To you all I have told;

[1] *Ha-si-ly*—hastily.

[2] [I cannot explain the placing of this stanza in parenthesis. There is no text in the MS—D. K. W.]

I hope you will all live honest,
And never be so bold.

Hiram Hubbert [48]
[Laws A 20]

This song is an echo of guerrilla warfare in the Highlands during
the Civil War. Contributed by Mrs. Margaret Green, Smithsboro,
Knott Co., Kentucky.

A sad and mournful story
'T's unto you I now will tell,
Concerning of Hiram Hubbert,
And abou' the way he fell.

He was traveling through the country,
Through sorrow and distress;
The rebels overhauled him,
With chains they bound him fast.

They driv him on before them,
Till the road was stained with blood;
They swore so hard against him,
They took his precious life.

They took him to Cumberland River
To try him for his life;
They swore so hard against him
They took his precious life.

They driv him up the holler,
They driv him up the hill
To the place of execution,
He begs to write his will.

"Come all my friends and neighbors,
Likewise my little child;
I'll leave this letter with you,
For I am going to die.

"Come all my friends and neighbors,
Who I do love so well;

I'll leave this letter with you,
For 'tis my last farewell."

They lashed the cord around him,
They bound him to a tree;
Eleven balls went through him,
His body shrunk away.

Hiram Hubbert was not guilty,
I've heard great many say;
He was not in this country,
He was ninety miles away.

The C. & O. Wreck [73]
[Laws G 4]

If all folk-songs opened in this fashion, their origin, and certainly
their age, would not be shrouded in mystery. Contributed by William
Back, Red Fox, Knott Co., Kentucky. [Ballet, procured 1924.]

It was on a New Year's morning,
Nineteen hundred and thirteen,
Engine Eight Hundred and Twenty
Went down with fire and steam.

It was on this sad morning
At about eleven o'clock,
The C. & O. bridge at Guyandott[1]
Began to tremble and rock.

When the train reached Guyandott
The engineer was there;
Ed Webber was his name,
He had dark and wavy hair.

He pulled his engine to the bridge,
But the flagman he was there;
He held out the red as if to say,
"You may cross here if you dare."

[1] In West Virginia.

Ed sat in his cab window
So peaceful and so fair;
He did not know that on the bridge
That death awaited him there.

Fireman Cook walked across the bridge
And stopped on the other side;
He did not know that Webber
Was taking his last ride.

Rufe Medders was the bridge foreman,
A kind good hearted man;
He stood there giving orders
And signals with his hands.

His crew was working on the bridge,
But this I think you know,
A-working for their families,
And for the C. & O.

Brakeman Williams gave the signal
And the engine started on;
But when she hit the trestle,
He knew that Webber was gone.

The bridge rocked for a moment,
And then went tumbling down;
They heard the engine crash below
With a sad and mournful sound.

Conductor Love looked across the bridge,
Then turned and bowed his head;
He knew that faithful Webber
Was numbered with the dead.

Thirteen men were on the bridge,
And when the bridge went down,
Six of them were rescued,
While seven of them were drowned.

Ed Webber was the engineer,
A brave and faithful man;
He went down on his engine
With the throttle in his hand.

His body was recovered
And placed beneath the sod;
We trust that he is resting
With our Savior and our God.

Ed Webber left a loving wife
And eight little children dear;
May God protect and comfort them
While they remain down here.

Were those men religious?
This I do not know;
But when our Savior calls us
We surely have to go.

God bless their families,
Their dear old mothers, too;
God bless their brothers and sisters
As they journey onward through.

Now all of us that see this song,
Be good and be true;
For God has said in His own words
That death will visit you.

Pearl Bryan [63D]
[Laws F 1B]

This song is evidently modeled on "Florella," but does not constitute a variant, for the circumstances of the murder of Miss Pearl Bryan are well known; two dental students of Louisville, Kentucky, seduced and killed Miss Bryan, near Fort Thomas, Kentucky, in 1896; they were hanged for the crime the following year. This song offers a good example of the facility of the folk in the technique of the ballad. Contributed by Lona Woofter, Glenville, West Virginia [1924].

Down in a lonely valley
Where the fairest flowers bloom,
There's where poor Pearl Bryan
Lies mouldering in her tomb.

Chorus:

While the banners waved above her,
The shrill was a mournful sound,
A stranger came and found her,
Cold, headless on the ground.

She died not broken hearted,
Nor by disease she fell,
But in a moment's parting,
From the one she loved so well.

One night when the moon was shining,
The stars were shining too,
Softly to her dwelling
Walling and Jackson drew.

They said, "Come, Pearl, let us wander
Down by these woods so gay;
Come, love, and let us ponder
Upon our wedding day."

The way seemed dark and dreary,
She was afraid to stay;
She says, "I am so weary,
Let us retrace our way."

"Retrace our way? No, never,
Among these woods to roam;
You bid farewell forever
To parents, friends and home."

Down on her knees before them
She pleaded for her life;
Into her snowy-white bosom
They plunged a fatal knife.

"Dear Jackson, I'll forgive you,
Though this be my last breath;
You know I never deceived you,
Now close my eyes in death."

The Auxville Love [116]
[Laws P 25]

Contributed by Mrs. Robin Cornett, Hindman, Knott Co., Kentucky.

In Auxville town of Delaware
My father lived, a merchant there;
I had a love, a true-love there,
Which filled my heart with sad despair.

Down through the green meadow a fence row there went,
Where she gathered red flowers with deep content;
She gathered of all, she plucked, she pulled,
Till at length she rolled her apron full.

On yonder's high mountain there grew a green pine,
The only one that she could find;
The only one that she could find
To ease her heart, her troubled mind.

Down on the green grass she made her a bed,
A pillow of sweet flowers lie under her head;
And as she lie down, these words she did say:
"I will rise no more till the judgment day."

No sooner did her blood it run cold,
Than unto him the news was told;
"I'm glad, I'm glad, I'm glad," said he,
"I'm glad she's in eternity."

Come all ye young maids, wherever you be,
And I pray, take advice from me:
And to a young man don't ever give way,
For if you do, they will lead you astray.

Sweet Jane [51]
[Laws B 22]

Contributed by Mrs. Richard Smith, Smithsboro, Knott Co., Kentucky.

> Farewell, sweet Jane, I now must start
> Across the waving sea;
> My ship is now on Johnson's Bar,
> With all my company.
>
> I see the sails upon the bar,
> They are ready now;
> Just one sweet kiss before I go,
> 'Tis mighty deep to plow.
>
> For seven weeks we sailed alone
> Across the billows wide;
> The crowd was filled with mirth and glee,
> Still at my bosom side.
>
> One morning at the break of day
> We landed on the shore;
> Each one of us made up our minds
> To dig the golden ore.
>
> For seven years we labored hard,
> A-digging for our wealth;
> We lived on bread and salty lard,
> And never lost our health.
>
> I loaded up my trunk with gold,
> And then I thought of Jane;
> My awful thoughts no tongue could tell,
> As I recrossed the Main.
>
> For seven weeks we sailed alone,
> Across the mighty deep;
> At last I thought we were all lost,
> Our captain was asleep.
>
> At last we came in sight of land,
> Of our own native town;
> I heard the captain give command,
> "Go take the rigging down."

I saw a crowd of pretty girls
Come marching to the ship;
I saw sweet Jane, with all her pearls,
And I begin to skip.

I flew and met her on the walks,
Our hearts were filled with charm;
Both were so full we could not speak,
I caught her in my arms.

We walked along the marble walk
Up to her father's door;
The crowd was all so nice and neat
While standing on the floor.

Someone then read the marriage law,
Which bound us both for life;
Now Jane is mine without one doubt,
My sweet and loved wife.

I'm Going To Join the Army [109]
[Laws O 33]

This song is an echo of the Spanish-American War (1898); it was very popular during this period. Pensacola, Florida, was a port of embarkation for soldiers bound for Cuba. Stanzas 5 and 6 have been borrowed from "Jack Went A-Sailing" [Laws N 7]. Contributed by Mrs. Rachel Stidham, Jackson, Breathitt Co., Kentucky.

"So fare you well, my darling,
So fare you well, my dear;
I'm going to join the army,
I'm going to volunteer.

"It's been my sad misfortune
A soldier for to be;
O be contented, darling,
And don't you weep for me.

"I'm going to Pensacola
To tarry for awhile;
So far from you, my darling,

About five thousand mile."

She wrung her lily-white hands,
So mournfully she cried:
"You're going to join the army,
And in that war you'll die.

"Your waist it is too slender,
Your fingers long and small,
Your cheeks too red and rosy
To face a cannon ball."

"I know my waist is slender,
My fingers long and small;
But it would not make me shudder
To see ten thousand fall.

"I hear the cannons roaring,
The balls are flying high;
The drums and fifes are sounding
To drown the dreadful cry."

"In the center you'll be wounded,
In the center you'll be slain;
It'll break my heart asunder
If I never see you again.

"The ships all stand at anchor,
The boys all dressed in blue,
You're going away to join them,
And love, what shall I do?"

"I'll sail around the enemy
My fortune for to try,
I'll think of you, my darling,
And oft sit down and cry.

"If you'll portray a single life
Throughout the great campaign,
I'll marry you, my darling,
When I return again.

"Then fare you well, my darling,
Then fare you well, my dear;
I'm coming back to see you,
If 't takes ten thousand year."

Jack Combs [49]
[Laws B 1]

This song is modeled on "The Dying Cowboy." Contributed by H. Cody, Hindman, Knott Co., Kentucky.

> As I passed by where Jack Combs was murdered,
> As I passed by there so early one day,
> I spied a cold corpse wrapped up in fine linen,
> Wrapped up in fine linen, as cold as the clay.

> *Chorus:*

> Go pick up your drums as if I were with you,
> Go beat your dead marches while carrying me along;
> And each one of you a bunch of red roses,
> To keep me from smelling while carrying me along.

> .   .   .   .
> .   .   .   .

> My head it is aching, my poor heart is breaking,
> With sad limitation I surely must die.

> So cruel was the man that committed this murder,
> So cruel was he that held to my arm;
> I might have applied to some friend all near me,
> To have saved my life before it was gone.

> Go take me to the graveyard and throw the dirt o'er me,
> And all that can sing must sing my song;
> Go take me to the graveyard and throw the dirt o'er me,
> For I have been murdered, and you know they've done wrong.

The Black Mustache [154]

An old manuscript [ballet], Knott Co., Kentucky.

> It's O once I had a charming beau,
> I loved him dear as life;
> I longed and longed some future day
> To be his charming wife.

His pockets they were filled with gold,
And he could cut a dash,
With a diamond ring and a watch and chain,
And a darling, black mustache.

He came to see me last Sunday night,
And stayed till almost three;
He said he never loved a girl
As well as he loved me.

He said we'd live in grandest style,
For he had lots of cash;
And then he pressed upon my lips
That darling, black mustache.

And then there came a sour old maid,
She's worth her weight in gold;
She had false teeth, and wore false hair,
She's forty-five years old.

So cruel he deserted me
For this old maid and her cash;
And now I know I've lost my beau
With a darling, black mustache.

Then take my advice, ye thoughtless girls,
And do not be too rash;
But leave alone those stylish chaps
That wear the black mustache.

The Married Man [177]

Contributed by Mrs. Edwin Daniel, Hindman, Knott Co., Kentucky.

I married me a wife, O then (*bis*),
I married me a wife, she's the plague of my life,
    And I wish I was single again.

Chorus:
I wish I was single again (*bis*),
If I was single, my pockets would jingle,
    And I wish I was single again.

She beat me, she banged me, O then,
She beat me, she banged me, she swore she would hang me,
   And I wish I was single again.

My wife got sick, O then,
My wife got sick, not any too quick,
   For I wanted to be single again.

My wife she died, O then,
My wife she died, and I laughed till I cried,
   To think I was single again.

I married me another, O then,
I married me another, she's the devil's grandmother,
   And I wish I was single again.

I made up my mind, O then,
I made up my mind to leave her behind,
   O then I was single again.

Davy Crockett [168]

Contributed by Wiley Parks, Hindman, Knott Co., Kentucky [*ca.* 1900].

I knew a little boy whose name was Davy,
He wouldn't eat meat, but he did like the gravy;
And when he eat his bread, O then he went to bed,
He would double up his feet and put 'em under his head.

I met a man one day, he says, "Where are you going?"
I looked at him, says, "I'm going out a-cooning";
And he says, "Where's your gun?" Says I, "I hain't got none."
"Well, you can't kill a coon unless you had one."

Went on a piece further and there I saw a squirrel
Sitting on a pine log, eating sheep and sorrel;
And he says, "Black calf, you had better not laugh,
For if you do, I'll bite you two in half."

Throwed down my gun and all my ammunition,
He'd bit off my tail and I'd swallowed his'n;

(I says to Col. Davy, "I'll cool his ambition").[1]
When we both locked horns I thought my breath was gone,
I was never squeezed so hard since the hour I was born.

We fit on a half a day, and then agreed to stop it,
I was badly whipped, and so was Davy Crockett;
And then we agreed to let each other be,
I was hard enough for him, and so was he for me.

[1] [I cannot explain the parenthesis. The text is not in the MS—D. K. W.]

The Bugaboo [107]
[Laws O 3]

Contributed by Tom Kelley, Hazard, Perry Co., Kentucky.

> I am a jolly boatsman,
> I plainly know the trade;
> And all the harm I ever did,
> Was courting a pretty fair maid.
>
> I courted her long summer days
> And winter nights also,
> And when I gained her free good will,
> I didn't know what to do.
>
> She came unto my bedside,
> Where I was lying asleep;
> She came unto my bedside,
> So bitterly she did weep.
>
> She wept, she mourned, she wrung her hands,
> Crying, "Love, what shall I do!"
> O then she jumped in the bed with me,
> For fear of the bugaboo.
>
> All in the first part of that night
> We lay in sport and play;
> All in the second part of that night
> She lay in my arms till day.
>
> The night being gone, the day coming on,
> "Kind sir, I am undone";

"Arise, pretty maid, and don't be afraid,
For the bugaboo is gone."

All in the first part of that year
She looked both slim and pale;
All in the second part of that year
She looked both fresh and gail' (gaily).

All in the third part of that year
She brought to me a son;
O now you can see, as well as I,
What the bugaboo has done.

I took that girl, I married her,
I loved her as my life;
I took that girl, I married her,
She made me a virtuous wife.

I never told her of her faults,
Nor d--- me if I do;
For every time the baby cries,
I think of the bugaboo.

The Rich and Rambling Boy [90]
[Laws L 12]

Contributed by Tom Kelley, Hazard, Perry Co., Kentucky.

I am a rich and rambling boy,
To many a show that I have been;
And a pretty fair miss for to pay my way,
She caused me to rob on the broad highway.

My mother sits and she watches and she mourns,
My sister says she is left alone;
My sweetheart sits in deep despair,
With her pink silk ribbon and her curly hair.

Hush up, hush up, dear darling,
Don't you watch and mourn;
For I'll be back some lonesome day,
For the eastern train will bring us home.

I'll buy me a ticket in Greenville town,
I'll get on the train and I'll sit down;
The whistle will blow and the wheels will roll,
In five more days I'll be at home.

I know I am condemned to die,
And all the girls for me will cry;
But all of their cries won't set me free,
For I'm condemned to the gallows-tree.

The rose is red, the stem is green,
The time is past that I have seen;
It may be more, it may be few,
But I hope to spend them all with you.

Bob Sims [59]
[Laws E 17]

Contributed by Tom Kelley, Hazard, Knott Co., Kentucky.

O once I had a partner,
Bob Sims was his name,
And everything that he would do,
I always was to blame.

His threatening and his quarreling
Was never known to fail;
At last he had me lock-ed up
In the Lincoln County jail.

They took me off to prison,
Locked me up in number four;
They gave me grub enough to eat,
But I always wished for more.

The beds were all the finest,
But sleeping I did fail;
I'll tell you what was troubling me
In the Lincoln County jail.

One night when I was sleeping
I dreamed a pleasant dream:

I thought I was a rich merchant,
All on some golden stream.

But I woke up broken hearted,
Locked up in Stanford jail;
My friends was all around me,
And none could go my bail.

So early next morning
A note to my love did write;
I asked her if she would bail me
If I'd quit getting tight.

She walked right down to Stanford,
Drew fifty dollars down;
She walked right down to prison house,
And she led me out of town.

Now my song is ended,
I've one more word to say:
Quit your drinking whisky, boys,
And throwing your money away.

You'll drink the poison whisky,
And throw your money about,
And when you get in these old jails,
Your friends won't bail you out.

Charles J. Guiteau [58]
[Laws E 11]

The source of this song is the assassination of President James A.
Garfield in 1881. Contributed by R. H. Johnson, Morgantown, West
Virginia.

But little did I think,
While in my youthful bloom,
I'd be taken to the scaffold
To meet my fatal doom.

Chorus:

My name is Charles Guiteau,
My name I'll never deny,
Though I leave my aged parents
In sorrow for to die.
(To climb the scaffold high.)[1]

'Twas down at the depot
I tried to make my escape,
But the people were against me,
It proved to be a mistake.

They took me to the prison
While in my youthful bloom;
And now unto the scaffold
To meet my fatal doom.

[1] [Probably an alternate line. The text is not in the MS—D. K. W.]

Bad Tom Smith [162]

"Bad" Tom Smith, one of the most dangerous gunmen of the Kentucky mountains, composed this song, words and music, and sang it in a loud, clear voice on the scaffold. Contributed by H. Cody, Hindman, Knott Co., Kentucky.

I am passing through the valley here in peace,
I am passing through the valley here in peace;
O when I am dead and buried in the cold and silent tomb,
I don't want you to grieve after me.

Chorus:

I don't want you to grieve after me,
I don't want you to grieve after me,
O when I am dead and buried in the cold and silent tomb,
I don't want you to grieve after me.

I am leaving all my friends here in peace,
I am leaving all my friends here in peace;
O when I am buried in the cold and silent tomb,
I don't want you to grieve after me.

Ellen Smith [65]
[Laws F 11]

Contributed by Dan Gibson, Lackey, Knott Co., Kentucky.

Come all you young people, both far and near,
I'll relate you a history of June, last year.

Last Monday morning about the break of day,
They captured poor Ellen and carried her away.

Where was she shot, and where was she found?
She's shot through the heart, lying cold on the ground.

Who would be so brave, and who would be so bold,
To murder poor Ellen for a handful of gold?

Who would be so brave, and who would have the face,
To murder poor Ellen in such a lonesome place?

Now poor Ellen's dead, with her hands upon her breast;
The high sheriffs and bloodhounds will give me no rest.

Poor little Ellen, she's harmless as a dove;
She's always stayed at home, for home she did love.

O now I am married and roaming in the East,
The police and bloodhounds will let me see no peace.

O now I am married and roaming in the West,
The sheriffs and bloodhounds will give me no rest.

O now I am married and living alone,
The sheriffs and bloodhounds won't leave me alone.

They gathered their Winchesters, they hunted me down,
They found me a-sailing in Monterey town.

It's true they have got me, and I'm a prisoner now,
But the Lord, He is with me and hears every vow.

O now they have caught me, they'll hang me if they can;
I'm sure if they hang me, they'll hang an innocent man.

O now I am a prisoner, and I'm confined in jail;
My friends all gathered round, but none was worth my bail.

Now I am a-praying, a-praying all the time,
A-praying for the man that committed this crime.

If I were a free man and back home today,
I'd scatter red roses on sweet Ellen's grave.

Sometimes I have a dollar, sometimes two and three;
My wife's off a-gamblin', she don't care for me.

Sometimes I have a dollar, sometimes five and six;
I want to be a-shooting, my pistol's out of fix.

Moonshiner [187]

Contributed by Monroe Combs, Hindman, Knott Co., Kentucky.

I've been a moonshiner for eighteen long year';
I've spent all my money for whiskey and beer.
I buy my own whiskey, I make my own stew,
If I get drunk, madam, it's nothing to you.

I'll get up on some mountain, I'll put up my still;
I'll sell you one quart, boys, for a one dollo bill.
I'll get up on some mountain, the mountain so high;
As the wild geese fly over, I'll bid them goodbye.

Pretty Betsy, pretty Betsy, would you think it unkind
For me to sit down by you and tell you my mind?
My mind is to marry and never to part,
For the first time I saw you, you wounded my heart.

Oftimes I have wondered how women love men;
Then again I have wondered how men could love them.
They'll cause your heart trouble, and a many downfall;
They'll cause you to labor in many a stone wall.

The bluebirds are flying from branch to each tree,
A-chirping and singing their sorrows away.
The breath smells so sweet-ly, like the dew on the vine—
God bless those moonshiners, I wish they were mine!

The Gambler [184]

Contributed by Rob. Morgan, Emmalena, Knott Co., Kentucky.

My moments are lonesome, no pleasure I find,
My true-love is a gambler, it troubles my mind.

My true-love is gone, I know not where;
Perhaps he is off gambling—I know he is not here.

He is taken a prisoner, in prison he is bound,
While other poor gamblers lie mouldering in the ground.

Young ladies, young ladies, some counsel to you:
Don't marry a gambler, whatever you do.

They will pull out their pistols, they'll swear they will kill,
Perhaps they will kill you to gain some small bill.

They brag on your beauty, like the lily of the west,
But drinking and gambling, they like it the best.

Jacob's Ladder [320]

This song, as well as the three following, are Negro spirituals. They furnish excellent examples of group improvisation. Contributed by Mrs. John W. Combs, Hindman, Knott Co., Kentucky.

I'm a-climbin' up Jacob's ladder,
And I won't be troubled any more,
I'm a-climbin' up Jacob's ladder, Lord,
And I won't be troubled any more.

Chorus:

And I won't be troubled any more (*bis*),
As soon as my feet strikes Zion's walls,
I won't be troubled any more.

Goin' to meet my father in the kingdom, etc.

Goin' to meet my mother in the kingdom, etc.

Goin' to meet my brother in the kingdom, etc.

Goin' to meet my sister in the kingdom, etc.

The Ship That Is Passing By [316]

Contributed by Mrs. John W. Combs, Hindman, Knott Co., Kentucky.

> I once had a father, but now I have none,
> He's gone to that beautiful home;
> O Lord, let me sail on that beautiful ship,
> The ship that is passing by.
>
> *Chorus:*
> The days seem so sad, and the night seems so long,
> And I am so lonely here;
> O Lord, let me sail on that beautiful ship,
> The ship that is passing by.
>
> I once had a mother, but now I have none, etc.
>
> I once had a brother, but now I have none, etc.
>
> I once had a sister, but now I have none, etc.

We Have Fathers Gone to Heaven [318]

Contributed by Mrs. John W. Combs, Hindman, Knott Co., Kentucky.

> We have fathers gone to heaven,
> O do tell me if you know,
> Will those fathers know their children,
> When to heaven they do go?
>
> We have mothers gone to heaven,
> O do tell me if you know,
> Will those mothers know their children,
> When to heaven they do go?
>
> We have brothers gone to heaven,
> O do tell me if you know,
> Will those brothers know each other,
> When to heaven they do go?

We have sisters gone to heaven,
O do tell me if you know,
Will those sisters know each other,
When to heaven they do go?

We have children gone to heaven,
O do tell me if you know,
Will those children known their parents,
When to heaven they do go?

Who Am Dat a-Walkin' in de Co'n? [325]

Contributed by Mr. Carey Woofter, Gilmer Co., West Virginia
[1924].

Who am dat a-walkin' in de co'n?
I hab look to east an' I hab look to west,
But nowhar cud I find Him dat walks
Marster's co'nfield in de mawnin'.

Chorus:
How long O Lawd, nobody knows,
I pray I'll rise on judgment day,
How long, O Lawd, nobody knows.

Who am dat a-walkin' in de co'n?
Am dat Joshua, de son ob Nun?
Er King David come to fight Goliar,
Neath de co'nfield in de mawnin'?, etc.

Who am dat a-walkin' in de co'n?
Am dat Petuh a-jinglin' hebben's keys?
Er ol' Gabriel come to blow his hawn,
Neath de co'nfield in de mawnin'?

Who am dat a-walkin' in de co'n?
I hab look to east an' I hab look to west,
But nowhar cud I find Him dat walks
Marster's co'nfield in de mawnin'.

APPENDIX

AN ANNOTATED LIST OF
THE JOSIAH H. COMBS COLLECTION
OF SONGS AND RHYMES

In the following list is outlined the—to my knowledge—complete corpus of the Josiah H. Combs Collection of songs and rhymes (a few riddles are omitted). Registered here are 325 songs or rhymes plus more than 100 additional variants. The attempt has been made to notice all items, published and unpublished, even to the indication of songs which seem to have been once in the collection, but have since disappeared. The inventory is based on (1) material published by Combs himself or by others on the basis of manuscript material he furnished them; and (2) The Josiah H. Combs Collection in the Western Kentucky Folklore Archive, University of California, Los Angeles. The manuscript collection was deposited by Combs 1957–1959 and augmented by B. A. Botkin, July, 1965, from material Combs had supplied him in the late 1920's.

The basic purpose of the following list is to describe and locate the material. Reference to the printed appearance of an item is normally deemed sufficient. An unpublished song is identified by citation of an analogue in print, in recent and readily available collections in so far as possible. No attempt has been made to furnish a full bibliography or discussion of individual songs. In a few instances, however, texts have been deemed of sufficient importance or interest to be printed and briefly discussed here. The usual entry, however, merely indicates to the student that a text exists and is available for future study.

Most material in the Combs Collection was acquired from 1909 to 1924, although a few texts are earlier and one is as late as 1959. Slightly more than half of the items were secured in Kentucky, more than a third are from West Virginia, and the remaining were collected from Oklahoma, Texas, Arkansas, Missouri, Michigan, Tennessee, and Illinois. Despite careful examination of the manuscripts and of printed reports, the geographical source of nineteen items is unknown. A number of the stated sources in the following list are based on probability and are so indicated.

The list is ordered for convenience on the basis of the numbered items of Francis James Child (*The English and Scottish Popular Ballads*) and of G. Malcolm Laws, Jr., (*Native American Balladry* and *American Balladry from British Broadsides*), followed by a listing based primarily on a descending scale of the narrative element in the texts. (Texts with analogues in the Child collection are also classified according to the story types established by Tristram P. Coffin, *The British Traditional Ballad in North*

America.) Some attempt has been made to group items of similar theme, tone, or function, but such categories are so illogical and overlapping that divisional labels would be of little help. Most play songs are found as Nos. 280–314, followed by a concluding section of religious songs. An index of titles and first lines cited is part of the general index of titles and first lines for the entire volume.

Each entry includes a standard title, if one exists; the local title or first line; the number of stanzas, whether single, double (d), or triple (t), and the chorus (ch) if present; the source and date of collection, if known; and a reference to any printed appearance of the variant. References to *Folk-Songs du Midi des États-Unis* (*FSMEU*) are to this edition; the pagination of the 1925 edition follows in brackets. Citation of analogues for identification are placed in parentheses, unless more extended discussion is necessary. A list of references cited precedes the inventory of the collection.

—D. K. W.

References

Belden, Henry Marvin. *Ballads and Songs Collected by the Missouri Folk-Lore Society.* Columbia, Missouri, 1940; rpt. 1955.

Botkin, B. A. *The American Play-Party Song* (University Studies of the University of Nebraska, XXXVIII), Lincoln, Nebraska, 1937; rpt. New York, 1963.

Brewster, Paul G. *The Two Sisters.* Folklore Fellows Communications No. 147. Helsinki, 1953.

Brown. *The Frank C. Brown Collection of North Carolina Folklore.* Vols. II, III, IV, V, ed. Newman I. White, Paull F. Baum, Henry M. Belden, Arthur Palmer Hudson, and Jan P. Shinhan. Durham, North Carolina, 1952–1962.

Browne, Ray B. "Alabama Folk Songs." Unpublished Ph.D. thesis, University of California, Los Angeles, 1956.

Cambiaire, Celestin Pierre. *East Tennessee and West Virginia Mountain Ballads.* London, 1934.

Chappell, Louis W. *John Henry: A Folk-Lore Study.* Jena, Germany, 1933.

Child, Francis James. *The English and Scottish Popular Ballads.* 5 vols. Boston and New York, 1882–1898.

Coffin, Tristram P. *The British Traditional Ballad in North America.* Rev. ed., Philadelphia, 1963.

Combs, Josiah H. " 'Cornstick Fiddle and a Buckeye Bow'," *Folk-Say: A Regional Miscellany,* 1930, pp. 239–250. (Ed. B. A. Botkin, Norman, Oklahoma, 1930.)

———. *Folk-Songs du Midi des États-Unis.* Paris, 1925.

———. *Folk-Songs from the Kentucky Highlands.* New York, 1939.

Cook, Davidson. "The Gypsy Laddie and the Fair Lady of the Ballad," *Journal of the Gypsy Lore Society,* 3d ser., XV (1936), 100–107.

Cox, John Harrington. *Folk-Songs of the South*. Cambridge, Massachusetts, 1925; rpt. Hatboro, Pennsylvania, 1963.

———. *Traditional Ballads and Folk-Songs Mainly from West Virginia*, ed. George Boswell. Philadelphia, 1964. (Rpt. from eds. of 1939.)

Cunningham, Allan. *The Songs of Scotland*. 4 vols. London, 1825.

Folk-Say. (See Combs.)

FSKH. (See Combs.)

FSMEU. (See Combs.)

Fuson, Harvey H. *Ballads of the Kentucky Highlands*. London, 1931.

Gilchrist, John. *A Collection of Scottish Ballads, Tales, and Songs*. 2 vols. Edinburgh, 1815.

Heart Songs. New York, 1909.

Hecht, Hans. *Songs from David Herd's MSS*. Edinburgh, 1904.

Henry, Mellinger E. *Folk-Songs from the Southern Highlands*. New York, 1938.

———. *Songs Sung in the Southern Appalachians*. London, 1934.

Herd, David. *Ancient and Modern Scottish Songs*. 2 vols. Glasgow, 1869.

———. *Antient and Modern Scotish Songs*. 2 vols. Edinburgh, 1791.

Johnson, James. *The Scots Musical Museum*. Edinburgh, 1787–1803; rpt. from 1853, Hatboro, Pennsylvania, 1962.

JAF. Journal of American Folklore, 1888–.

KFPM. Kentucky Folk-Lore and Poetry Magazine, 1927–1931.

KFR. Kentucky Folklore Record, 1955–.

Knapp, Andrew, and William Baldwin. *The Newgate Calendar*. London, 1824.

Knoblock, Judith Ann. " 'The Gypsy Laddie' (Child 200); An Unrecognized Child of Medieval Romance," *Western Folklore*, XIX (1960), 35–45.

Laws, G. Malcolm, Jr. *American Balladry from British Broadsides*. Philadelphia, 1957.

———. *Native American Balladry*. Rev. ed., Philadelphia, 1964.

Linscott, Eloise Hubbard. *Folk Songs of Old New England*. New York, 1939.

Lives of the Most Remarkable Criminals. 2 vols. Ed. Arthur Haywood. London, 1927.

Loesser, Arthur. *Humor in American Song*. New York, 1942.

Lomax, Alan. *Folk Songs of North America*. New York, 1960.

Lomax, John A., and Alan Lomax. *American Ballads and Folk Songs*. New York, 1934.

———. *Cowboy Songs*. New York, 1938.

———. *Our Singing Country*. New York, 1941.

Lunsford, Bascom Lamar, and Lamar Stringfield. *30 and 1 Folk Songs (from the Southern Mountains)*. New York, 1929.

McDowell, Lucien L., and Flora Lassiter. *Memory Melodies*. Smithville, Tennessee, 1947.

Mutzenberg, Charles G. *Kentucky's Famous Feuds and Tragedies*. Hyden, Kentucky, 1899.

Newell, William Wells. *Games and Songs of American Children.* New York, 1883; 2d ed., 1903; rpt. New York, 1963.

Odum, Howard W., and Guy B. Johnson. *Negro Workaday Songs.* Chapel Hill, 1926.

Owens, William A. *Texas Folk Songs.* Austin and Dallas, 1950.

PTFS. Publications of the Texas Folklore Society, 1916–.

Ramsay, Allan. *The Tea Table Miscellany.* 2 vols. Rpt. from the 14th ed., Glasgow, 1871.

Randolph, Vance. *Ozark Folksongs.* 4 vols. Columbia, Mo., 1946–1950.

Reeves, James. *The Everlasting Circle.* London, 1960.

———. *The Idiom of the People.* New York, 1958.

Richardson, Ethel Park. *American Mountain Songs.* New York, 1927; rpt. 1955.

Ritchie, Jean. *A Garland of Mountain Song.* New York, 1953.

Sandburg, Carl. *The American Songbag.* New York, 1927.

Sharp, Cecil J. *English Folk-Songs from the Southern Appalachians,* ed. Maud Karpeles. 2 vols. London, 1932.

Skean, Marion H. *Circle Left!* Ary, Kentucky, 1939.

SFQ. Southern Folklore Quarterly, 1937–.

Spaeth, Sigmund. *Read 'em and Weep.* New York, 1926.

Struthers, John. *The Harp of Caledonia.* 3 vols. London, 1819–1821.

TFSB. Tennessee Folklore Society Bulletin, 1935–.

Williams, Alfred. *Folk-Songs of the Upper Thames.* London, 1923.

WF. Western Folklore (originally *California Folklore Quarterly*), 1942–.

Wolford, Leah Jackson. *The Play-Party in Indiana.* Indianapolis, 1916; new ed., Indianapolis, 1959.

Index to the Combs Collection

1. THE ELPHIN KNIGHT (Child 2).
    A. "As I walked out in yonder dell." 8. William Bush, Index, Gilmer Co., W.Va. (Carey Woofter, 1924?) (Coffin A.) In an article to appear in *Western Folklore*, Bernth Lindfors demonstrates that this is a fraudulent text plagiarized from Child, V, 284, and subjected to alterations that would not have occurred in a traditional text.
    B. Lost text. From the singing of John Rafferty, Withers, W.Va., who heard his mother, born in Ireland, sing the song.

2. LADY ISABEL AND THE ELF KNIGHT (Child 4).
    A. "May Collins." 14. F. C. Gainer, Tanner, Gilmer Co., W.Va. Contributed by Carey Woofter, 1924. (Coffin A.)
    B. Fragment titled "Chorus to Six Kings Daughters." (Berlin B. Chapman, Webster Co., W.Va., 1924?)

3. EARL BRAND (Child 7). Lost text of more than 14 stanzas. Kentucky.

4. THE TWA SISTERS (Child 10). "The Miller's Two Daughters." 10. F. C. Gainer, Tanner, Gilmer Co., W.Va. Contributed by Carey Woofter, 1924. Text summarized in Brewster, FFC No. 147, p. 50.

5. THE CRUEL BROTHER (Child 11). 23. David Chenoweth, Minorra, Calhoun Co., W.Va. [Chenoweth's address is given as Gip in No. 38.] Contributed by Carey Woofter, 1924. " 'Doctored' by one Daniel De Weese." Perhaps the "doctoring" is responsible for the apparently unique refrain.

> There's three fair maids went out to bleach the cloth,
>   All along the chip-yard so clean;
> There's three rich men came to court them all,
>   As plainly it could be seen.
>
> The first rich man was dressed in red,
> He asked if the oldest would him wed.
>
> The second rich man was dressed in yellow,
> He asked the second if he wasn't a proper fellow.
>
> The third rich man was dressed in white,
> He asked the youngest to be his own dear wife.

"But you must ask of my father so dear,
And of my mother, who'll be near.

"And you must ask of my sister Sue,
Or else your favor you will rue.

"And don't forget my brother Harry,
Of all men he's the most contrary."

The rich man asked of her father dear,
He asked the favor of her sister Sue,

And sought of her mother fairly,
But forgot her brother so contrary.

And all the neighbors far and near
Came to wish the bride good cheer.

Her father led her through the hall,
Her mother danced before them all.

Her sister Sue at her gown did pluck,
And wished her all of the best good luck.

Her brother Harry waited by the stile
To greet her for a long, long while.

He had a knife both sharp and stout,
With it he cut her fair white throat.

The blood ran down upon her breast,
She knew that hour would be her last.

They carried her back to her father's hall,
There she made her will before them all.

"And I leave to my father so dear
All the lands that I hold here.

"And I leave to my old mother there
All the clothes I have to wear.

"And I leave to my sweet sister Sue
My rich husband for her view.

"And I leave to my brother Harry's wife
Shame and disgrace the rest of her life.

"And I leave to my brother Harry's son
To pay the debt his father has won.

"And I leave to my brother Harry himself
The gallows in payment of his deed;

"And may my husband throw the trap
Before he stops his tears to shed."

6. LORD RANDALL (Child 12).

A. "Sweet Harry." 4. Frank Reaser, Revel, W.Va., who learned it in
the lumber camps on Cherry River, W.Va. Contributed by Carey
Woofter, 1924. (Coffin A.)

B. Lost text, apparently mentioning a "small green serpent." Kentucky.

7. EDWARD (Child 13). 16. Mrs. Rosa Pierce, Annomoriah, Calhoun Co., W.Va. Contributed by Carey Woofter, 1924. See D. K. Wilgus, "The Oldest(?) Text of 'Edward'" *WF*, XXV (1966), 77 ff.

8. SIR LIONEL (Child 18). Lost text, fragmentary, with "chorus borrowed from 'The Frog and the Mouse.'" Berlin B. Chapman, Marion Co., W.Va., 1924.

9. THE CRUEL MOTHER (Child 20). "There was a duke's daughter lived at New York." 16. D. H. Purdue, Switchback, McDowell Co., W.Va. (1924?). (Coffin A.)

10. THE THREE RAVENS (Child 26).
    A. "There were two crows sat on a tree." 4. F. C. Gainer, Tanner, Gilmer Co., W.Va. (Contributed by Carey Woofter, 1924?) (Coffin A.)
    B. "There were three crows sat on a tree." 3. George O. Humphries, Morgantown, W.Va., who learned it as a boy in Michigan. (Contributed by Carey Woofter, 1924?) (Coffin A.)

11. THE BROOMFIELD HILL (Child 43). "Green Broom." 10. Louis Waugh, Clarksburg, Harrison Co., W.Va. Contributed by Carey Woofter, 1924. *FSMEU*, pp. 113 f. [127 ff.]. (Notes in the Combs MSS indicate that this is the variant referred to on p. 65 [83] as imported from Michigan and surpassing all British texts in vulgarity. As the printed text does not fit the description and Combs refers specifically to stanzas 17–20, one must conclude that a large part of the original text is lost.)

12. CAPTAIN WEDDERBURN'S COURTSHIP (Child 46). Lost text. Kentucky. Contributed by Cecil Sharp.

13. THE TWO BROTHERS (Child 49). "Brother, won't you pitch a shoe?" 7. Mrs. Narcissa Woodyard, Glenville, Gilmer Co., W.Va., who learned it from her mother. Contributed by Carey Woofter, 1924. (Coffin C.)

14. YOUNG BEICHAN (Child 53).
    A. "The Turkish Lady." 17. Samuel Lowden, age 81, Latonia, Gilmer Co., W.Va., who learned the words from his father, who learned them when a boy in Albemarle Co., Va. Contributed by Carey Woofter, 1924. (Coffin A.)
    B. "Lord Wetram." 15 with tune. Emma Hewitt, Morgantown, Monongalia Co., W.Va. Contributed by Carey Woofter, 1924. Cox, *Traditional Ballads*, pp. 29 ff., where the notation of the music is credited to Miss Frances Sanders. (Coffin A.)
    C. "Lord Bateman was a noble lord." 19. Source unknown. (Coffin A.)

15. THE CHERRY-TREE CAROL (Child 54).
    A. "Joseph was an old man." 7. Mae Ellyson, Cowen, Nicholas Co., W.Va., 1924. Contributed by Carey Woofter. (Coffin A.)
    B. "Joseph was an old man." 2. An old Negro woman. Contributed by Miss Forrest Hatfield, Charleston, W.Va. (1924?). (Fragment.)

C. "Joseph and Mary." 11. Bessie Fidler, Linn, Gilmer Co., W.Va., who learned it from her mother, who was born in Culpepper Co., Va. Contributed by Carey Woofter, 1924. "This ballad was given to me under protest, and with the agreement that I would not show it to any of the others here, because it was not what a decent girl ought to say. The two stanzas which open and close the ballad are peculiar. I have a sort of remembrance of an old song which went in part:

> To-day is the day we give babies away,
> With half a pound of tea;
> If you see any ladies without any babies,
> Just send them around to me.
>
> Oh all you young ladies,
> From near and from far;
> Beware of the sailor
> With the bright morning star.

I cannot recall any more of this jig; and do not know to what it refers, or of what it may be a part; but I am inclined to think it is part of an old blackguard river song we used to sing when running timber"— C. W.

Woofter's inclination seems correct—the blackguard song "Jimmy Taylor-O" has not to my knowledge been published. Roger D. Abrahams has pointed out to me that since the "bright morning star" refers to a flower in the West Indies, the reference in the shanty may be to defloration. The "Today is the day we give babies away" portion seems widespread as a rhyme or song, as a number of persons from various sections of the United States recall it from their youth. I knew it in Ohio coupled with "I like to go swimming with bowlegged women." Rosalie Sorrels performs a version from Utah on *Rosalie's Songbag*, Prestige/International 13025.

Otherwise, this variant is essentially Coffin B.

> Come all ye young ladies
> From near and from far;
> And I'll tell you the story
> Of the bright morning star.
>
> When Joseph was married
> And Mary had home brought,
> Mary was got with child
> And Joseph knew it not.
>
> Mary and Joseph
> Went walking one day,
> And saw the cherries red
> On all the little trees.
>
> Mary asked of Joseph,
> With words meek and mild,

"Joseph, bend down the limb,
For I am with child."

Joseph made her a reply,
In words very tart,
"Let him bend the limb down
That got thee with brat."

The Lord spoke in Heaven,
Saying these words,
"Bend over, little cherry tree,
While Mary gathers some."

The cherry tree bent down,
All low to the ground,
And Mary gathered cherries
While Joseph stood around.

As Joseph stood a-gawking,
He heard an angel sing,
"Soon shall be born
Our heavenly King.

"He shall not lay
In bed nor in crib,
But his head shall rest
Upon the oxen's rib.

"He shall not be wrapped
In silk nor satin bright,
But his didy will be pinned
By the lantern light."

Now all ye young ladies,
From near and from far;
You have heard the story
Of the bright morning star.

16. FAIR ANNIE (Child 62). "The Sister's Husband." 31. J. R. Umstead, Mt. Zion, Calhoun Co., W.Va. Probably contributed by Carey Woofter, 1924. *FSMEU*, pp. 114 ff. [129 ff.]. (Coffin B.)

17. YOUNG HUNTING (Child 68).
   A. "Loved Henry." 13. Lincoln Co., W.Va. Contributed by Carey Woofter, 1924. (Coffin A.)
   B. Lost variant. Kentucky. Possibly the source of the four stanzas quoted on p. 32.

18. LORD THOMAS AND FAIR ANNET (Child 73). Lost variant. Kentucky.

19. FAIR MARGARET AND SWEET WILLIAM (Child 74).
   A. "Sweet William." 15. Hindman, Knott Co., Ky. *JAF*, XXIII, 381 f. (Coffin E.)

B. "Sweet William rose, one morning bright." 18. No source given. This seems to be the same variant printed as G in Cox, *Folk-Songs of the South*, pp. 75 ff., communicated by Carey Woofter. The MS text differs only in 4.4: "That was seen no more in there." (Coffin A.)

C. "Sweet William rode one morning bright." 19. Mrs. Effie Rhinehart, Gilmer Co., W.Va.; originally from Randolph Co. before the Civil War. Contributed by Carey Woofter, 1924. (Coffin A.)

20. LORD LOVEL (Child 75).
   A. "Lord Lovel he stood at his castle gate." 10. Contributed by Carey Woofter, Gilmer Co., W.Va., 1924. (Coffin A.)
   B. Lost tune. Belle Fortney, Morgantown, Monongalia Co.. W.Va. Contributed by Carey Woofter, 1924.

21. THE LASS OF ROCH ROYAL (Child 76). "Sweet Annie of Roch Royal." 27. From Dora, W.Va. Contributed by Carey Woofter, 1924. *FSMEU*, pp. 118 ff. [134 ff.] (Coffin A.)

22. THE WIFE OF USHER'S WELL (Child 79). "There was a lady fair and gay." 6. Mrs. Catherine Wigner, Latonia, Gilmer Co., W.Va. Contributed by Carey Woofter, 1924. (Coffin A.)

23. LITTLE MUSGRAVE AND LADY BARNARD (Child 81). "Lord Daniel's Wife." 9. Mrs. Margaret Green, Smithsboro, Knott Co., Ky., 1910. Cox, *Folk-Songs of the South*, pp. 94 f. (Coffin C.)

24. BONNY BARBARA ALLEN (Child 84).
   A. "Barbara Allen." 9. Newton Gaines, Fort Worth, Tex., Aug. 13, 1933. "Learned from my wife's mother, who was born in Mississippi about 1875"—N. G. An aluminum recording of Gaines' singing is lost. Gaines recorded the ballad for the Victor Recording Co. in 1930, and it was issued as Victor V–40243.
   B. Lost text. Kentucky.

25. LADY ALICE (Child 85).
   A. "Young Collins roved out one evening." 13. Communicated by Berlin B. Chapman, Webster Co., W.Va. (1924?). (Coffin A.)
   B. "John Collins said to his mother one day." 9. Communicated by Carey Woofter, Gilmer Co., W.Va., 1924. (Coffin C.)
   C. "Giles Collins." 8 with tune. *FSKH*, pp. 8 f. The MS notation in Combs' hand, "Woofter, Toledo Blade," may have no reference to the source. (Coffin C.)

26. PRINCE ROBERT (Child 87). "Harry Saunders." 11. F. C. Gainer, Tanner, Gilmer Co., W.Va. Probably contributed by Carey Woofter, 1924. *FSMEU*, pp. 121 ff. [138 f.].

27. LAMKIN (Child 93). "False Lamkin." 19. Mr. George Tomblin, Rudkin, Gilmer Co., W.Va., who learned it when a boy from his grandmother. Communicated by Carey Woofter, 1924. (Coffin A.)

28. THE MAID FREED FROM THE GALLOWS (Child 95).
. "Hangman, O hangman, hold your rope." 15. S. E. Lowden, Gilmer Co., W.Va., who learned it from his father, Pocahontas Co., W.Va. Contributed by Carey Woofter, 1924. (Coffin A.)

   B. "O ropeman, ropeman, stop your rope." 15. Source unknown. (Coffin A.)

   C. "Ropeman, ropeman, slack your rope." 1 and prose gloss. Communicated by Berlin B. Chapman, Webster Co., W.Va. (1924?).

29. WILLIE O WINSBURY. (Child 100). "There was a lass in the north countrie." 7. L. P. Williams, De Kalb, Gilmer Co., W.Va. (1924?). *FSMEU*, pp. 123 f. [140 f.].

30. THE BAILIFF'S DAUGHTER OF ISLINGTON (Child 105). Lost text. Kentucky.

31. SIR HUGH (Child 155).
   A. "It rained a mist, it rained a mist." 9. Martin Bennet, Tanner, Gilmer Co., W.Va., who learned it from his grandfather, Ananias Stalnaker. Communicated by Carey Woofter, 1924. (Coffin A.)

   B. "It rained a mist, it rained a mist." 8. S. Wise Stalnaker, Clarksburg, W.Va., who learned it from his grandmother on the Little Kanawha River, Gilmer Co., W.Va. "His grandmother was a Goff, and a lineal descendant of the exile Goff"—C. W. Contributed by Carey Woofter, 1924. (Coffin A.)

   C. "It rained a mist, it rained a mist." 9. F. R. Power, Hampshire Co., W.Va. (1924?). (Coffin A.)

32. MARY HAMILTON (Child 173). "Word has gone to the kitchen." 13. George Burris, Grantsville, Calhoun Co., W.Va. "Brought to America by ancestors of the Burris family, who in Scotland were Davisson and took part in the rebellion of 1745 and fled for their lives. For safety, name changed to Burris"—C. W. Contributed by Carey Woofter, 1924. *FSMEU*, pp. 124 ff. [141 ff.]. (Coffin A.)

33. THE GYPSIE LADDIE (Child 200).
   A. "Gypsy Davy." 11. Clifton Danley, formerly of Gilmer Co., W.Va., who learned the ballad while working as a farm hand in corn cutting time along the Scioto River in Ohio. Contributed by Carey Woofter, 1924. (Coffin A.)

   B. "Amos Furr." Contributed by Carey Woofter, October, 1925. This localized version concerns a Gilmer Co., W.Va., veteran of the Civil War. Woofter wrote that Amos Furr "was noted for his fighting, his prayers, and his fondness for women." Old Amos "ran after" a woman named Lizzie Collins for years. "The man who gave me the song said it was made over from an old song which his father used to sing, for the purpose of tormenting 'Uncle Amos' when he would go to mill."

      There is another localized form of Child 200 in West Virginia (Coffin F; Cox, *Folk-Songs of the South*, D). In fact, the ballad may have begun as a piece of local satire. Judith Ann Knoblock (*WF*, XIX, 35 ff.) has pointed out that "The Gypsie Laddie" seems to derive from and possibly parody "King Orfeo" (Child 19). Davidson Cook (*Journal of the Gypsy Lore Society*, 3d ser., XV, 100 ff.) finds the basis for the parody in the alleged seduction by the gypsy Francie Faa of Elizabeth Douglas, daughter of the eighth Earl of Angus, early in the seventeenth century.

For *spruncin'*, see No. 128.

> Old Amos Furr came down the road
> A-hunting for his Lizzie-O;
> He pounded and banged on the door,
> But got no answer-O.
>
> Old Amos Furr banged on the door,
> A-calling to his Lizzie-O;
> Her daughter made him an answer,
> "She's gone with a spruncin' laddie-O."
>
> "Go saddle me the Canada gray,
> Go saddle me the bright-brown stallion-O;
> I'll ride all night, and I'll ride all day,
> To overtake my Lizzie-O."
>
> He rode till he came to Paddy's Run,
> And the water was muddy and swift-O;
> He crossed his feet on the saddle-horn,
> And crossed Cedar Creek so steady-O.
>
> He rode till he came to Wellington's,
> In search of his Lizzie-O;
> He rode till he came to Willseat Ford,
> A-hunting for his Lizzie-O.
>
> Old Amos Furr did find his Lizzie
> With that spruncin' laddie-O,
> A-setting there on the river bank,
> By the mouth of Willseat-O.
>
> "And have you left your house and home
> To sport with a spruncin' laddie-O?
> And have you left your feather beds
> To sport on the river bank-O?"
>
> "And to sit on the river bank
> With a spruncin' laddie-O
> Is no worse than to be whacked with a broom
> By old Jim Shiflett's wife-O.
>
> "Yes, I have left my house and home
> To sport with a spruncin' laddie-O;
> And I have left old Amos behind,
> To hold his bag for the snipes-O.

"And I have left my feather beds,
The horse-weeds are much softer-O;
Tonight I'll lag [lay?] at the Willseat Ford
With my spruncin' laddie-O."

34. BONNIE JAMES CAMPBELL (Child 210).
  A. "Bonnie Johnnie Campbell." 4 couplets. Lloyd Miller, Letter Gap
  [Gilmer Co.], W.Va., (1924?). *FSMEU*, p. 126 [144]. (Coffin A.)
  B. "Booted and saddled and bridled rode he." 3 couplets. Mrs. Nora Ed-
  man, Big Springs, Calhoun Co., W.Va. (1924?). *FSMEU*, pp. 126 f.
  [144 f.]. (Coffin A.)

35. THE RANTIN LADDIE (Child 240). 13. Mrs. Nora Edman, Big
  Springs, Calhoun Co., W.Va. (1924?). *FSMEU*, pp. 127 f. [145 ff.]. (Coffin A.)

36. JAMES HARRIS (THE DAEMON LOVER) (Child 243).
  A. "Well met, well met, my own true love." 17. Clarice Bailes, Clay
  Co., W.Va., 1924, whose grandmother sang it in Virginia. Communi-
  cated by Carey Woofter. (Coffin A.)
  B. "Well met, well met, my own true love." 13. Source unknown. (Cof-
  fin A.)

37. OUR GOODMAN (Child 274).
  A. "The old man came home the other night." Morgantown, Monongalia
  Co., W.Va. Brought from Canada. Communicated by Carey Woofter,
  1924. (Coffin A.)
  B. "Mr. Goody Goody." 9. Mrs. John W. Combs, Hindman, Knott Co.,
  Ky., 1910. (Coffin B.)
  C. "Old wife, false wife." 8. Mrs. Polly B. Smith, Hindman, Knott Co.,
  Ky., 1921. (Coffin B.)

38. GET UP AND BAR THE DOOR (Child 275). "Old John Jones." 10.
  David Chenoweth, Gip, Calhoun Co., W.Va. [1924? Chenoweth's address
  is given as Minorra in No. 5.] *FSMEU*, pp. 128 f. [147 f.]. An almost
  identical text is printed in Cox, *Folk-Songs of the South*, pp. 516 f., contributed by Carey Woofter, Sept., 1924, as from the recitation of Mrs.
  Sarah Clevenger, Briar Lick Run, Gilmer Co., W.Va. (Coffin A.)

39. THE WIFE WRAPPED IN WETHER'S SKIN (Child 277). "There's
  a little old man lives in the West." 8. George Tomblin, Rudkin, Gilmer
  Co., W.Va., who learned it in the Union Army in Tennessee. Contributed
  by Carey Woofter, 1924. (Coffin A.)

40. THE FARMER'S CURST WIFE (Child 278).
  A. "There was an old man who owned a large farm." 13. George O.
  Humphrey, Morgantown, Monongalia Co., W.Va., who learned it
  in Michigan. Contributed by Carey Woofter, 1924. (Coffin A.)
  B. "The old black devil came one stormy night." 9. Elbert Carpenter,
  Minnora, Calhoun Co., W.Va., 1924. Contributed by Carey Woofter.
  (Coffin A.)

C. "There was an old man lived under the hill." 8. Albert Williams, De Kalb, Gilmer Co., W.Va., 1924. Contributed by Carey Woofter. This version differs from the usual story of the ballad in that the wife does not get past the gates of hell.

> There was an old man lived under the hill,
> And if he ain't dead yit he lives there still.
>
> One day this old man went out for to plow,
> Along came the old devil saying, "And how are you now?
>
> "I didn't come for your oldest son,
> But to take your old woman for to have some fun."
>
> He shouldered her up all across his back,
> And walked off as though she were an old meal-sack.
>
> But when he got a right smart piece up the road
> He grunted and said, "Old woman, you sure are a load."
>
> He set her down on a big old stump to rest;
> She picked up a stick and hit him her best.
>
> He toted her on, all the way to hell's open gate,
> But when he got there it was all too late.
>
> So this old man he had to keep his wife,
> And keep her he did for the rest of his life.

41. THE SWEET TRINITY (Child 286). Lost text. Kentucky

42. THE MERMAID (Child 289). Lost text. Kentucky.

43. BRAVE WOLFE (Laws A 1). 19. School children on Bear Fork of the right hand fork of Steer Creek, Calhoun Co., W.Va., who sang it to the tune of "Yankee Doodle." Contributed by Carey Woofter, 1924. *FSMEU*, pp. 153 ff. [176 ff.].

44. MAJOR ANDRÉ'S CAPTURE (Laws A 2). "John Paulan." 13d. Source unknown.

45. THE TEXAS RANGERS (Laws A 8). "Roving Ranger." 7d. Bill Cornett, Hindman, Knott Co., Ky.

46. THE DRUMMER BOY OF SHILOH (Laws A 15). "On Shiloh's dark and bloody ground." 5. Mrs. Robin Cornett, Hindman, Knott Co., Ky., 1910.

47. THE LAST FIERCE CHARGE (Laws A 17). "The Battle of Gettysburg." 20. Ballet. Mrs. Robin Cornett, Hindman, Knott Co., Ky., 1910.

48. HIRAM HUBBERT (Laws A 20). 9. Mrs. Margaret Green, Smithsboro, Knott Co., Ky. (1909?). *FSMEU*, pp. 171 f. [199 f.].

49. THE COWBOY'S LAMENT (Laws B 1).
A. "The Dying Cowboy." 6. Mrs. John W. Combs, Hindman, Knott Co., Ky., 1912.

B. "Jack Combs." 6 ch. H. Cody, Hindman, Knott Co., Ky. *FSMEU*, p. 180 [209 f.].

50. THE DYING COWBOY (Laws B 2). "The Lone Prairie." 6. ch. Contributed by Carey Woofter, Gilmer Co., W.Va., 1924.

51. SWEET JANE (Laws B 22). 12. Mrs. Richard Smith, Knott Co., Ky. *FSMEU*, pp. 177 f. [206 f.].

52. THE ROLLING STONE (Laws B 25). "Away to California." 6 ch. Mrs. J. W. Combs, Hindman, Knott Co., Ky., 1910.

53. THE JAM AT GERRY'S ROCK (Laws C 1). "The Jam at Jerry's Rock." 10. Contributed by Carey Woofter, Gilmer Co., W.Va., 1924.

54. THE SHIP THAT NEVER RETURNED (Laws D 27). 3d. ch. Source unknown.

55. JESSE JAMES I. (Laws E 1). "Jesse James." 8. Knott Co., Ky.

56. SAM BASS (Laws E 4). 6. C. E. Elliott, Welch, W.Va. (1924?).

57. WILD BILL JONES (Laws E 10). 7 plus variant stanza, with tune. Roscoe Back, Jackson, Breathitt Co., Ky., 1915. *FSKH*, pp. 24 f. [In my opinion, the "variant stanza" is a shift in person effected in a stanza of incremental repetition. Consequently, the text is of eight stanzas.]

58. CHARLES J. GUITEAU (Laws E 11). 3 ch. R. H. Johnson, Morgantown, Monongalia Co., W.Va. (1924?). *FSMEU*, p. 186 f. [218].

59. LOGAN COUNTY JAIL (Laws E 17). "Bob Sims." 10. Tom Kelley, Hazard, Perry Co., Ky. *FSMEU*, pp. 185 f. [216 f.].

60. J. B. MARCUM (Laws E 19). 13 ch. Mr. Noble, Jackson, Breathitt Co., Ky. *FSMEU*, pp. 159 f. [182 ff.].

61. THE ROWAN COUNTY CREW (Laws E 20). "The Tolliver Song." 13d. Hattie Rowland, Cliff Top, Fayette Co., W.Va. (1924?). *FSMEU*, pp. 161 f. [185 ff.].

62. TALT HALL (Laws dE 42). 8. Rob. Morgan, Emmalena, Knott Co., Ky. (1908?). *FSMEU*, pp. 157 f. [181 f.].

63. THE JEALOUS LOVER (Laws F 1 A–B).
A. "Florella." 11 with tune. Mrs. Lizzie Combs, Hindman, Knott Co., Ky., 1910. *FSKH*, pp. 38 f.
B. "Florella." 8. F. R. Power, Hampshire Co., W.Va., 1924.
C. "One eve the moon shone brightly." 4d. Wolfe Co., Ky. Student at Transylvania College, 1912.
D. "Pearl Bryan." 8. ch. Lona Woofter, Glenville, Gilmer Co., W.Va., 1924. *FSMEU*, pp. 174 f. [203 f.].

64. POOR OMIE (Laws F 4).
A. "I will tell you a story about little Oma Wise." 18. Source unknown.

B. "Little Anna." 16. Rob. Morgan, Emmalena, Knott Co., Ky., 1909.

65. ELLEN SMITH (Laws F 11). 18. Dan Gibson, Lackey, Knott Co., Ky. *FSMEU*, pp. 188 f. [219 ff.]

66. McAFEE'S CONFESSION (Laws F 13). 12. Rachel Pickens, De Kalb, Gilmer Co., W.Va. (1924?).

67. THE VANCE SONG (Laws F 17). 9. Hattie Rowland, Cliff Top, Fayette Co., W.Va. (1924?). *FSMEU*, pp. 163 f. [189 ff.].

68. FLOYD FRAZIER (Laws F 19). 16. Mrs. Margaret Green, Smithsboro, Knott Co., Ky. (1909?). *FSMEU*, pp 155 ff. [179 ff.].

69. POOR GOINS (Laws F 22). "Poor Goens." 4½d. Rob Morgan, Emmalena, Knott Co., Ky. (1908?). *FSMEU*, pp. 167 f. [195 f.].

70. THE PEDDLER AND HIS WIFE (Laws F 24). "The Irish Peddler." 7. Jesse Green, Smithsboro, Knott Co., Ky. *FSMEU*, pp. 166 f. [194 f.].

71. WILLIAM BAKER (Laws dF 48). 13. Mrs. John W. Combs, Hindman, Knott Co., Ky. *FSMEU*, pp. 169 ff. [197 ff.]. "This song was composed by William Baker, while he was in prison, condemned to death for the murder of one Prewitt, in Clay County, Kentucky. He gave it to his wife, who also was said to have been a party to the murder—for his friends to sing. She kept the song till she was an old woman, then gave it to her friends. Baker is said to have married an Indian, which in some way was said to have been connected with the Baker-Howard feud in Clay Co."—J. H. C.

72. THE DEATH OF SAMUEL ADAMS (Laws dF 62). 12. Contributed by A. B. Combs, Prestonburg, Floyd Co., Ky., 1931. *KFR*, VI, 123 f.

73. THE C. & O. WRECK (1913) (Laws G 4). 18. Ballet signed by William Back, Red Fox, Knott Co., Ky. Procured 1924. *FSMEU*, pp. 172 ff. [200 ff.].

74. SPRINGFIELD MOUNTAIN (Laws G 16).
     A. "In Springfield Mountain there did dwell." 5 ch. Raymond Beall, Cedarville, Gilmer Co., W.Va.; and Storf Shock, Orndorff, Webster Co., W.Va., 1924. Contributed by Carey Woofter.
     B. "Father Maggard had a son." 5. L. S. Vannoy, Ritchie Co., W.Va., 1924. Contributed by Carey Woofter.

75. YOUNG CHARLOTTE (Laws G 17).
     A. "Young Charlotte lived by the mountain side." 24. R. L. Stalnaker, Withers, W.Va. Contributed by Carey Woofter, 1924.
     B. "Fair Charlotte lived in a mountain side." 15. F. R. Power, Hampshire Co., W.Va., 1924.
     C. "Fair Charlotte." 18. Sent January, 1959, by R. Lee Stewart, Morehead, Rowan Co., Ky. Copied from ballet or print, including note: "This original copy was written in 1871 near Damsville, Michigan.

The event occurred over 20 years before. This was sent to me by W. H. Gardner, an Evangelist, from Ohio, who was visiting his cousin in Michigan in 1864. Contributed by Laura M. Klinefetter, North Dakota." Combs informed me that Stewart, aged 85 at the time, had grown up in Knott Co. I suspect that the text was copied from an "Old Songs" section in a weekly newspaper.

76. THE SILVER DAGGER (Laws G 21). "Once there was a young man who loved a lady." 9. Mrs. Richard Smith, Smithsboro, Ky., 1909.

77. THREE PERISHED IN THE SNOW (Laws G 32). 3d ch. Source unknown.

78. AN ARKANSAS TRAVELER (Laws H 1). "My name is Joe Cephas, I came from Buffalo Town." 2. Contributed by Berlin B. Chapman, Webster Co., W.Va. (1924?).

79. THE LITTLE FAMILY (Laws H 7). 8d. Contributed by D. L. Thomas, Centre College, Danville, Ky., 1915.

80. THE LITTLE MOHEA (Laws H 8). "Pretty Maumee." 7 with tune. Mrs. Edwin Daniel, Hindman, Knott Co., Ky. *FSKH*, pp. 22 f.

81. JOHN HENRY (Laws I 1). 12. Jesse Green, Smithsboro, Knott Co., Ky. (1909?). *FSMEU*, pp. 164 f. [191 ff.]; Cox, *Folk-Songs of the South*, pp. 185 f., with alterations apparently made by Cox. (See Chappell, *John Henry*, pp. 2–3.)

82. JOHN HARDY (Laws I 2).
    A. "John Hardy was a brave little man." 13. Knott Co., Ky., 1909. Cox, *Folk-Songs of the South*, pp. 186 ff.
    B. "John Hardy was a-standing by the Dark Sea Bar." 5 and prose summary. Rachel Hays (later Stidham), Jackson, Breathitt Co., Ky., *ca.* 1900.
    C. "John Hardy was a-standing at the bar-room door." 11. Dr. Waitman T. Smith, who learned it in Roane Co., W.Va., *ca.* 1899. Communicated by Carey Woofter, 1924.
    D. "John Hardy was a little farmer boy." 10. Ruby Mick, Ireland, Lewis Co., W.Va. Communicated by Carey Woofter, 1924. (Cf. text from Walter Mick printed by Cox, *Folk-Songs of the South*, pp. 182 f.)
    E. "John Hardy was only three years old." 5. Contributed by Berlin B. Chapman, Webster Co., W.Va., 1924.

83. FRANKIE AND ALBERT (Laws I 3).
    A. "Frankie." 8. Ballet. Red Fox, Knott Co., Ky., 1924.
    B. "Frankie." 13. C. E. Elliott, Welch, McDowell Co., W.Va. (1924?).
    C. "Frankie and Johnnie." 10. Contributed by James R. Masterson, Michigan, *ca.* 1943.

84. JOSEPH MICA (Laws I 16). "Wreck of the Six-Wheeler." 5 ch. Newton Gaines, Fort Worth, Tex., Aug. 13, 1933, who learned it in 1910

from a young man at the University of Texas, who in turn had "learned it from negroes working in the fields around Paris, Texas, some years previous to the appearance of the popular song, 'Casey Jones.' " Gaines recorded it for the Victor Recording Co. in 1930. Issued on Timely Tunes C–1564 under the pseudonym of Jim New.

85. JAY GOULD'S DAUGHTER (Laws dI 25). "John White." 2. Richmond, Madison Co., Ky. Contributed by D. L. Thomas, Centre College, Danville, Ky., 1915. In my opinion, the following text should be considered a form of "Joseph Mica" (Laws I 16), as should all other texts of dI 25.

> Jay Goul' gave his youngest son
> A bran' new en-gine that had never been run.
> He said, "Son, son, if you listen to me,
> You'll run this en-gine to Santa Fe."
>
> Tuesday morning came a shower of rain,
> 'Round the curve I spied a passenger train.
> On the boiler laid Hobo John,
> He's been a good ole hobo, but he's dead an' gone.

86. THE SAILOR BOY I (Laws K 12). "Sweet William." 9. William C. Lemley, Preston Co., W.Va., 1924.

87. A GAY SPANISH MAID (Laws K 16). "The Spanish Maid." 10. Contributed by Berlin B. Chapman, Webster Co., W.Va., 1924. *FSMEU*, pp. 134 f. [153 ff.].

88. MARY'S DREAM (Laws K 20). "Mary and Sandy." 7. H. F. Watson, Marion Co., W.Va., 1924. Contributed by Berlin B. Chapman (1924?).

89. THE YORKSHIRE BITE (Laws L 1). "Selling the Cow." 21. F. C. Gainer, Tanner, Gilmer Co., W.Va. Probably contributed by Carey Woofter, 1924. *FSMEU*, pp. 130 ff. [149 ff.].

90. THE RAMBLING BOY (Laws L 12).
   A. "The Rich and Rambling Boy." 6. Tom Kelley, Hazard, Perry Co., Ky. *FSMEU*, pp. 184 f. [215 ff.].
   B. "Jack Wilson" ("James Irving"). 9 with variation and tune. Mrs. Martha Smith, Smithsboro, Knott Co., Ky., 1909. *FSKH*, pp. 10 f.

91. THE BOSTON BURGLAR (Laws L 16B). 12. Source unknown.

92. EARLY, EARLY IN THE SPRING (Laws M 1).
   A. " 'Twas early, early in the spring." 8. Student, West Virginia University, 1924.
   B. " 'Twas early, early in the spring." 7 with tune. Belle Fortney, Morgantown, Monongalia Co., W.Va. Cox, *Traditional Ballads*, pp. 79 f., where it is credited to the collection of Miss Frances Sanders, June, 1914 [1924?].

93. THE DROWSY SLEEPER (Laws M 4). Lost text from Kentucky or West Virginia; or possibly two lost texts.

94. BETSY IS A BEAUTY FAIR (Laws M 20). "Betsy Brown." 10. Mrs. John W. Combs, Hindman, Knott Co., Ky., 1910.

95. THE BANKS OF DUNDEE (Laws M 25).
   A. "The Banks of Sweet Dundee." 20 with tune. Wiley Parks, Knott Co., Ky., 1913. *FSKH*, 26 f.
   B. "There was a fair maiden." 10d. H. F. Watson, Marion Co., W.Va., 1924. Contributed by Berlin B. Chapman.

96. FAREWELL, DEAR ROSANNA (Laws M 30). "Rosanna." 10d couplets. Rob. Morgan, Emmalena, Knott Co., Ky. (1908?). *FSMEU*, pp. 168 f. [196 f.].

97. WILLIAM AND DINAH (Laws M 31A). 6 with tune. Mrs. Martha Smith, Smithsboro, Knott Co., Ky., 1909. *FSKH*, pp. 5 ff.

98. THE BRAMBLE BRIAR (Laws M 32).
   A. "In yonder's forth town there lived a margent." 17. Mrs. Margaret Green, Smithsboro, Knott Co., Ky., 1909.
   B. "There was a rich man lived near Bridgewater." 15. Agnes Polling, Tucker Co., W.Va., who learned it from her grandmother. Contributed by Berlin B. Chapman, Webster Co., W.Va., 1924.

99. JACK MONROE (Laws N 7).
   A. "Jackie Frazier." 7 plus another 5 apparently given as variations known to the contributor. Albro Thomas, Knott Co., Ky.
   B. "Poor Jack's gone to war." 8. Patrick Starcher, Webster Springs, W.Va., who learned it from an old woman. Contributed by Carey Woofter, 1924.

100. THE GOLDEN GLOVE (Laws N 20).
   A. "There was a young squire in London did dwell." 11. F. R. Power, Hampshire Co., W.Va., 1924.
   B. Lost text. Contributed by Berlin B. Chapman, Webster Co., W.Va., 1924. (This may, however, be the A text.)

101. KATE AND HER HORNS (Laws N 22). "Kate and the Clothier." 10. Mrs. Martha Smith, Smithsboro, Knott Co., Ky. (1909?). *FSMEU*, pp. 137 f. [157 f.].

102. WILLIAM HALL (Laws N 30).
   A. "There was a brisk and gay young farmer." 11. Mrs. John W. Combs and her brother, H. Cody, Hindman, Knott Co., Ky.
   B. 11. *Ibid.*

103. JOHN (GEORGE) RILEY II (Laws N 37).
   A. "George Reilly." 7. Knott Co., Ky.
   B. "Soldier Boy." 7. An Arkansas student in the Oklahoma Northeastern State Normal School, Tahlequah, 1917.

104. THE MANTLE SO GREEN (Laws N 38). "William O'Riley." 10. Leslie Co., Ky.

105. THE BANKS OF CLAUDY (Laws N 40).
    A. "It was all on a summer's morning." 10. Knott Co., Ky.
    B. "All on the Banks of Claudy." 7d. Knott Co., Ky.

106. PRETTY FAIR MAID (Laws N 42). "Soldier Boy." 7. Knott and Letcher Cos., Ky.

107. THE FOGGY DEW (Laws O 3). "The Bugaboo." 10. Tom Kelley, Hazard, Perry Co., Ky. *FSMEU*, pp. 183 f. [214 f.]. (Cf. No. 180.)

108. THE LADY OF CARLISLE (Laws O 25). "The Lady and the Fan." 12. Old ballet contributed by H. H. Smith, Hindman, Knott Co., Ky., 1921.

109. THE GIRL VOLUNTEER (Laws O 33). "I'm Going to Join the Army." 12. Mrs. Rachel (Hays) Stidham, Jackson, Breathitt Co., Ky. *FSMEU*, pp. 178 f. [207 ff.].

110. MOLLY BAWN (Laws O 36). "Mollie Vaughnders." 7. F. R. Power, Hampshire Co., W.Va., 1924.

111. THE GIRL I LEFT BEHIND ME (Laws P 1).
    A. (P 1A) "My parents treated me tenderly." 12. Knott, Perry, and Leslie Cos., Ky.
    B. (P 1B) "I had a kind old father." 12. West Virginia (1924?).

112. THE NIGHTINGALE (Laws P 14). 7 with tune. Will Wooton, Knott Co., Ky., 1921. "Edited" text, *FSKH*, pp. 20 f. Original readings follow:
    2.1   With hugging and kissing, they walked together.
    3   With hugging and kissing he caught her 'round the middle,
          And out of his knapsack he drew a fine fiddle;
          He tun-ed her up to the heighth of her string, etc.
    4.3   He tuned up his fiddle to the heighth of her string.
    7.4   They leave you a baby to trot on your knee.

113. RINORDINE (Laws P 15). "Ryner Dine." 8. H. F. Watson, Marion Co., W.Va. Probably contributed by Berlin B. Chapman, 1924. *FSMEU*, pp. 143 f. [165 ff.].

114. BLOW THE CANDLE OUT (Laws P 17). "The Jolly Boatsman." 10. Mrs. Margaret Smith, Smithsboro, Knott Co., Ky. (1909?). *FSMEU*, pp. 140 f. [161 f.].

115. THE BUTCHER BOY (Laws P 24).
    A. "In london city a lady did dwell." 8½. A ballet signed Bernard B. Smith, Spider, Ky., and Brax Combs, Sassafras, Ky. The text differs sufficiently from the printing (with tune) in *FSKH*, pp. 30 f., that it is given in full below.

In london city a lady did dwell
that Railroad boy she love so well
he corted me my life away
and with me he would he would not stay.

He go out in some old town
find some girl and he sit down
he take her up all on his knee
and tell her something he wouldent tell me

Can you tell me the reason why because
she was more gold than I
her gold will melt and silver will fly
then she will be just as poor as I.

She went up stairs to fix her bed
not one word had her Mama said
Papa come home all from his work
crying where is my daughter dear.

Mama went out the stair way to
crying daughter what troubles you
Mama mama I dare you tell
that railroad boy I love so well.

Papa went up stairs the door he broke
he found her hanging by a rope
he drew his knife and cut her down
up on her breast these words he found.

Go dig my grave both wide and deep
place marble stone at my head and feet
up on my breast place a turtle Dove
and to the world that I died for love.

When I wore my apron low he follow
me through frost and snow
now I wear them to my chin
He'll pass right by and he wont come in.

Around my grave you can build a fence
to show the world I had no sence.

B. "The Brown-Eyed Boy." 6. Knott Co., Ky.
C. "In Jersey City there once did dwell." 9. Contributed by Carey Woofter, Gilmer Co., W.Va., 1924.
D. "The Butcher Boy." 3 ch. Glendale (Marshall Co.?), W.Va., 1924. Contributed by Carey Woofter.

116. LOVE HAS BROUGHT ME TO DESPAIR (Laws P 25). "The Auxville Love." 6. Mrs. Robin Cornett, Hindman, Knott Co., Ky. *FSMEU*, p. 176 [205].

117. CAROLINE OF EDINBURGH TOWN (Laws P 27). Lost Kentucky text.

118. THE CRUEL SHIP'S CARPENTER (Laws P 36B).
    A. "Oh Polly, pretty Polly, Oh, yonder she stands." 12 with tune. Knott Co., Ky. *FSKH*, pp. 35 f.
    B. Tune and stanza 1 as in A. *FSKH*, p. 37.
    C. "Pretty Polly." 8½d. H. H. Smith, Hindman, Knott Co., Ky.

119. THE OLD LADY OF SLAPSADAM (Laws Q 2). "The Old Lady of London." 8 ch. Knott Co., Ky.

120. THE BOATSMAN AND THE CHEST (Laws Q 8). "There was a wealthy merchant." 14. Aubrey Goff, Revel, W.Va., 1924. Contributed by Carey Woofter.

121. THE SEA CAPTAIN AND THE SQUIRE (Laws Q 12). "There was a sea captain who was married of late." 13. George O. Humphrey, Morgantown, Monongalia Co., W.Va. (Learned in Michigan? Contributed by Carey Woofter, 1924?) *FSMEU*, pp. 138 ff. [159 ff.].

122. THE MILLER'S WILL (Laws Q 21). "The old man called up his eldest son." 9. Aubrey Goff, Revel, W.Va. Contributed by Carey Woofter, 1924. Text (identical except *derned* for *damned* in stanza 9) printed in Cox, *Traditional Ballads*, pp. 164 f., with note that Goff learned it from H. C. Stalnaker (contributed June, 1925).

123. THE ROMISH LADY (Laws Q 32). 22. F. R. Power, Hampshire Co., W.Va., 1924.

124. THE CHILDREN IN THE WOOD (Laws Q 34). "Now ponder well, ye parents dear." 8 (but many lines forgotten) with tune. Emma Hewitt, Morgantown, Monongalia Co., W.Va. Cox, *Traditional Ballads*, pp. 89 ff., where it is credited to the collection of Miss Frances Sanders, June, 1924.

125. WILLIAM BLEWITT. 10. Bill Cornett, Hindman, Knott Co., Ky. *FSMEU*, pp. 151 f. [174 f.].
    A William Blewitt—pickpocket, housebreaker, and accomplice to murder—was executed at Kingston, in Surrey, England, April 12, 1726, after his capture in Holland. (See Knapp and Baldwin, *The Newgate Calendar*, I, 218 ff.; *Lives of the Most Remarkable Criminals*, II, 143 ff. There is no mention of the dove hovering over his head.) Another text of the ballad is printed in *KFPM*, II, No. 4, pp. 4 f.

126. PRETTY PEGGY-O. 9. Mrs. John W. Combs, Hindman, Knott Co., Ky. Differing texts from the same informant are printed in Sharp, II, 59, and *Sewanee Review*, XIX, 14. (Cf. Brown, III, 456; V, 254.)

127. LONELY NAN. 4. A student in the Oklahoma Northeastern State Normal School, Tahlequah, 1917.
    A 9-stanza text of this apparently imported ballad may also be found in *KFPM*, II, No. 4, pp. 2 f.

There was a lady in our land,
We all did know as Lonely Nan;
In stature she was very tall,
And around her waist was rather small.

A noble squire living near,
Who chanced to fall in love with her,
And I suppose by her consent
Picked up her shawl and away they went.

She said that she was my best friend,
And would remain till time did end;
But now I see how she, my friend,
Has acted until time did end.

So now, Miss Nan, fare you well,
I wish you well, no tongue can tell;
I bid you now a long farewell,
Farewell, Miss Nan, fare you well.

128. THE OLD WIFE. 12. Mrs. Mag Perkins, Cedarville, Gilmer Co., W.Va. Communicated by Carey Woofter, 1924. *FSMEU*, pp. 135 f. [155 ff.].

This occurs as "The auld Wife beyont the Fire" in Allan Ramsay's *Tea Table Miscellany*, I, 103 ff., as an old song with additions. Whether the West Virginia text (which substitutes *spruncin* for *snishing* as a term for sexual intercourse) derives from Ramsay's or represents a parallel tradition is difficult to determine. (See also Johnson's *Scots Musical Museum*, No. 435; Gilchrist, II, 155 f.; Herd, *Antient and Modern Scottish Songs*, II, 151 ff., *Ancient and Modern Scottish Songs*, II, 16 ff.) Paul Clayton (*Unholy Matrimony*, Elektra 147, 12" LP) has recorded a similar text with no indication as to source.

129. PETER GRAY. 8. Theodore Stalnaker, De Kalb, Gilmer Co., W.Va., who learned it when a boy in Randolph Co. Contributed by Carey Woofter, 1924. (Cf. Lomax, *Our Singing Country*, pp. 252 f.)

130. THE ALLEGHENY. 6. Perry and Leslie Cos., Ky. *KFR*, VI, 129. (Cf. *PTFS*, XXXII [1964], 68 f.)

131. THE HAPPY STRANGER. "Stranger in the Desert." 7. Knott Co., Ky. (Cf. Brown, II, 372 ff.)

132. THE LOWLANDS OF HOLLAND. "The Soldier Bride's Lament." 8. Air: "William Baker." Mrs. John W. Combs, Hindman, Knott Co., Ky. *FSMEU*, p. 150 [173 f.]. (Cf. Randolph, I, 339 f.)

133. PRETTY POLLY. 6. Contributed by Berlin B. Chapman, Marion Co., W.Va., 1924. *FSMEU*, p. 144 [166 f.]. (Cf. Randolph, IV, 242.)

134. "Once a farmer and his wife had cause for disputation." 3. H. N. Taylor, Morgantown, Monongalia Co., W.Va., 1924.

Once a farmer and his wife had cause for disputation,
They were used to noisy strife, and wordy altercation;
"Good man," she said, "you are too free and too open handed."
"Good wife," said he, "you let me be, I will not be commanded."

Then when harvest time came 'roun', and boys with girls were racin',
Oft the farmer's wife had foun' he would the girls be chasin'.
"Good man," cried she, "you are too free, and too open hearted."
"Good wife," said he, "you let me be, or we will soon be parted."

Long, long years did pass away, and still they kep' on railin'
Till at last one winter's day, she said when she was ailin',
"I am too old always to scold, I think your ways are mended."
Said he, "You're right, good wife." And so the matter ended.

135. "Come all ye false lovers." 13. Mrs. John W. Combs, Hindman, Knott
Co., Ky. *FSMEU*, pp. 147 f. [170 f.].

136. THE FROG'S COURTSHIP. (Cf. Brown, III, 154 ff.; V, 85 ff.)
   A. "A frog went a-courting and he did ride." 14 ch. Contributed by Carey
      Woofter, Gilmer Co., W.Va., 1924.
   B. "A frog went a-courting, he did ride." 12. F. R. Power, Hampshire Co.,
      W.Va., 1924.
   C. "There was a frog lived in a rill." 7. H. F. Watson, Marion Co., W.Va.,
      1924. (Probably contributed by Berlin B. Chapman.)
   D. "A frog went a-courting and he did ride." 12 ch. Contributed by Lily
      Bell Sefton, West Virginia University. The variant came originally
      from Pennsylvania.
   E. "A frog he went a-courting and he did ride." 8. Mrs. Radcliff in the
      Negro settlement on the waters of Steer Creek, Calhoun Co., W.Va.
      Contributed by Carey Woofter, 1924. (This is clearly the text sum-
      marized in Cox, *Folk-Songs of the South*, p. 473, No. 162 G.)
   F. "Mr. Mouse went a-courting and he did ride." 2 with tune. Cox, *Tra-
      ditional Ballads*, p. 174, where the informant is given as Carey Woof-
      ter, Gilmer Co., W.Va., with the notation of the music and the com-
      munication of the variant credited to Miss Frances Sanders, Morgan-
      town, June, 1924. (Cf. Nos. 14B, 92B, 124, 142D, 226, 227, 310.)
   G. "A frog went a-courting he did ride." 4. Source unknown.
   H. "Froggie Would A-Wooing Go." 20. Newton Gaines, Fort Worth,
      Tex., Aug. 13, 1933. "The tune and most of the verses are those learned
      from my aunt who learned them from my grandmother, who was
      born in South Carolina about 1839. Several of the verses I had added
      from time to time, notably some from the paper on 'Froggie's Courting'
      by Dr. Payne of the University of Texas. The variations from 'unhu'
      are my own which have grown with the years, as they pleased better
      the little children that listen to me, especially when I imitate the
      various animal sounds"—N. G. The aluminum record of Gaines'
      performance has been lost.

137. KITCHIE KI-MO. "Kitty Kimo." 8 ch. Source unknown. (Cf. Brown, III, 165 ff.; V, 94 ff.)

138. THE DERBY RAM. (Cf. Brown, II, 439 ff.; IV, 233 ff.)
A. "O I went down to Darby Town." 9 ch. H. H. Smith, Hindman, Knott Co., Ky., *ca.* 1910.
B. "Darby's Ram." 2. Source unknown
C. "As I went down to Darby." 7 ch. Judge Daniel Walker, Beaumont, Tex., 1941.

139. FAIR NOTAMAN TOWN. 8. H. H. Smith, Hindman, Knott Co., Ky., *ca.* 1910. (Cf. Randolph, III, 201 ff.)

140. THE GOWANS ARE GAY. 12. Charles McIntosh, Walkersville, Lewis Co., W.Va. (1924?). *FSMEU*, pp. 142 f. [163 f.]. (Cf. Allan Ramsay, *The Tea Table Miscellany*, I, 214 ff.)

141. BARNEY McCOY. 6. Tahlequah, Okla. (1917?). The original seems a ballet or a student exercise. (Cf. Brown, II, 346 ff.; IV, 202.)

142. MY BOY BILLY. (Cf. Brown, III, 166 ff.; V, 97 ff.)
A. "O where are you going, Billy boy, Billy boy?" 6. Mrs. John W. Combs and Mrs. Rhoda Kelly, Hindman, Knott Co., Ky.
B. "O where have you been, Billy boy?" 11. Aubrey Goff, Revel, W.Va. Contributed by Carey Woofter, 1924.
C. "Where have you been, Billy boy, Billy boy?" 7. Mrs. Annie Lorenz, Glenville, W.Va., 1924. Contributed by Carey Woofter.
D. "Oh, where have you been, Billy-boy, Billy-boy." 7 with tune. Monongalia Co., W.Va. (This seems to be one of the items contributed by Miss Frances Sanders, June, 1924. Carey Woofter was probably involved in the collection. Cf. Nos. 14B, 92B, 124, 136F, 226, 227, 310.)

143. THE KEYS OF HEAVEN. (Cf. Brown, III, 6 ff.; V, 3 ff.)
A. "I'll give to you a paper of pins." 20. Knott Co., Ky.
B. "I'll give to you a paper of pins." 16. Mrs. E. G. Rohrbaugh, Glenville, Gilmer Co., W.Va. Contributed by Carey Woofter, 1924.

144. RANTING ROVING LAD. "My Love was born in Aberdeen." 4 ch. George Burris, Grantsville, Calhoun Co., W.Va. (See No. 32.) Contributed by Carey Woofter, 1924. *FSMEU*, p. 149 [172].
This text is almost identical with that in Allan Cunningham, *Songs of Scotland*, III, 208 f. For Burns' version, "The White Cockade," see Johnson's *Scots Musical Museum*, No. 272. See also Hecht, p. 124; Herd, *Antient and Modern Scotish Songs*, II, 131; Struthers, III, 149 f.; Gilchrist, II, 277 f.

145. SAID THE BLACKBIRD TO THE CROW. "The Woodpecker." 4. Sung by an 85-year-old woman in central Kentucky in 1875 and said to have been brought from Virginia in 1812. Contributed by D. L. Thomas, Centre College, Danville, Ky. (1915?).

146. OLD KING COLE. "Old King Coal was a merry old soul." 1½. Berlin B. Chapman, Webster Co., W.Va. (1924?). (Cf. Lomax, *Our Singing Country*, 204 f.; Ritchie, *Garland*, 34 f.

147. HUSTLING GAMBLERS (DARLING COREY). 10. Tom Kelley, Hindman, Knott Co., Ky., 1913. (Cf. Henry, *Songs*, pp. 102 ff. Full references in my notes to *The Doc Watson Family*, Folkways FA 2366 12" LP.)

148. GROUNDHOG. "Groun' hog." 43 with 2 tunes. Tom Kelley and Dan Gibson, Hindman, Knott Co., Ky., 1915.

Two variants have been combined and reconstruction is not possible. The following differences may be noted among the text in MS and the texts printed in *Folk-Say*, 1930, 246 ff., and in Lomax, *American Ballads and Folk Songs*, pp. 271 ff.: The tune in Lomax and consequently the refrain ("Ground hog!") are not from the Combs Collection. The MS refrain is "To my rang tang a whaddle linkey day," and the *Folk-Say* printing adds two variant refrain lines. The *Folk-Say* text includes 39 stanzas and the Lomax text 33. The MS adds:

> Rousted and they rousted, they couldn't git 'im out,
> Took 'm by the tail and they pulled 'im out.

Folk-Say adds the following which is not in the MS:

> Oh, mam, look at Sam,
> He eat all the 'hog 'n a-soppin' out the pan.

149. THE BLACK HILLS. 6. Gerald McIntosh, Bromide (Johnston Co.?), Okla., 1924. (Cf. Belden, 349 f.)

150. BONNIE LITTLE GIRL. 5. Knott and Letcher Cos., Ky. (Cf. Williams, p. 209; Reeves, *The Idiom of the People*, p. 158; *JAF*, LII, 33 f.; Cambiaire, p. 158.)

151. AULD ROBIN GRAY. 9. Contributed by Berlin B. Chapman, Marion Co., W.Va., 1924. (Cf. *Heart Songs*, p. 445.)

152. THE GYPSY'S WARNING. "Trust him not, O gentle lady." 2. Contributed by Berlin B. Chapman, Webster Co., W.Va., (1924?). (Cf. Randolph, IV, 219 ff.)

153. THE FATAL WEDDING. 6d ch. Tahlequah, Okla. (1917?). The MS is a ballet or a student exercise. (Cf. Spaeth, *Read 'em and Weep*, pp. 172 ff.)

154. THE LITTLE BLACK MUSTACHE. "The Black Mustache." 7. Old ballet, Knott Co., Ky. *FSMEU*, pp. 180 f. [210 f.]. (Cf. Brown, II, 479; IV, 260.)

155. ANNIE LEE. "I have finished him a letter." 7 ch. "As sung in the 'parlors' by the young ladies at Hindman, Ky., 1898"—J. H. C. (Cf. Brown, II, 376 f.; IV, 212.)

156. TIME ENOUGH YET. 5 ch. Tahlequah, Okla. (1917?). The MS is a ballet or a student exercise. (Cf. Randolph, III, 75 ff.)

157. WHEN THE BEES ARE IN THEIR HIVE. 2d ch. Tahlequah, Okla. (1917?). The MS is a ballet or a student exercise. This is an Alfred Bryan-Kerry Mills song of 1904.

158. LITTLE JIM. Tahlequah, Okla. (1917?). 5. The MS is a ballet or a student exercise. This is probably a Paul Dresser song of 1890.

> I am little Jim an orphan boy
> My mother dead and gone yes
> She was my only joy has left me all alone.
> Little Jim Little Jim he is poor little orphan boy.
>
> My father too is far away
> his face no more I see,
> perhaps he is dead I hear them say
> For he would come to me.
>
> The world seems dark and dreary to me.
> Since I am left alone
> No loving Mother's voice to cheer
> how sad without a home.
>
> Dear friends can be to me
> as kind as friends to friends can be,
> but still I'll never never find
> what mother bore to me
>
> But Ile try to do the best I can
> and and in the favor grow
> with all around between God and man
> and then to mother go.

159. WHY DID THEY DIG MA'S GRAVE SO DEEP? "Poor Little Nellie." 3d ch. Tahlequah, Okla. (1917?) MS is a ballet or student exercise. (Cf. Spaeth, *Read 'em and Weep*, pp. 102 f.)

160. DON'T GO TOMMY. 2d ch. Talequah, Okla. (1917?). MS is a ballet or student exercise. (Cf. Randolph, IV, 385 f.)

161. BROTHER GREEN. 8. Knott Co., Ky. (Cf. Brown, III, 468 ff.; V, 261 f.)

162. BAD TOM SMITH. 2 ch. H. Cody, Hindman, Knott Co., Ky. (MS credits Mrs. John W. Combs, sister of Cody.) *FSMEU*, p. 187 [218 f.].
" 'Bad' Tom Smith composed this song, words and music, and sang it just before he was hanged at Jackson, Ky., *ca.* 1895. He was my mother's first cousin . . . worst man in the Kentucky mountains. His death was brought about by the sudden collapse of a scaffold upon which he was standing and upon which he was the principal actor. But he had taken time to compose and sing his own death song before the collapse"— J. H. C.

"Bad" Tom Smith was hanged June 28, 1895, for the murder of Dr. John E. Rader in Breathitt Co., Ky. Mutzenberg's contemporary history of Kentucky feuds fails to mention either the farewell song or the collapse of the gallows. Smith's "goodnight" is based on an old spiritual song, "Don't You Grieve After Me" (see Brown, III, 585 f.; V, 333).

163. THE CHURCH ACROSS THE WAY. 2t ch. Source unknown. (Cf. Randolph, IV, 345.)

164. THE KING'S DELIGHT. 2d. Given by an Englishman on a train to H. N. Taylor, a student in West Virginia University, 1924.

> On this day our King was born,
> Let harp be sounded, fill'd the Morn;
> With me-theg-lin to the brim,
> For ev'ry heart beats high for him.
> Bards with voices clear and strong,
> Pour freely forth a joyous song,
> Cheering day and gladd'ning night,
> And call the song the "King's Delight."
>
> For the King well pleased will be,
> While list'ning to the melody,
> Rising from his subject all,
> In lowly cot or lofty hall.
> May he live a thousand years,
> And may this song salute his ears;
> May his smile be ever bright,
> When he has heard the "King's delight."

165. BENDING THE SHOE. Given by an Englishman on a train to H. N. Taylor, a student in West Virginia University, 1924.

> Oh, whence these emotions of anguish and fear?
> This throb of the bosom, and fast falling tear?
> The sound of the anvil, that forge's loud roar
> Ne'er woke these sad feelings within me before.
>
> How oft have I heard them a far thro' the vale,
> With Howell's blithe song ringing sweet in the gale,
> And my bosom was glad and r'joic'd while I knew,
> For the wars of his prince he was "bendin' the shoe."
>
> O happy those dreams, when dreamin' no ill,
> I watched him still wielding the iron at will;
> For the war steeds o' others, those days are now flown,
> And Howell is bending the shoe for his own.
>
> Llewellyn hath summon'd with bugle and bow,
> The brave of his country, to combat the foe;
> And Howell, with all who are valiant and true,
> Must quit for the battlefield "bendin' the shoe."

166. THE JOVIAL TINKER (JOAN'S ALE IS NEW). "When I was a little boy I walked up and down." 7. Ballet in the possession of John Wolverton, Hardman, W.Va., who said that he wrote the song down from hearing his mother sing it at the close of the Civil War. Contributed by Carey Woofter, 1924. *FSMEU*, pp. 132 f. [152 f.]. (Cf. Cox, *Folk-Songs of the South* pp. 492 f.; Reeves, *The Idiom of the People*, pp. 133 ff.)

167. KIND BETTY. (Cf. Reeves, *The Idiom of the People*, pp. 113 f.)
A. "I laid my hand down on her toe." 8. Perry Co., Ky., 1951.
B. "A maid and a man settin' in a corner." 1. Hickory Co., Mo., 1940.

168. DAVY CROCKETT. 5. Wiley Parks, Hindman, Knott Co., Ky., *ca.* 1900. *FSMEU*, pp. 182 f. [213]. (Cf. Randolph, III, 165 ff.; Owens, 244 ff.; *TFSB*, XIII, 81 f.)

169. THE COWBOY'S DREAM. 2½d ch. An itinerant Baptist evangelist named Hornsby, from Texas, at Hindman, Knott Co., Ky., *ca.* 1900. *KFR*, VI, 134.

170. PRETTY SARO. 10. Mrs. John W. Combs, Hindman, Knott Co., Ky., 1910. (Cf. Brown, III, 285 ff.; V, 166 ff.)

171. THE GOVERNMENT CLAIM. 5d ch. Dr. Ernest Smith of Oklahoma at Hindman, Knott Co., Ky., 1907. *FSKH*, 32 ff. MS glossed "B. County" as "Beaver County." (Cf. Randolph, II, 190 f.)

172. "Darling Cloe, my darling Cloe." Berlin B. Chapman, Webster Co., W.Va. (1924?). Browne, pp. 394 ff., reports a text from Alabama, 1961.
    Darling Cloe my darling Cloe
    Your sweet face I soon shall see I know.
    It's been twenty years or more, since I left the cabin door
    And I'm going home to see my darling Cloe.

173. GRANDMOTHER'S ADVICE. "Grandmother lives on yonder little green." 5 ch. Student in the Oklahoma Northeastern State Normal School, Tahlequah, 1917. (Cf. Brown, II, 476 ff.; IV, 254 f.)

174. THE SWAPPING SONG. "The Foolish Boy." 13 ch. Knott Co., Ky. (Cf. Brown, II, 471 ff.; IV, 196 f.)

175. THE KICKING MULE. 4d. Knott Co., Ky. "Probably clipped from some newspaper"—J. H .C.

176. WHOA MULE (Cf. Brown, III, 567 f.; V, 328). Both of the following variants were sung by Cullie Williams, Red Fox, Knott Co., Ky., *ca.* 1902.

A. There was a man in Possum town,
    His hair was long and thick;
    He had a mule with streamy eyes—
    O how that mule could kick!

Chorus:
W'o' mule when I tell you,
W'o' mule when I say,
Never mind you, w'o' mule,
Just hold on to the sleigh.

He kicked the ice all over the frog,
He broke the elephant's back;
He met a Texas railroad train,
And kicked her off the track.

I'm a-goin' down to Possum town,
Miss Lizy, you keep cool;
I hain't got time to kiss you now,
For I'm busy with this mule.

Miss Lizy, git your bonnet,
Come and take your seat,
And bring that board you're settin' on,
To cover up your feet.

The sleigh bells they are ringing,
The snow is falling fast;
Go put the harness on that mule,
I've got him up at last.

B.   Massa had a little gray mule,
His name was Simon Broad;
Kick a chaw o' terbacker out o' yo' mouf,
And never touch yo' jaw.

Chorus:
W'o' (there) mule, I tell you,
W'o' mule I say!
W'o' mule I tell you,
Feed that mule more hay.

(or: W'o' mule, I tell you,
   W'o' mule I say!
   Don't go to kickin' little Lizy Jane,
   But hold on to the sleigh.)

Rode that mule to town one day,
Hitched him by hisself;
Kicked both hindlegs down his throat,
And kicked hisself to death.

I'm a-goin' down to Possum town,
Miss Lizy, you keep cool;
Ain't got time to kiss you now,
I'm boun' to hold this mule.

In addition to being a folk performer, Cullie Williams was (or is) the
subject of a ballad. Among the folksong texts deposited in the Western

Kentucky Folklore Archive in 1956 by Alice M. Childs is the following, collected from Dora Blair, near Pippa Passes, Ky., in the 1930's:

Young people all I pray draw near;
Listen a while and you shall hear
How Cullie Williams did so bad,
He shot his wife in jealous mad.

They carried her to the graveyard
And put her away,
And there to sleep with Jesus
Until the Judgment Day.

The people all did gather
To see what had been done.
Cullie had shot and killed her
And never tried to run.

The sheriff arrested Cullie
And took him to jail.
The crime he had committed,
They wouldn't allow him bail.

The news came to his children,
And they never shed a tear
That Cullie had gone to the pen for life
And ought to have the chair.

"Now children you all know what is right,
You ought to do the best.
Your dad had gone to the pen for life,
And your mother has gone to rest."

They carried her to the graveyard,
And they put her away,
And there to sleep with Jesus
Until the Judgment Day.

The preachers all did gather
To funeralize the dead,
And to comfort the poor children
When the crime was done, they said.

They had eleven children,
And some of them were small.
They had a good old mother,
And had no dad at all.

"Now, girls, don't forget your mother.
I hope the Lord will bless you all.
Pray the Lord for His forgiveness
And meet Him when He calls.

"Now, boys, while you are young and blooming,
Your father has gone far beyond the way,

Your mother is in the graveyard sleeping,
Pray the Lord your mother to meet.

"You all know what caused the trouble,
What took your mother's life,
Because he loved some other,
And didn't love his wife."

Old Cullie is now in trouble.
He brought it on himself.
It would have been much better,
If'd he took old Cordie and left.

In 1959 Combs furnished the following information concerning Cullie Williams:

> If he is still living, he must be beyond 75 years old. When I was a boy, "Cull" stayed at our house and worked for us at Hindman, Knott County, about the turn of the century. He was a great "banjer" picker. He married a "woods colt" daughter of another negro who used to work for us. On a casual visit to Knott County, in 1923, ... we saw Cull, who was living at the mouth of Breeding's Creek of Carr's Fork, with wife and family. I spent the night with him. We made our way back to a mountain cove, to a cornfield, where Cull pulled out a gallon of moonshine from a shock of corn and gave it to me to take back home, to my mother's, at Hindman. Breeding's Creek is about eight or nine miles from Hindman, and the post office is Red Fox, Ky. To make the story short, Cullie was dabbling with moonshine, and drinking. Shortly after our visit over there, that is, sometime after 1923, he came home one night drunk, and shot and killed his wife, who was in bed. He waived trial, and accepted life imprisonment in the State prison. After a few years he was pardoned on good behavior, and came home. I saw him again in 1933. . . . He was an intelligent, industrious, and withal a likeable fellow. When he killed his wife, under the influence of "hootch," he was said to be "running around" with another woman. . . . I didn't know a song had been written about the murder.

177. I WISH I WAS SINGLE AGAIN. (Cf. Brown, III, 37 ff.; V, 21.)
    A. "The Married Man." 6 ch. Mrs. Edwin Daniel, Hindman, Knott Co., Ky. *FSMEU*, pp. 181 f. [211 f.].
    B. "O when I was single, I'd make the money jingle." 7. Contributed by Berlin B. Chapman, Webster Co., W.Va., (1924?).

178. I WISH I WERE A SINGLE GIRL AGAIN. "When I were married no pleasure could I see." 5. Albro Thomas, Knott Co., Ky., 1911. (Cf. Brown, III, 54 ff.; V, 28 f.)

179. TO CHEER THE HEART. 4d ch. Mrs. John W. Combs, Hindman, Knott Co., Ky. *FSMEU*, pp. 146 f. [168 ff., where it is printed as 9]. (Cf. Randolph, IV, 236 ff.)

180. SLAGO TOWN. 6 ch. Mrs. John W. Combs, Hindman, Knott Co., Ky. *FSMEU*, p. 145 [167 f.]. 4 and variant stanza printed with tune in *FSKH*, pp. 16 f., with note that the "text has been slightly 'toned down', to allow publication." (Related to Laws 03. Cf. Randolph, I, 105 ff.)

181. LAST GOLD DOLLAR. 7 ch. Tom Kelley, Hindman, Knott Co., Ky., 1913. *KFR*, VI, 131 f. (Cf. Randolph IV, 114 f.)

182. THE LOVER'S LAMENT. "Loving Hanner." 9. Mrs. John W. Combs, Hindman, Knott Co., Ky., 1909. (Cf. Brown, II, 279 ff.; IV, 156.)

183. THE INCONSTANT LOVER. (Cf. Brown, III, 271 ff.; V, 154 ff.)
    A. "A-walking and a-talking." 13. Mrs. John W. Combs, Hindman, Knott Co., Ky.
    B. "Come all ye pretty fair maidens." 6. Knott Co., Ky.

184. THE GAMBLER. 6 couplets. Rob. Morgan, Emmalena, Knott Co., Ky. (1908?). *FSMEU*, p. 190 [223 f.]. Sung (with alterations) to his own tune by Logan English, *Gambling Songs*, Riverside RLP 12–643. (This song may be considered a form of No. 183.)

185. "Trouble, trouble on my mind." 1. Source unknown. *KFR*, VI, 134. (Cf. Brown, III, 344 ff.; V, 209 f.)

186. RYE WHISKEY (FOR WORK I'M TOO LAZY). 9 ch. Newton Gaines, Fort Worth, Tex., Aug. 13, 1933. Recorded in 1930 for the Victor Recording Co. and issued on Timely Tunes under the pseudonym of Jim New. Tune and partial text printed in *PTFS*, VII, 153 f.

187. MOONSHINER. 5. Monroe Combs, Hindman, Knott Co., Ky. *FSMEU*, p. 189 [222 f.]. (Cf. Lomax, *Folk Songs of North America*, p. 257; *SFQ*, II, 160 f.)

188. LITTLE SPARROW. 6. Mrs. John W. Combs, Hindman, Knott Co., Ky., 1910. (Cf. Brown, III, 290 ff.; V, 173 ff.)

189. THE FALSE TRUE LOVER. (Cf. Brown, III, 299 ff.; V, 181 ff.)
    A. "The True Lover's Farewell." 5. Knott Co., Ky.
    B. "Turtle Dove." 2 ch. Knott Co., Ky. Botkin, p. 284.

190. FOND AFFECTION. "The Dear Companion." 4 ch. with tune. Mrs. Margaret Green, Knott Co., Ky. *FSKH*, pp. 12 f. (Cf. Brown, II, 398 ff.; IV, 222 ff.)

191. MY DEAREST DEAR. "O now to me the time draws near." 12. Knott Co., Ky. (Cf. Sharp, II, 13.)

192. THE PRISONER'S SONG. (Cf. Brown, III, 411 ff.; V, 246.)
    A. "New Jail." 5 ch. Tom Kelley, Hindman, Knott Co., Ky., 1913.
    B. "New Jail." 4 ch. A patient from Pike and Martin Counties, Ky., in the government clinic at Hindman, Ky., 1913.

193. A PRISONER FOR LIFE. "Farewell, ye old green fields, soft meadows, adieu." Knott Co., Ky. (Randolph, II, 147 ff.)

194. ON THE BANKS OF THAT LONELY RIVER. 4 ch with tune. Learned from Mrs. John W. Combs (his mother) when J. H. C. was two or three years old; heard later in Logan Co., W.Va. *FSKH*, pp. 14 f. (Cf. Brown, II, 433 f.; IV, 232 f.)

195. WHITE WINGS. 3 ch. Student in the Oklahoma Northeastern State Normal School, Tahlequah, 1917. (Cf. Randolph, IV, 295.)

196. WE HAVE MET AND WE HAVE PARTED. "We are parting now forever." 4. Roger Cornett, Hindman, Knott Co., Ky., *ca.* 1900. (Cf. Brown, III, 410 ff.)

197. LITTLE PINK. 9 with tune. A patient from Pike Co., Ky., in the government clinic at Hindman, *ca.* 1915. *FSKH*, pp. 18 f. (Cf. Brown, III, 342.)

198. KITTY CLYDE. (Cf. Brown, III, 293 ff.; V, 175 ff.)
   A. 5 ch. Wayne Co., Ky.
   B. "If I was a little turkle dove." 2 ch. Mrs. John W. Combs, Hindman, Knott Co., Ky., 1910.

199. JINNY, GIT YO' HOE CAKE DONE. Source unknown. (Chorus missing?)

> The biggest fool I ever saw
> Come from the state of Arkansaw;
> He put his shirt on over his coat,
> And buttoned his breeches around his throat.

200. LITTLE BUNCH OF ROSES. 1. Source unknown. *KFR*, VI, 134.

201. JINNY GIT AROUND. 1 ch. Knott Co., Ky. *KFR*, VII, 72 f.; Botkin, p. 235.

202. SHADY GROVE. 11 with tune. Knott Co., Ky. *Folk-Say*, 1930, 241 ff. (Cf. Brown, III, 339 ff.; V, 318 f.)

203. SOURWOOD MOUNTAIN. (Cf. Brown, III, 251 ff.; V, 162 ff.)
   A. "Chickens a-crowin' in the Sourwood Mountain." 7. Knott Co., Ky.
   B. "I got a gal at de head o' de holler." 2. From a contributor named Felder. Probably Kentucky.
   C. "Old man, old man, can I have your daughter?" 1. Berlin B. Chapman, Webster Co., W.Va. (1924?).

204. CUMBERLAND GAP. "Big Stone Gap." 7 plus 4 possibly from another source. Knott Co., Ky. (Cf. Brown, II, 381; V, 229 f.)

205. RIVER SONG. 12. Contributed by Carey Woofter. "Sung by the men who ran timber down the little Kanawha River on their way home."

Pork and beans and eggs to fry,
Doughnuts, kraut and apple pie—
We'll hit Gilmer by and by.

I'm nothing but a riverman,
A riverman, a riverman,
I'm nothing but a riverman,
Mudding it from Creston.

Creston is a sorry town, etc.
Girls, who'll take the posy?

Creston won't give us feather beds,
No, we'll bunk by the fire.

Annamoriah has an old ferry,
Ring around the rosy.

Brooksville has no use for us,
But they have "white hoss."

Widder Betts has a big tin pan
To mix the "white hoss" in.

Grantsville don't give a damn,
If in hell we're roasted,

But Doc Dye has a store,
And he can write a scrip.

White Pine is a slinking place,
Bid the sassafrax (*sic*) goodbye.

I'm nothing but a riverman,
Mudding it from Creston.

Pork and beans and eggs to fry,
Doughnuts, kraut and apple pie,
We'll hit Gilmer by and by.

206. THE BANK OF THE ARKANSAS. 1. Contributed by Berlin B. Chapman, Webster Co., W.Va. (1924?). The following stanza seems to belong to a song collected in Texas in 1937 (Lomax, *Our Singing Country*, pp. 68 f.). The Texas variant employs a chorus compounded (?) of "Cornstalk Fiddle" and "Cotton-Eyed Joe" (see Nos. 207, 208).

Ma, Pa, and me they came from Arkansas;
My girl *she* came from Arkansas.
She can saw more wood than my ma can saw,
And chaw more 'backer than my paw can chaw.

207. "Corn stalk fiddle and buckeye bow." 1. (Kentucky?) *Folk-Say*, 1930, p. 239; *KFR*, VII, 73. (See No. 206.)

208. COTTON-EYED JOE. 2. Marion Co., Ark. (1917?). (Cf. Lomax, *Our Singing Country*, p. 99; see also No. 206 above.)

209. "Gee whiz! Boys, Pa's maul and wedge is gone." 1. Berlin B. Chapman, Webster Co., W.Va. (1924?).

> Gee whiz! Boys, Pa's maul and wedge is gone.
> And here's the stump he laid her on.
> Now boys, the devil will have to pay
> When Pa comes along this way
> And hears us say, "Yer maul and wedge is gone,
> And here's the stump, by gosh, you laid her on."

210. GOING DOWN THE RIVER 2. Searcy Co., Ark. (1917?).

> Boat begin to rock
> And your heart begin to quiver,
> Oh my little girl,
> You're a-goin' down the river.
>
> Massa killed a hog,
> And the puppy got the liver,
> And the last I saw of him
> He's a-goin' down the river.

211. HOOK AND LINE. 14. Knott Co., Ky. (Cf., *JAF*, XXVI, 127; Fuson, p. 157.)

212. ROCKY ISLAND. 6. Dan Gibson, Hindman, Knott Co., Ky., 1915. *KFR*, VII, 63 f.

213. SHOESTRINGS. 7 ch. Tom Kelley, Hindman, Knott Co., Ky., 1915. *KFR*, VII, 64 f.

214. OLD VALISE. 5. Tom Kelley, Hindman, Knott Co., Ky., 1913. *KFR*, VI, 133.

215. OLD BLACK BETZ. 3 ch. Tom Kelley, Hindman, Knott Co., Ky., 1913. *KFR*, VI, 135.

216. BEEFSTEAK. 2. Knott Co., Ky. (Cf. Brown, III, 344 ff.; V, 209 f.)

217. "I won't go home till morning." 2. Knott Co., Ky. *KFR*, VII, 66.

218. CRAWDAD. (Cf. Lomax, *Our Singing Country*, pp. 298 ff.; McDowell, *Memory Melodies*, p. 75.)
A. 7 with tune. *Folk-Say*, 1930, pp. 245 f. (Kentucky?)
B. "Crawfish he don't stan' no show dis mawnin'." 5. From a contributor named Felder. Probably Kentucky.

219. THAT LONESOME ROAD. 7 with tune. Tom Kelley, Hindman, Knott Co., Ky. *FSKH*, pp. 28 f. (Cf. Brown, III, 347 f.; V, 210.)

220. LIZA JANE (Cf. Henry, *Folk-Songs*, pp. 430 ff.)
A. "Kitchen Door." 11. Marion and Searcy Cos., Ark., 1917.
B. "Sugar Hill." 11. Student in the Oklahoma Northeastern State Normal

School, Tahlequah, 1917; apparently as heard in Marion and Searcy Cos., Ark.

221. "I went down the new-cut road." 2. Wayne Co., Ky. Those stanzas might well be considered with Nos. 213 or 220. (But cf. Brown, III, 494 ff.; V, 413 f.)

222. HOG-EYED MAN. "Sally in the garden sifting sand." 1 ch. Knott Co., Ky. (Cf. Brown, III, 261.)

223. OLD JOE CLARK. (Cf. Brown, III, 120 ff.; V, 61 f.)
A. 6 ch. Tom Kelley, Hindman, Knott Co., Ky., 1915.
B. 6 ch. Student from Marion Co., Ark., in the Oklahoma Northeastern State Normal School, Tahlequah, 1917.

224. CRIPPLE CREEK. 6 ch. with tune. Knott Co., Ky. *Folk-Say*, 1930, pp. 340 f. (Cf. Brown, III, 354 ff.; V, 213 ff.)

225. "When I get on my bran'-new suit." 1. Source unkown. *KFR*, VII, 66.

226. ARKANSAS TRAVELER. (Cf. Brown, III, 381 ff.; *PTFS*, XVIII, 11 ff.)
A. Dialogue. Knott Co., Ky.
B. Tune and prose tale. Cox, *Traditional Ballads*, p. 210, where it is credited to the collection of Miss Frances Sanders, Morgantown, W.Va., June, 1924.

227. OFF SHE GOES. Fiddle tune and legend. Cox, *Traditional Ballads*, p. 211, where it is credited to the collection of Miss Frances Sanders, Morgantown, W.Va., June, 1924.

228. IDA RED. 30 ch. Knott Co., Ky. (Cf. Randolph, III, 442.)

229. WHAT'LL I DO WITH THE BABY-O? "Georgy-O." 1 ch. Knott Co., Ky. (Cf. Sharp, II, 336.)

230. SUSIE. 3 ch. Knott Co., Ky. (Cf. Brown, III, 366 f., 555; V, 320.)

231. LYNCHBURG TOWN. 6 ch. Tom Kelley, Hindman, Knott Co., Ky., 1913. (Cf. Brown, III, 498 ff., 549; V, 277 ff.)

232. WALK, GEORDIE-RO. 1 ch. Knott Co., Ky. Botkin, pp. 236–237. (Cf. Brown, III, 143 ff.; V, 79 f.)

233. THE DEVIL IS DEAD. 4 ch. Knott Co., Ky. *KFR*, VII, 65 f.; stanza 3 in Botkin, p. 284.

234. CLUCK OLD HEN. 7. Tom Kelley and Dan Gibson, Hindman, Knott Co., Ky., 1915. (Cf. *JAF*, LII, 50, No. 55.)

235. HOUN' DOG. 8. Kentucky. (Cf. Randolph, III, 278 ff.)

236. "Roosters lay eggs in Kansas." 3. "Heard at a circus in Knott Co., Ky. . . . 1897"—J. H. C. (Cf. Randolph, III, 17 ff.)

237. PEGGIN' AWL. 1. Knott Co., Ky. *KFR*, VI, 135. (Cf. Lunsford and Stringfield, pp. 30 f.)

238. GIT ALONG LITTLE DOGIES. 4 ch. Newton Gaines, Fort Worth, Tex., Aug. 13, 1933. Recorded in 1930 by the Victor Recording Co. and released on Victor V–40253 as "A-Walkin' the Streets of Laredo." Tune and portion of text printed in *PTFS*, VII, 149.

239. I'M WILD AND WOOLY or IT'S MY NIGHT TO HOWL. 1. Newton Gaines, Fort Worth, Tex., Aug. 13, 1933. Recorded in 1930 as a prelude to "A-Walkin' the Streets of Laredo," Victor V–40253—see No. 238. (Cf. Lomax, *Cowboy Songs*, p. 133; *American Ballads and Folk Songs*, p. 382.)

240. "Today is the day we give babies away." 1d. Carey Woofter, Gilmer Co., W.Va. (1924?). See No. 15 C.

241. "Raccoon's tail has rings all around." 1. Boone Co., Ky., Negro. Contributed by D. L. Thomas, Centre College, Danville, Ky. (1915?). (Cf. Brown, III, 209 f.; V, 122 f.)

242. CHARMING BETSY. 6 ch. A Pike Co., Ky., patient in the government clinic, Hindman, Ky., *ca*. 1915. (Cf. Brown, III, 297 f., 544 f.; V, 180 ff., 315 f.)

243. SHORTNIN' BREAD. 8 ch. Knott Co., Ky. (Cf. Brown, III, 535 ff.; V, 305 f.)

244. LINK FOL DEY. 6. Knott Co., Ky. *KFR*, VII, 67.

245. TURKEY IN DE STRAW. 3 ch. (Kentucky?) (Cf. Sandburg, p. 97, B, C.)

246. OLE FERGINNY NIGGER. 5. Joseph Williams, Smithsboro, Knott Co., Ky., 1895. *KFR*, VII, 67 f.

247. "Did you ever see the Devil?" 2. (Kentucky?) (Cf. Henry, *Songs*, p. 252.)

248. TWO SONG. 4 ch. Fleming Co., Ky. Contributed by D. L. Thomas, Centre College, Danville, Ky. (1915?). *KFR*, VII, 68 f.

249. GIT DA. 2. Boone Co., Ky., Negro. Contributed by D. L. Thomas, Centre College, Danville, Ky. (1915?). *KFR*, VII, 69.

250. "De sole of my shoe's mos' gone." 3. From a contributor named Felder, who learned it from John Fox, Jr. Presumably Kentucky. *KFR*, VII, 69 f.

251. I MET MISS DINAH. 4. From a contributor named Felder. Probably Kentucky. *KFR*, VII, 70.

252. "I wisht I had a little wife." 5. From a contributor named Felder. Probably Kentucky. *KFR*, VII, 70 f.

253. COON DOG. 1. Boone Co., Ky., Negro. Contributed by D. L. Thomas, Centre College, Danville, Ky. (1915?). *KFR*, VII, 71.

254. "Chickens on my back." 1. Boone Co., Ky., Negro. Contributed by D. L. Thomas, Centre College, Danville, Ky. (1915?). (Cf. Odum and Johnson, *Negro Workaday Songs*, p. 128.)

255. ROLL ON, JOHN. 8. Knott Co., Ky. (Cf. Brown, III, 267; V, 151 f.)

256. NINE-POUND HAMMER. "The Yew-Pine Mountains." 8. Harley Townsend, Dusk, W.Va., "whose brother heard it years ago in the coal camps near Fairmont." Contributed by Carey Woofter, 1924. *FSMEU*, p. 166 [193 f.]. (See comment on this text in Chappell, *John Henry*, pp. 3 f. Cf. Brown, II, 626 f.; IV, 300 ff.)

257. JIM CROW. "Wheel around, turn around, do this so." 1. Knott Co., Ky. (Cf. Randolph, II, 323.)

258. THE LITTLE BROWN JUG. 7 ch. with tune. Gilmer Co., W.Va. Contributed by Carey Woofter (1924?). (Cf. Brown, III, 62 ff.; V, 35.)

259. LITTLE MORE CIDER. 4d ch. Tahlequah, Okla., (1917?). MS is a student exercise or a ballet. (A published song credited to Austin Hart, 1852. Cf. Brown, III, 75 ff.; V, 41 f.)

260. UNCLE NED. "Dere wuz a ole nigguh by de name of Uncle Ned." 1 ch. Boone Co., Ky., Negro. Communicated by D. L. Thomas, Centre College, Danville, Ky. (1915?). (Cf. Brown, 505 f.; V, 208 f.)

261. SUSANNAH! "It rained all night the day I left." 1. Knott Co., Ky. (Cf. Brown, III, 488 ff.; V, 271 f.)

262. BEAR WENT OVER THE MOUNTAIN. 1d. Kentucky. (Cf. Linscott, pp. 164 ff.)

263. SARO JANE. 2 ch. "Heard at a circus in Knott Co., Ky. . . . 1897"— J. H. C. (Cf. Sandburg, p. 307.)

264. "You ought to see your dear aunt laugh." 1d. Knott Co., Ky. *KFR*, VII, 72.

265. THE HOLE IN THE BOTTOM OF THE SEA. 4 ch. Air: "Sweet Bye and Bye." (Kentucky?) (Cf. Brown, III, 186; V, 109 f.)

266. TEN LITTLE BOYS. 10. Knott Co., Ky. (Cf. Richardson, pp. 84 f.)

267. "Constantinople, lake-a-lo lake along." 1. Knott Co., Ky. *KFR*, VI, 136.

268. "I went to milk and I didn't know how." 1. Knott Co., Ky. (Cf. *JAF*, XLIX, 234.)

269. "Away down yonder in the Scioto bottom." 1. (Kentucky?) *KFR*, VII, 71.

270. "Away to the West the gray goose flew." 1. (Kentucky?) *KFR*, VII, 71.

271. "Chicken in the bread-tray pickin' up dough." 1. (Kentucky?) *KFR*, VII, 71.

272. "Hell's a-floatin'," the river's a risin'." 1. (Kentucky?) *KFR*, VII, 71.

273. "Rye-chick-a-noodin, noodin, noodin." 1. (Kentucky?) *KFR*, VII, 71.

274. "A nigger and a mule." 1. Knott Co., Ky. *KFR*, VII, 72.

275. GREASE MY HEELS. 1. Knott Co., Ky. (Cf. Brown, III, 69 ff.; V, 38 ff.)

276. OLD GRAY HORSE. 1. Knott Co., Ky. (Cf. Brown, III, 216 f.)

277. RYE STRAW. 1. Knott Co., Ky. *KFR*, VII, 72.

278. "Way down yonder in Kalamazine." 3. Knott Co., Ky. Botkin, p. 143; *KFR*, VII, 72.

279. A Dance Set. 9. Source unidentified. Indicated tune: "Reuben, I've Been Thinking." "Reuben and Rachel" was copyrighted 1871, words by Harry Bush and music by Wm. Gooch. (Cf. Loesser, pp. 254 f.)

280. OLD AS MOSES. 1. Knott Co., Ky. *KFR*, VII, 73.

281. THE BORDERS OF THE LILY. 2. Knott Co., Ky. *KFR*, VII, 73.

282. "Long came a lady with a rosy in her hand." 1. Knott Co., Ky. *KFR*, VII, 73.

283. OLD BETTY LARKIN. 4. Knott Co., Ky. Botkin, p. 144 (Cf. Randolph, III, 262 ff.; Ritchie, *Garland*, pp. 38 f.)

284. GREEN GROW THE RUSHES. 4. Knott Co., Ky. (Cf. *JAF*, XLIX, 257, No. 16.)

285. I'LL SAIL ON THE SEA. 6 ch. Knott Co., Ky. *KFR*, VII, 73 f.; Botkin, pp. 255 f.)

286. KING WILLIAM WAS KING JAMES' SON. (Cf. Randolph, III, 344 ff.)
    A. "King William was King James' son." 3 with tune. J. E. Woofter, Morgantown, W.Va., formerly of Gilmer Co. Contributed by Carey Woofter (1924?).
    B. "Here stands a lovely creature." 3. Gilmer Co., W.Va. Contributed by Carey Woofter (1924?). Stanza 1 printed by Botkin, p. 357.

287. THREE DUKES. (Cf. Brown, III, 101.)
    A. "Here come two dukes a-rovin." 7. Knott Co., Ky.
    B. "Here comes an old lady from Newfoundland." 5. Gilmer Co., W.Va. Contributed by Carey Woofter (1924?).

288. MY LOVE SAT DOWN.
    A. "My love sat down in a sad condition." 3. Knott Co., Ky. Botkin, pp. 216 f.
    B. "Sad Station." Lost text and tune from Gilmer Co., W.Va.

289. SWEETHEART A-HUNTING. "Sail Around the Ocean." 5. Knott Co., Ky. Botkin, p. 320.

290. "Here we sit all in this ring." 1. Knott Co., Ky. (Cf. Botkin, p. 186; Skean, p. 24.)

291. ROUND AND ROUND THE VILLAGE. 7. (Kentucky?) (Cf. Brown, III, 108 f.; V, 55.)

292. NEEDLE'S EYE. (Cf. Brown, III, 107 f.; V, 54.)
    A. "Needle's eye that doth supply." 1. Knott Co., Ky.
    B. "The needle's eye it doth supply." 2 ch. with tune. J. E. Woofter, Morgantown, W.Va., formerly of Gilmer Co. Contributed by Carey Woofter (1924?).

293. THE MILLER BOY. (Cf. Brown, III, 108; V, 54.)
    A. "The Jolly Miller." 1. Knott Co., Ky.
    B. "The Dusty Miller." 1 ch. with tune. J. E. Woofter, Morgantown, W.Va., formerly of Gilmer Co. Contributed by Carey Woofter (1924?).
    C. "The Dusty Miller." Lost text from Gilmer Co., W.Va. Cited in Botkin, p. 212.
    D. "There stands a jolly old miller all alone by himself." 4. Gilmer Co., W.Va. Contributed by Carey Woofter (1924?).

294. MARIAH. 6. Knott Co., Ky. (Cf. Sharp, II, 369.)

295. BIG BALD EAGLE. 5. Knott Co., Ky. (Cf. Sharp, II, 374.)

296. THE GOOSEBERRY BUSH. 5. Knott Co., Ky. (Cf. Sharp, II, 373.)

397. GOING TO BOSTON. 9 ch. Knott Co., Ky. (Cf. Randolph, III, 526 f.; Ritchie, *Garland*, pp. 40 f.)

298. SKIP TO MY LOU. (Cf. Randolph, III, 287 f.)
    A. 15. Knott Co., Ky.
    B. 14 ch. with tune. Gilmer Co., W.Va. Contributed by Carey Woofter (1924?).

299. WEEVILY WHEAT. (Cf. Brown, III, 100 f.; V, 50 f.)
    A. "Charlie." 6 ch. Knott Co., Ky.
    B. "Weevily Wheat." 6 ch. with tune. J. E. Woofter, Morgantown, W.Va., formerly of Gilmer Co. Contributed by Carey Woofter (1924?).
    C. "I won't have none of your weevily wheat." 5. Callaway Co., Mo.
    D. "Charlie he's a nice young man." 3. Illinois.
    E. "Charlie he's a nice young man." 2. Missouri.
    F. "Charlie loves good ale and brandy." 1. Missouri.

G. "There's news from Modart came yester e'en." 3. Pike Co., Ky. "Old Scotch rallying song upon the landing of Charles Stuart, the Young Pretender, at Moldart in Inverness Shire, July, 1745"—J. H. C. Botkin, pp. 345 f.

300. THE PIG IN THE PARLOR. 4 with tune. J. E. Woofter, Morgantown, W.Va., formerly of Gilmer Co. Contributed by Carey Woofter (1924?). (Cf. Brown, III, 80; V, 56 f.)

301. LONDON BRIDGE. (Cf. Randolph, III, 388.)
   A. "London Bridge is falling down." 3 with tune. J. E. Woofter, Morgantown, W.Va., formerly of Gilmer Co. Contributed by Carey Woofter (1924?).
   B. "London Bridge is falling down." 1. Northern part of W.Va. Contributed by Carey Woofter (1924?).
   C. "London Bridge is falling down." 1. W.Va. Contributed by Carey Woofter (1924?).

302. THE FARMER IN THE DELL. 8 with tune. J. E. Woofter, Morgantown, W.Va., formerly of Gilmer Co. Contributed by Carey Woofter (1924?). (Cf. Wolford, *Play-Party*, pp. 209 f.)

303. GREEN GRAVEL. (Cf. Randolph, III, 532 f.)
   A. 1 with tune. J. E. Woofter, Morgantown, W.Va., formerly of Gilmer Co. Contributed by Carey Woofter (1924?).
   B. 1. Gilmer Co., W.Va. Contributed by Carey Woofter (1924?).

304. SHEEP'S CLOTHING. 1 with tune. J. E. Woofter, Morgantown, W.Va., formerly of Gilmer Co. Contributed by Carey Woofter (1924?).

305. RED BIRD. (Cf. Skean, p. 7.)
   A. 2 with tune. Gilmer Co., W.Va. Contributed by Carey Woofter (1924?).
   B. 1. Knott Co., Ky.

306. THREE CHILDREN SLIDING ON THE ICE. "Four Young Ladies." 2 with tune. Gilmer Co., W. Va. Contributed by Carey Woofter (1924?). (Cf. Randolph, III, 588.)

307. IN AND OUT THE WINDOW. "We're marching round the window." 7 with tune. Gilmer Co., W.Va. Contributed by Carey Woofter (1924?). (Cf. Brown, III, 76 f.; V, 55.)

308. LAZY MARY. 8 with tune. Gilmer Co., W.Va. Contributed by Carey Woofter (1924?). (Cf. Newell, p. 96.)

309. CAPTAIN JINKS. 3 with tune. Gilmer Co., W.Va. Contributed by Carey Woofter (1924?). (Cf. Brown, III, 119; V, 60 f.)

310. BUFFALO GALS. "Jim Town Girls." 2 with tune. Monongalia Co., W.Va. (Cf. Brown, III, 114; V, 57 ff.) This seems to be one of the items contributed by Miss Frances Sanders, June, 1924. Carey Woofter was

probably involved in the collection. (Cf. Nos. 14B, 92B, 124, 136F, 142D, 226, 227.)

311. MARCHING DOWN TO OLD QUEBEC. 2 ch. Knott Co., Ky. (Cf. Randolph, III, 296 f.)

312. JOHN BROWN HAD A LITTLE INDIAN. 11. Knott Co., Ky. (Cf. Randolph, III, 594.)

313. WILLIAM TRIMMEL TRAN (Counting out rhyme). 1 plus variant lines. Knott Co., Ky. (Cf. Newell, p. 203, No. 30; *JAF*, LXIII, 427.)

314. "Eeny meeny miny mo" (Counting out rhyme). 1. Knott Co., Ky. (Cf. Newell, p. 199, No. 9; *JAF*, LXV, 319.)

315. THREE SHIPS CAME SAILING BY. 8. A. E. Harris, Little Birch, Braxton Co., W.Va. (1924?). *FSMEU*, pp. 141 f. [163]. (Cf. Brown, II, 210.)

316. THE SHIP THAT IS PASSING BY. (Cf. Randolph, IV, 95.)
A. "I once had a father, but now I have none." 4 ch. Mrs. John W. Combs, Knott Co., Ky. *FSMEU*, p. 191 [225].
B. "I once had a father, but now I have none." 3. (Kentucky?)

317. SHAKING OF THE HAND. Tahlequah, Okla. (1917?). MS is a student exercise or a ballet.

At a brightly beaming eye or gently winning smile, may entice us to betray and allure us to beguile even the language of the tongue. We may fail to understand but there nothing like deceit in the shaking of the hand.
Set the fashion ables meet with a smile upon the lips and so lightly touch the hand with their dainty finger tips, but it never warms the heart like a good old fashion shake, with the hands so tightly grasped that the feverish fingers ache.
So we'll give a hearty grasp when we go and when we stay and in silence press the hand as the loved ones pass away with the sure and steadfast hope. When the master bids us come with the shaking of the hands they will shout us welcome home.

Chorus:
Oh the shakings of the hand speaks the language of the heart ever joyful when we meet ever hopeful when we part. Oh the shaking, shaking, shaking the shaking of the hand. Oh the shaking of the hand speaks the language of the heart.

318. WE HAVE FATHERS GONE TO HEAVEN. 5. Mrs. John W. Combs, Hindman, Knott Co., Ky. *FSMEU*, pp. 191 f. [225 f.]. (Cf. *PTFS*, X, 177 f.)

319. HEAVEN BELLS. 1 ch. Mrs. John W. Combs, Hindman, Knott Co., Ky., 1910. (Cf. *New England Magazine*, XIX, 612.)

320. JACOB'S LADDER. 5 ch. Mrs. John W. Combs, Hindman, Knott Co., Ky. *FSMEU*, p. 190 [224]. (Cf. Brown, III, 536 f.; V, 335 f.)

321. STAY ALWAYS AND I CANNOT. 4 ch. Marion Combs, Smithsboro, Knott Co., Ky., 1898. *KFR*, VII, 74 f.

322. GOOD LORD LEND ME THE WINGS. 4. Mrs. John W. Combs, Hindman, Knott Co., Ky., 1910. *KFR*, VII, 75.

323. THE PRODIGAL SON. 6. From a contributor named Felder who "heard the roustabouts singing it on the Chattahoochie River in 1897." *KFR*, VII, 75 f.

324. I GOT A ROBE. 4. Prof. Morelock of Tennessee, at Paintsville, Ky., 1912. (Cf. Brown, III, 607 f.; V, 550 f.)

325. "Who am dat walkin' in de co'n?" 4 ch. Contributed by Carey Woofter, Gilmer Co., W.Va., 1924. *FSMEU*, p. 192 [226].

INDEX OF TITLES AND FIRST LINES
OF SONG TEXTS

Italic references after titles refer to song texts in this collection.